Mindfulness in Nature

84 Nature-Oriented Exercises & Theoretical Foundations

Copyright © Michael Huppertz and Verena Schatanek, 2017.

1st English Edition.

Translation by Garry Zettersten.

First published in German by Junfermann Verlag in Paderborn, Germany, 2015.

www.junfermann.de

All images © Verena Schatanek.

Content

Table of Exercises   4

Acknowledgments   9

Introduction   11

Part 1: Fundamentals   31

1. The Attitude of Mindfulness   31

1.1. Definition   31

1.2. The Dimensions of Mindfulness   39

2. Mindful Approaches to Nature   45

2.1. Nature and Approaches to Nature   45

2.2. The Mindful Approach to Nature   46

2.3. Forms of Mindful Approaches to Nature   47

3. Recommendations for the Practice of Mindfulness in Nature   60

3.1. General Recommendations   61

3.2. Recommendations for Group Leaders   63

3.3. Recommendations for the Practice of Mindfulness with Children   67

Part 2: The Exercises   72

4. Receptive Exercises   81

5. Exploratory Exercises   122

6. Empathic Exercises   158

7. Playful Exercises   167

8. Shaping Exercises   185

9. Contemplative Exercises   221

Part 3: Background

10. Mindfulness in Nature Education (Verena Schatanek)   242

10.1 Mindfulness in Different Teaching Traditions of Nature Education 247

10.2. Education for Sustainable Development   258

10.3. Environmental Psychology Perspectives   261

10.4. Mindfulness in Nature Education – Practical Experiences   265

10.5. The Contribution of Mindfulness in Nature to Education for
Sustainable Development   270

11. The Importance of Mindfulness in Nature to Well-Being and Mental
Health (Michael Huppertz)   281

12. Mindfulness and Nature Ethics (Michael Huppertz)   299

12.1. The Ethical Aspect of Mindfulness   299

12.2. Mindfulness and the Intrinsic Value of Nature   300

12.3. The Necessity of Moral Reflection   302

12.4. Nature Ethical Positions   304

12.5. Nature Ethics from the Perspective of Being in Nature and
Mindfulness   313

13. The Spiritual Search in Nature (Michael Huppertz)   319

13.1. Spirituality   319

13.2. Mindfulness and Spirituality in Nature   320

13.3. Interpretations of Spiritual Experiences of Nature   331

14. Bibliography   350

Table of Exercises

Flashlight   73

Sharing   74

And-Techniques   75

Which Nature Type are You? - Round of Introductions   77

One's Own Place   78

Meeting Place   80

4. Receptive Exercises

1. Calling-Out Suggestions   81

2. 90-Degree Turn   83

3. Hearing a Place   85

4. Perceiving with the Inner Picture   88

5. Near-Far Exercise   90

6. Opening the Horizon   91

7. Walking on Uneven Ground   94

8. 3-2-1-Exercise   96

9. Three Focuses   97

10. Two-Trees Exercise   98

11. Natural Points of Contact   100

12. Touches of Nature   102

13. Touching in a Circle   103

14. Three Stage Touching   105

15. Body Journey with Tree   107

16. Freezing   108

17. Tasting   110

18. Smelling and Sniffing   112

19. By the Water   114

20. Observing Impulses and not Following Them   116

21. Observing Yourself – Being in Nature   117

22. Lying on the Ground   118

23. Wide Mindfulness   120

5. Exploratory Exercises

24. Panorama Exercise   122

25. Exploring a Place as an Animal   124

26. Change in Scenery   125

27. Exploring the Weather   127

28. Aimless Exploration   128

29. Time Dimensions   129

30. Blindly Feeling a Tree and Finding it Again   130

31. Exploring the Seasons   131

32. Searching and Gathering   133

33. Mirror Walk   136

34. Observing the Surface   138

35. Gaps   139

36. Exploring the Environment with the Body   141

37. Photographer and Camera   142

38. Claiming Space for Oneself   145

39. Nature as a Place to Breathe   146

40. Where does it Come From?   148

41. Being Guided Blindly   150

42. Cloth Exercise   152

43. Nomad Exercise   154

44. Searching for Opposites in Nature   156

6. Empathic Exercises

45. Listening to Animals in Nature   158

46. Microcosm   160

47. Following an Animal   162

48. Approaching an Animal   164

7. Playful Exercises

49. Touch Memory   167

50. More and Less   169

51. Leading with Sounds   171

52. Sneaking   174

53. Forming a Snake   176

54. Speed Variations   177

55. Tree Telephone   178

56. Climbing a Steep Slope 180

57. Experimenting with Water 183

8. Shaping Exercises

58. Staging the Unremarkable 185

59. Sketching 187

60. Shaping Lines in the Landscape with Movements 189

61. Miniature Landscape 190

62. Color Palettes 192

63. Juicing 195

64. Arrangement on the Water 197

65. Lighting 199

66. De-familiarize 201

67. Forrest Net or Mandala 203

68. Three Dimensions 206

69. Connecting 206

70. Cleaning Up 209

71. Archaeological Field 211

72. Forest Art 212

73. My Barefoot Path 214

74. Coloring Bark Beetle Branches 216

75. Nature Concerts 218

9. Contemplative Exercises

76. Contemplations in Nature   221

77. Nature Experiences   226

78. Sunset or Sunrise, Twilight and Night   228

79. Fire   231

80. Small World   234

81. Water   235

82. Bridge Exercise   237

83. Underneath Trees   238

84. Seasons   240

Acknowledgments

Michael Huppertz

I wish to thank my colleagues from the "AG Achtsamkeit" (i.e. mindfulness work group) in Darmstadt. Without your love for experimentation, your idealism, and your friendship this book would not have been possible. I would also like to thank the attendants of our group sessions and workshops for skepticism, criticism, feedback, and suggestions.

Verena Schatanek

I wish to thank my husband Marcel who was always a critical and curious conversational partner and reviewed my work. I wish to thank Barbara Gugerli for her invigorating feedback. I also thank my colleague Rita Schneider for our shared experiences of mindfulness in nature. Finally, I wish to thank the entire team of the Nature Schools of the Office of Parks and Open Spaces in Zurich for their constructive and daily advice while "mindfully experimenting."

We both wish to thank our publisher, Dr. Stephan Dietrich, for his trust in this topic and the smooth cooperation.

In this text we switch between male and female designations. The opposite gender is always meant as well.

Of course it is of no use to direct our steps to the woods, if they do not carry us thither. I am alarmed when it happens that I have walked a mile into the woods bodily, without getting there in spirit. In my afternoon walk I would fain forget all my morning occupations and my obligations to Society. But it sometimes happens that I cannot easily shake off the village. The thought of some work will run in my head and I am not where my body is – I am out of my senses. In my walks I would fain return to my senses. What business have I in the woods, if I am thinking of something out of the woods?
(Thoreau, n.d. [1851], p. 11)

I think that the man of science makes this mistake, and the mass of mankind along with him: that you should coolly give your chief attention to the phenomenon which excites you as something independent on you, and not as it is related to you. The important fact is its effect on me...The philosopher for whom rainbows, etc. can be explained way never saw them. With regard to such objects, I find that it is not they themselves (with which the men of science deal) that concern me; the point of interest is somewhere between me and them (i.e. the objects). (Thoreau, 2009 [1857], p. 475-476)

My life and the world´s life are deeply intertwined; when I wake up one morning to find that a week-long illness has subsided and that my strength has returned, the world, when I step outside, fairly sparkles with energy and activity: swallow are swooping by in vivid flight; waves of heat rise from the newly paved road smelling strongly of tar; the old red barn across the field juts into the sky at an intense angle. Likewise, when a haze descends upon the valley in which I dwell, it descends upon my awareness as well, muddling my thoughts, making my muscles yearn for sleep. The world and I reciprocate one another. The landscape as I directly experience it is hardly a determinate object; it is an ambiguous realm that responds to my emotions and call forth feelings from me in turn." (Abram 1996, p. 33)

Introduction

Mindfulness is easiest in nature and nature is reliant on the mindfulness of humans. Mindfulness is the art to be in the present, in alert contact with the surroundings, and with oneself without pursuing any further purpose. It is the art of just being there. This attitude allows us to contemplate nature in peace and to explore its effect on us without any effort, while being open to new experiences, and not pursuing any purpose. The more we let nature affect us, the more mindful we become. But the more mindful we move in nature, the more differentiated we will experience it.

The connection between many of our spontaneous nature experiences and the attitude of mindfulness is so close that it can be asked if it is even worth, or rather disrupting, to speak of "mindfulness" and even write a workbook on the topic. We provide our book because we have made the experience that the conscious adoption of the attitude of mindfulness can be of great help and that this attitude takes practice for most people in our society. This is true in general, but also in nature. It is helpful to consciously adopt the attitude of mindfulness because we gain more influence on our life: we know what we do when and why, and can therefore shape our life accordingly. We can discuss this attitude and its consequences and pass them on. But we can especially contrast the undertow of our daily lives, which often leads in a different direction, with an energetic and patient practice of exercises, as well as a private and social vision.

Many people enjoy being in nature and its effect, but in nature they are first and foremost not *in contact with nature.* In nature they engage in ideas, conversations, picnics, hikes, sports etc. Nature is often just a backdrop for other activities. A specification of the practice of mindfulness in nature is: engage only in nature and what it provokes in you. Our exercises are suggestions on establishing this connection. Everything that goes beyond that (gaining knowledge, feeling comfortable, wanting to experience something, being productive, resting, developing oneself further) plays a secondary role, if at all. We therefore do not present any exercises in this book where nature is just a backdrop. We have – with few exceptions – only chosen exercises that are exclusively or substantially better practicable in nature.

"What does it mean to you to be in nature?"

You can gladly answer this question for yourself, before continuing to read. For this book we posed this question to our colleagues, friends, and the participants of our "mindfulness in nature" groups. When we review the answers and add the findings of environmental psychology a relatively clear and simultaneously many-sided picture is the result, which can be summarized in 17 points:

1. *Distance*: Nature makes it possible to gain "distance from everyday life", "to flee from everyday life during that time."[1] Environmental psychologists speak of "being away" (Kaplan 1989, p. 189) and by this mean having a "conscious distance from everyday life and its requirements and restrictions" (Flade, p. 94).

2. *Carefreeness*: Nature is a "place where worries lessen."

3. *Non-Responsiveness*: "There are no expectations to be met", "while being in nature it is not necessary to be responsive; one does not have to constantly interact and communicate with others, as is often expected in normal everyday life." (Flade, 94)

4. Nature is a place of *tranquility* and of rest ("island of tran-quility in a stressful daily routine", "unburdened tranquility", "doing nothing"). It leads to regeneration and relaxation. This point was named the most in our survey.

5. *Vastness*: In nature one can "enjoy vision and view". "I come to peace,

---

1. All (exemplary) citations in this paragraph stem from our survey if not specified otherwise. We have left the original spelling. Corresponding studies in environmental psychology can be found in Kaplan&Kaplan 1989, Kellert 2002, Flade 2010, Louv 2011 and 2012, and Gebhard 2013. Also see annotation 21.

especially in combination with water and vastness."

6. *Sensuousness*: "I have intense sensual experiences." People marvel at the diversity of nature, its steady alterability, its sensual intensity.

7. *Not having to think*: "Nature helps me (…) to let go of thoughts that are turning in circles." "For me it means to be able to clear my head."

8. *Being able to think well*: "In nature my thoughts are sorted, put to ease, and change to the positive." "My thoughts flow better." In nature it is easier to "let ideas develop".

9. *Gathering strength*: Nature is a "source of strength", a "place of energy and relaxation", and one can "gather strength" in it. Strength is taken from one's own relaxation, but also from the emanation of nature.

10. *Beauty*: "Nature gives me the possibility to concentrate on beautiful and fundamental things." "For me, being in nature means marveling at the beauty of the colors and forms of flowers." One participant spoke of "delight regarding the beauty, diversity, sadness regarding the destruction".

11. *Coherence*: Nature is experienced as "diversity in sensible cooperation", as "meaningful", and as an "idyllic world". Rachel and Stephan Kaplan (1989, p. 193) speak of "compatibility" in this regard, a special resonance between natural spaces and human tendencies. This coherence is a requirement in order for people to view the landscape as a recreational environment.

12. *The mysterious*: "I enjoy exploring and researching unknown landscapes, finding out new things, always being something of a detective. Nature is somehow always new and there are so many mysterious things to discover." A certain amount of manageability seems to be a part of well-being in nature. Studies in environmental

psychology show that people find the landscapes most enjoyable and relaxing that have a certain, but not too high, amount of "mystery": bent and unclear paths, alcoves and valleys that are not visible, mountains behind which things could be hidden. Diversity, complexity, fuzziness, and lack of clarity are positively experienced to a certain point, but too much of it makes a landscape aversive, as it seems menacing (Kaplan 1989, p. 55 et seq.).

13. *Nativeness, reality, existence*: "For me, being in nature means 'being on solid ground', coming out of my head and into reality, into 'the real world', to concentrate on what really matters, on things that really exist." "[In nature] I have the feeling of 'being there'." "For me, being in nature means experiencing the original, being able to grasp the element of being 'without' human interference. For example the sea: the waves come and go, following their rhythm, there is nothing to do."

14. *Connectivity*: "The more I can immerse myself in nature, the more I feel a part of it, the stronger the regeneration effect." "In happy situations I felt at one with it." "Connectivity with the essential, with 'creation' probably, because I find everything in it that makes up life for me: very touching beauty and simultaneously 'cruelty', transience, death and life, amazement/ admiration, together and alone, symbiosis and separation, development."

15. *Comfort*: "To me, nature means: tranquility, source of strength and comfort in regard to our mortality." "Often a distancing and relativizing of that which makes me become narrow in my thoughts, feelings, and actions by connecting it to what is still there and lastly is essential. Thereby freedom, tranquility, serenity, touched, comfort."

16. *Transience and trust in the future*: The reliability that nature will always change in its own rhythm can activate our consciousness for our own mortality, as well as give us trust that there is always a future and a new beginning. (Linden&Grut 2002)

17. *Freedom*: "I enjoy the freedom, the wildness of the landscape", "[being in nature to me means] freedom, island of peace in a stressful everyday life", "a feeling of freedom". Freedom in nature also plays a significant role for children, as it is a "grown-up free" zone (Gebhard, p. 90).

"Does the practice of mindfulness change something about your experience of nature?"

We also posed this question to our friends and acquaintances. The first question was intended for everyone who enjoys being in nature, this second one only for those who – not necessarily in nature – practice mindfulness. Here are many of the answers:

"My heart opens up [in nature] and I feel a lot of energy, and at the same time I feel calm, relaxed. Through the practice of mindfulness this experience has become stronger, takes hold more quickly, and I can even reach it when I have been in a bad mood. This change has come through mindfulness."

"For me, being in nature used to mean a form of setting or a backdrop for outdoor activities like hikes, conversations with friends, functionalized to a sort of enhanced gym. Nice to look at, but alien. Nature was the occasion, but not the main reason. Since practicing mindfulness in nature my relationship has greatly changed. I have become slower. I notice myself much more IN nature. I allow myself to stop and to regard it with sufficient time and open senses. It is how it is and it is not there for me. That means: the respect has also grown."

"Thanks to mindfulness, all my senses are open and I notice (I can go through nature pretty well and not notice any of it and let my thoughts turn in circles). Therefore, always come back to mindfulness."

"Yes! Nature is experienced much more consciously, I find things that I otherwise would not have noticed, the senses become more honed – the exercises I learned are very helpful."

"Mindfulness helps me not to become lost in unwanted troubling thoughts, to get out of mulling things over, and to consciously and much more intensely turn my attention to things, animals, plants, colors, smells and sounds, life, and the here and now."

"Yes! I am much more astute, I notice more, and therefore have the impression that nature influences me more, I feel more connected."

"The practice of mindfulness leads to diverse experiences. Smelling, tasting, feeling, and looking become more intense, I become slower. I do not project my feelings on nature as much and instead looking, feeling, tasting...create – in a dialogue so to speak – new experiences and emotions, sometimes insights as well."

"The practice of mindfulness helps with 'recognizing' what is there and thusly making the experience more 'intense'."

"The aspect of mindfulness has made my experience of nature more deep and intense, for example to use all senses to experience nature and to regard nature in more facets ('broader'). Through the practice of mindfulness in nature it has become much more clear to me that nature has more to do with our everyday life and our life experiences, and that much of what we experience in life is already present in nature."

"Through mindfulness I find that behind the foreground and the obvious there are more exciting dimensions and worlds to be experienced."

The practice of mindfulness seems to enhance and decelerate being in nature, to bring nature out of the background and into the foreground of perception, and to make a more direct and free contact with nature possible. Nature appears more diverse and sensual, and through this harmony participants feel more diverse and sensual themselves. Nature appears more important and the workshop participants seem to more intently trace what nature moves inside of them.

Who is this book for?

This book is for each individual who wishes to consciously practice mindfulness in nature, as well as for pedagogues, counselors, and psychotherapists who wish to start such groups of their own or incorporate individual exercises into their work.

Most exercises do not have any special requirements, so a garden or a corner of a park can be sufficient. Some require a certain environment (water, hills, darkness etc.). General recommendations for the practice of exercises in nature can be found in chapter three. There we also concern ourselves with the question of the practice of mindfulness in nature with children. The exercises that are especially suited for children are marked accordingly in chapter four.

We have also written this book for people who are interested in theoretical backgrounds, terms, and concepts. The last four chapters are for readers who not only wish to use the book in practice, but also to inform themselves on the theoretical problems of the research fields involved and to understand the theoretical foundation of the book. We drew up these chapters separately, because our competencies and the work was divided up very differently. Different responsibilities resulted out of this. Of course we also discussed these chapters, revised, and adjusted them together.

Is mindfulness a fad?

Mindfulness is not a new concept. It can be found in different aspects in many spiritual and philosophical traditions. Buddhism and the Humanist tradition, whose understanding of mindfulness goes back to the life reform movement at the beginning of the 20th century, are exemplary in the history of mindfulness, because mindfulness was explicitly developed as a way of practice in these traditions. More recent concepts of mindfulness have developed in the past 30 years and are founded mainly in Asian – especially Buddhist – traditions of mindfulness. These have a tendency towards inner mindfulness, sometimes also towards spiritualization, and work with rigid and often difficult exercise instructions (longer static exercises). The mindful confrontation with uncomfortable experiences and with the fathomless aspects of life (meditation on transience, loss, death etc.) is a major contribution of Buddhism to the concept of mindfulness. The western Mindfulness traditions – Jewish and Christian traditions, Gindler-Jacoby-Work, sensory awareness training, the practice of mindfulness in nature pedagogics, person-centered therapy and others – understand themselves as a more experimental form of contact with situations, things, people, and oneself. Their approach is individual and experimental and they prefer an eventful and body-friendly approach.[2] In regard to mindfulness, we believe that both traditions can be brought together to a plentiful, consistent, and broad in its practice concept of mindfulness.[3]

"Mindfulness" is currently a popular subject – so popular that it is making itself unpopular. Some cannot hear any more of it and some still have not heard of it. It is spreading among therapists and counselors, in clinics, doctor's offices and information centers, in magazines, on TV, the internet, etc. This popularity has something to do with a more manageable presentation of the subject currently, as well as good marketing. But that would hardly be successful, if the idea and practice of mindfulness did not answer to current social developments and challenges that may be as old as the industrial era, but have increased significantly, especially in the past few decades: pressure to perform, acceleration, fleetingness, alienation, addiction. Provided that survival and the protection of prosperity came first in the past – and that was the case for most people in the mainly catastrophic 20th century – and that it still comes first today – and this remains true for most of humanity - , mindfulness is not a subject for the masses. But when safety and prosperity become somewhat guaranteed, the consumption that is needed to maintain this accomplishment of civilization becomes clear. Mainly human and ecological resources are consumed. This consumption is not a law of nature, instead it is the result of economic principles that put abstract economic growth and the increase of wealth before collective goods and the orientation towards nature, health, or justice.

Many people feel that life rushes past them, are constantly tired, suffer from fears, as well as psychosomatic ailments, and the feeling of a pointless restlessness or a restless pointlessness. They are hurt by the same mechanisms that also lead to the ruthless exploitation of natural resources.

2. Huppertz 2011, p. 11 et seq.
3. Huppertz 2009, 2011, Huppertz et al. 2013.

Therefore, the interest in mindfulness and an ecological orientation are born allies and go hand in hand in the consciousness of many people. In the 19th century, authors such as Henry David Thoreau, who we gladly cite repeatedly in this book, already had a sense of the tight connection between the practice of mindfulness and human, as well as environmental, rights. In chapter twelve, on the importance of mindfulness for nature ethics, which is also always a human ethic, we explore this relationship in more depth.

What are the limitations and difficulties of mindfulness in nature?

Mindfulness, as many fundamental discoveries, is a very easy concept that we find in many interesting variations in different teachings and spiritual traditions. The basic principle of mindfulness is easy to explain and understand. Something simpler than just being there is hard to find or fathom in life. Mindfulness only becomes difficult in itself if we do not think it through consistently. This happens when we needlessly limit it (for example to our "inner processes" – thoughts, bodily feelings etc.) or when we only suggest difficult exercises like sitting still for a long time, long focuses for example on breathing, or complicated motion sequences. It also becomes difficult if we force heroic and questionable goals on it, such as not thinking or mystical expectations (see chapter 13). The practice of mindfulness in nature is especially suited for keeping things grounded. In nature it becomes clear how important it is that mindfulness is directed towards the outside *and* the inside *and* the connection that we have and create with nature. That is not harder, but easier, as we do not need to mask anything this way and can hold on to what we have always experienced – the way we experience it.

If the simple elementary stance of mindfulness still is not easy to practice and especially difficult to realize in everyday life, then not because it is complicated in itself, but because the social and personal contexts are complicated in which it is to be realized. The social head wind is considerable in terms of lack of time, excessive demands, acceleration, and stimulus satiation. Mindfulness does not require much, but it does require a little time. But there are also personal obstacles: an insufficient or false under-standing of mindfulness, lack of motivation, impatience, and the tendency to make an effort (see chapter 3). Those who experience nature as an environment in which they feel comfortable, can let their minds wander, or pursue certain activities, will find it strange if they are asked to, for example, focus their attention on a 15x15" piece of ground. But nature luckily is inviting. Mindfulness exercises create a win-win situation – nature experiences help the practice of mindfulness and the practice of mindfulness helps nature experiences. Our collaboration began from this intuition, when we met by chance some years ago in the wonderful landscape of the English Lake District and told each other of our completely different work experiences.[4] This book is full of recommendations to check this intuition.

Being mindful in nature

The effect of nature depends – though not exclusively – upon how we encounter it. Most approaches to nature have little or nothing to do with mindfulness because we follow a purpose with them. We want to use nature for food, the production of energy, relaxation, well-being, self-discovery, or self-improvement. Mindfulness in nature can lead to relaxation, rest, development, but we do not follow such goals while we are mindful in nature. We just want to be in nature and see what happens in nature and with us. This apparent paradox is central to the practice of mindfulness (see chapter 1). Part of the practice of mindfulness is noticing how we experience nature, what it provokes in us, how it affects us, and how we are in nature at this moment. We cannot directly experience nature "how it is". Our perceptions are shaped by our practices and our cultural and personal interpretations. In cooperation with the environment they form what we call "perception". Nature, with its specified properties, encounters our biological, personal, and social dispositions in different ways. "If perception is the sensual being in an environment, then the perceiving person does not only determine from a quasi outer world position what is happening in his

---

4. We would like to thank Liz and Tim Melling at this point, the founders and managers of the "nab cottage", a language school and a place of understanding and inspiration.

environment, he moreover is affectively concerned by the state of his environment and will become aware of a certain composition of the environment in his sensitivities." (Böhme 1989, p. 10) Despite these cultural and personal biographic imprints, our perceptions are not necessarily symbolic or metaphoric phenomenons. If we handle a spade or listen to a bird we do this with our practical and sensual skills. But we do not first represent our environment in ourselves in order to perceive it in ourselves. A perception and an activity are firstly interactions.[5]

The meaning of natural phenomena can be different every day and every minute. It depends on the mood, the expectations, and the fantasies that we face them with, as well as on how they reveal themselves. The attitude of mindfulness allows these changes and does without guidelines or limitations. Mindfulness is *a* form of interaction with nature. Of course it is not always appropriate, as often commitment and change are needed. Mindfulness is only an adequate attitude if we do not wish to or are unable to change a situation. But then it is not primarily interested in beautiful, pleasant, or harmonic nature experiences. It is certainly pleasing if nature shows us its kind face, but mindfulness is also directed towards the aspects of reality and life that we like to avoid: transience, suffering, disgust, ugliness, terror, want, death, eat or be eaten, cruelty, catastrophes. While in the attitude of mindfulness we do not avoid these experiences, inter-

---

5. Böhme 1995, Abram 2012 [1996], Rehman-Stutter 1998, Gallagher 2005, Gallagher&Zahavi 2008, on tradition and discussion: Fingerhut et al. 2013. Clearly babies already interact without needing symbolic representations. Humans interact from the beginning and are not primarily narcissistic. The priority of being in the world has long been known in philosophy (Husserl, Heidegger, Merleau-Ponty, Wittgenstein, Polanyi, Schmitz, just to name a few influential authors). Children, as do adults, develop psychomotor and interactive schemas that are part of scenes. The handling of things is based upon direct harmonization, just as communication and empathy are. Sensual and atmospheric experiences, bodily feeling and moving in nature are essentially not symbolic activities. In nature experiences symbolic meanings play an important role, but they build on interactive experiences (Lakoff& Johnson 2014 [1980]). Gebhard (2005, 2013 [1994]), who deals with this topic at length in reference to the perception of nature, is of a different opinion. He includes phenomenological and developmental psychological theories, but remains connected to traditional psychoanalytical conceptions of permanent and essential symbolizing (2005, p. 148 et seq., 2013, p. 28 et seq.). Gebhard makes it clear that despite all "feelings of relation (…) we do have a clear feeling that we are not one with it" (Gebhard 2013, p. 27). But he explains this feeling through the symbolic activity of humans and an inner reproduction of the outside world.

pretations, evaluations, and reactions, but we also do not reinforce or hold on to them, for example by fighting against them.

While in the attitude of mindfulness we take time to explore the different aspects of being in nature. We speak of "inner", "outer", and "relational" mindfulness (see chapter 1). It is possible to focus the "inner" processes (bodily feelings and mental processes like thoughts, memories, fantasies), or the objective/trans-subjective aspects (that which influences us, generally accessible reality), or the relational happenings (interaction, contact, communication) more intently. Ideally, we observe all three dimensions by letting our attention circulate between these aspects. When we climb a hill or come into contact with an animal we adapt our behavior and observe what is approaching, how we react, and how the contact develops.

We present and explain 84 exercises in nature in this book. In these nature-oriented exercises, nature is a part of mindful encounters and the result of mindful approaches to nature: nature creates sensuality, animates explorations, arrangements, existential considerations, and spiritual experiences. We dedicated chapters 4 and 9 to these approaches to nature. Our book shows how to open oneself to these possibilities of nature experiences.

The natural philosophy background

When we critically ask what "mindfulness", "nature", and "mindfulness in nature" are we come to the same philosophical questions as when we ask which "nature pedagogy", "practice of mindfulness", or "psychotherapy" we represent. Philosophy searches, among other things, for the meaning of terms and concepts. In the case of nature pedagogy: which idea of man is behind each concept? How is the relationship between nature and culture in humans regarded? How natural is nature? How is the relationship between humans and nature seen? Which goals are aspired to? What can realistically be expected from nature pedagogy?

We are concerned with "nature experiences" in this book and not with influences of nature that do not follow the path of subjective experience (such as the percentage of iodine in the air, the production of vitamin D, the effect of officinal plants etc.). Nature experiences are based on interactions between humans and nature. The interactive perspective of our relationship with nature has been formulated differently in recent years.[6] It is rooted in philosophical traditions that understand humans as beings that are in the world and who can only be understood by their relationships to nature and contemporaries.[7]

This natural philosophical position is not self-evident. There are two classic alternatives that both, though in different ways, abstract from this interactivity: the first position views all nature experiences as constructs of a subject, or rather society (of a social subject). In this interpretation, descriptions of landscapes such as "cheerful" or "majestic" and themes like "transience" or "security" are affixed by humans and society with neutral and in itself meaningless nature. This position can be called "radically contructivist". Yet it is unable to explain *why* we interpret nature this way and not another. It is clear that the composition of nature does not offer a definitive answer to our life in nature, but that it does not have a share in it seems improbable. Even social constructivist authors find that it plays a role in perception: "Nobody will deny that we perceive the Matterhorn aesthetically differently than a blooming mountain meadow. It is the diversity in appearance of outer nature which constitute its abundance and aesthetic allure" (Groh&Groh 1996, p. 131-132). They also accept "that it is not our subjective approach that first constitutes the object of experience" (Groh&Groh 1996, p. 132). However, they do not pursue the question of how this could occur further. Historic, environmental psychological, and phenomenological examinations, which also evaluate the objective

6. Böhme 1989, 1997, Rehmann-Stutter 1998, Großheim 1999, Mutschler 2002, Gebhard 2013.
7. Pragmatism, interactionism, phenomenology, existential philosophy, philosophy of dialogue (M. Buber), systems theory, as well as developments within the past few decades in the field of socialization research, of psychoanalysis, and cognitive science. A broad compilation of these traditions is offered by Gergen 2009, although it is incomplete and sadly also the content is excessively portrayed.

conditions of the impressions and atmospheres of nature, can help. It is also about how nature changes historically, the "sociality of natural conditions, or more precisely of nature itself" (G. Böhme 2005, p. 10).

The second position does not view the meaning of nature as reliant on subjects. Nature *is* beautiful, harmonious, diverse, and good, but also wild and chaotic. From this perspective all meaning is already decided in nature, "matter and mind" are "married" by "analogy" (Emerson 2003 [1836], p. 55). "A life in harmony with Nature, the love of truth and of virtue, will purge the eyes to understand her text. By degrees we may come to know the primitive sense of the permanent objects of nature, so that the world shall be to us an open book, and every form significant of its hidden life and final cause" (ibid., p. 54-55). This way, "the universe" becomes "transparent" and "the light of higher laws shines through it" (ibid., p. 46). Spiritual principles govern nature. "There seems to be a necessity in the spirit to reveal itself in material forms" (ibid., p. 46). Even morality can already be found in nature. "The axioms of physics translate the laws of ethics: 'The whole is greater than its part'." (ibid., p. 53)[8] This position is fruitful insofar that it can describe the meaning of nature for humans in many pictures. That is what makes Ralph Waldo Emerson's *Nature* or John Muir's descriptions powerful texts. But meaning here lies solely on the side of nature, or rather the "primal reason" (Emerson 2003 [1836], p. 52), or the "Original Cause" (ibid., p. 49).

This could be considered a purely historic position, as Ralph Waldo Emerson published it in 1836. It was not just very influential, but still remains current. "The image of the neural net conveys a major systems insight: mind is not separate from nature; it is in nature. However primitive, the mind pervades the natural world as the subjective dimension within every open system, says systems philosopher Ervin Laszlo. It is ubiquitous in the circuits of information, or feedback loops, guiding every relationship,

---

8. "All things are moral; and in their boundless changes have an unceasing reference to spiritual nature. Therefore is nature glorious with form, color, and motion; that every globe in the remotest heaven, every chemical change from the rudest crystal up to the laws of life, every change of vegetation from the first principle of growth in the eye of a leaf, to the tropical rainforest and the antediluvian coal-mine, every animal function from the sponge up to Hercules, shall hint or thunder to man the laws of right and wrong, and echo the Ten Commandments." (Emerson 2003, [1836], p. 58).

says Gregory Bateson," (Macy&Brown 1988, p. 43). The context has shifted with this citation and is no longer Christian as with Emerson, but Buddhist. There was and is little room in this perspective for genuine human and cultural creativity and freedom, for the complexity of nature ethical problems, or a spirituality that thrives on diversity. A detailed criticism of this thesis on identity can be found in chapters 7 and 8. In this book we will attempt to think of the relationship between humans and nature in terms of relation, not omnipotent subjectivity or nature. When we deal with the nature ethical importance of mindfulness in chapter 7 and follow the spiritual search in chapter 8 we will encounter both extremes of being uninvolved in and of being one with nature again and deal with them in more depth. We will take a position between the extremes of the sameness of humans and nature and their complete alienation. We are of the opinion, as many of the authors we cite, that the relationship between humans and nature can be described as a plurality of relations and forms of interaction.

Awareness for the relative autonomy of culture and the individual are needed to understand the socio-historical and individual dimensions of being in nature. Cultural worlds develop from the interactions of humans with each other and with nature, which cannot be described in appropriate terms for nature: language, norms, technology, institutions, reason, inter-subjective understanding, art, spirituality. The relative freedom of humans is based on these accomplishments. Culture creates space in contrast to the expectations of our inner and outer nature. This space allows us to not only continually formulate new goals, but to also deal with reality and nature without having to fight for our survival. It makes the creativity of art, play, mindfulness, and spiritual practices possible. With such activities we have freed ourselves of direct necessities for survival. The practice of mindfulness is itself rich in cultural requirements and an especially mature attitude, if one understands maturity as the ability to refrain from own interests and to take responsibility for others and other things. Without culture there is no term for "nature" and without that no care for nature and human rights, which are always also justified with human instinctiveness. Only through the recognition of one's own instinctiveness and dependence, by consciously recognizing the conditions of one's own existence and thereby inner and outer nature, do humans win their "sovereignty" (G. Böhme 1985, p. 287). We are not one with nature and due to that we can be enriched, inspired, and sometimes even healed by our encounters with it.

Mindfulness is often understood as having to pull one's own tuft out of the swamp. That is known to be difficult, but is unnecessary. Mindfulness in nature shows us another way. We can also take the help of reality, encounters with other people, with art, or with nature. We can use the effectiveness of reality to live a more animated, healthier, and perhaps spiritual life. We want to show in this book, how mindfulness can find its way through the reality of nature. We let nature be how it is and let ourselves be who we are in it. But we move in it, take in its effects, and *let* the effects take hold: its emanation, its atmosphere, its personal and existential meanings. All of these effects are not in nature itself, but the result of our encounters, resonance, and openness with it. To deal with nature more or less mindful is our responsibility – towards nature and ourselves. Mindfulness in nature means to engage it in different ways, to let ourselves be touched, and to respect and protect its otherness. Devotion is always a part of mindfulness, as this is the only way an encounter is possible and can enrich nature. If we can show how this is possible through the practice of mindfulness, then this book might be able to contribute to a better understanding of the attitude of mindfulness.

Those only following a practical interest can read the fundamentals (chapters 1-3) and use the exercise portion (chapter 4-9). They work without the following chapters 10-13. We hope to be able to show the most important roots and ramifications of "mindfulness in nature" with the chapters on nature pedagogy, well-being, spiritual health, nature ethics, and the spiritual search in nature. In these chapters, we reconstruct the efforts for mindful nature experiences in nature pedagogy so far, as well as in psychotherapy and counseling, while looking for possible developments. We try to show the benefits of mindfulness for individuals, our culture, our spiritual development, and nature. On the following pages of this introduction, we give a short overview of the third part of this book.

Mindfulness in nature pedagogy

Elements of mindful approaches to nature can be found time and time again in the history of nature pedagogy, or rather of "nature-oriented environmental education". After long discussions, we decided to use the term "nature pedagogy" for this book, as it is the most commonly used and the term "nature-oriented environmental education" is impractical, as well as only being commonly used in Switzerland. But this does not mean that nature pedagogy is only for children. "Nature pedagogy" is currently applied to adults more and more, in correspondence to the trend to "lifelong learning". In this book, we understand "nature pedagogy" as the plurality of nature-oriented educational endeavors for children and adults. Elements of mindfulness, which certainly exist in nature pedagogy, are not usually carefully worked out and differentiated from other, for example more knowledge transfer oriented, material. This mindful access to nature has not been defined as an approach of its own so far.

Nature pedagogy, an engaged discipline with different schools of thought, wishes to animate children and adults to be more mindful of the natural environment. Working with mindfulness can strengthen this educational work, by contrasting the disappearance of senses and making further forms of experience possible. One of the advantages of mindfulness is its openness to new experiences, perspectives on nature, and all personal reactions. Its goal of strengthening environmental awareness can only be reached in its typical indirect way, but perhaps therefore more effectively. Approaching nature in different ways and offering this possibility to children as well is being demanded more and more from modern nature pedagogy. Richard Louv suggests that children should just be in nature again and move and act freely: running, climbing, fishing, forming, meandering (or "strielen" as they say in Switzerland), playing, hiding, looking, plucking, laughing, and being curious – without fear, reverent distance, and too much regard for nature. This commitment is central to many environmental activists and nature pedagogues and to us as well. Ulrich Gebhard formulates this concern as follows:

"Moreover, I underline the psychological value of outer nature for the inner nature of humans: (…) experience-oriented nature pedagogy relies on the connection of inner and outer, subject and object, self and world insofar, as a change in the subject's treatment of nature is hoped to be reached through these nature experiences." (Gebhard 2005, p. 145)

70 years ago, a pioneer of environmental protection said:

"Wilderness areas are first of all series of sanctuaries for the primitive arts of wilderness travel, especially canoeing and packing. I suppose some will wish to debate whether it is important to keep these primitive arts alive. I shall not debate it. Either you know it in your bones or you are very, very old." (Leopold 1949, p. 193)

We do not suggest to saddle a horse, but we do suggest to contact nature and other lifeforms directly with movement, the senses, exploring, play, forming, or regarding. This does not replace the knowledge of ecological processes and problems, but it does compliment this knowledge through personal and often very emotional experiences closer to nature. It is only probable that nature will find enough supporters if more people continue to encounter nature in a direct sensual-practical, diverse, and emotional way and make it to a major part of their life.

The importance of mindfulness for quality of life and spiritual health

No one will deny that nature can heal in climatic, pharmaceutical, or physiological ways. But in this chapter we explain how nature *experiences* can improve quality of life and maintain or improve health. In this chapter – after a short review of the importance of nature in psychiatry, psychotherapy, and rehabilitation – we introduce different forms of therapy and, in an exemplary form, individual projects that are connected to mindfulness.

The importance of mindfulness for nature ethics

Mindfulness has ethical potential. This is shown, when we describe the idea of not judging as a part of mindfulness in more detail (see chapter 1). Developed through the attitude of mindfulness, a careful and always preliminary form of judgment is the result, which leads to the appreciation of people, things, and nature for themselves, and not due to functionality. We will address current nature ethical discussions in chapter 12 and present the possible contribution of the concept of mindfulness.

Mindfulness and the spiritual search in nature

Living in culture and self-reflection puts us in a state of worry, planning, anticipation, learning from past mistakes, and latent or manifest fear of death. The attitude of mindfulness allows us to distance ourselves from these demands and accompanying perceptions and thought patterns, even from the fear of death. People usually require an intense and extended practice of mindfulness to replace familiar existential habits like orientation along needs, wishes, worries, and actions, as well as to finally overcome fear in everyday life and replace it with focusing on the present, vitality, openness, and presence. This practice is not independent from a good conditions. Spending time mindfully in nature is especially good. Nature is alien and related to us at the same time. It challenges and carries us, lifts and roots us, shows us boundaries and unforeseen possibilities. Nature allows a distance to our familiar world and welcomes us, due to its special features, into a world where we can experience simplicity, connectivity, relaxation, trust, thankfulness, and happiness.

In chapter 13 we wish to show how the experience of the otherness of nature and the connection with nature can lead to the transcendence of familiar conditions of experience. The spiritual potential of nature is also easier to understand if it is understood as a possible specific correlation between the characteristics of nature and an equivalent orientation of the person who is searching. Spiritual experiences in nature need an interpretation or articulation. We deal with a number of significant interpretations in this chapter.

As exciting as all these questions are – mindfulness in nature is primarily a learnable practice. This is an immeasurable advantage in regard to education and appeals.

Part 1 | Fundamentals

1. | The Attitude of Mindfulness

1.1. Definition

Mindfulness is the art of being. Imagine you are awake, have energy and could do something, at least plan or think, but instead decide to just be there – in contact with the environment, maybe with other people, and yourself. You are ready to receive, open yourself to what is currently happening, and let it affect you. You do not change anything, but allow change to take place.

If you do not wish to change anything it also means that you let what is currently transpiring happen, without reinforcing, holding on to, or avoiding it. You do not fight anything either, as it would only be another form of holding on to something. This approach of letting things happen is often referred to as "acceptance". This term is useful and emphasizes a certain resolution, but should not be confused with approval (which is sadly implied by the literal meaning of accepting something).

If you are not pursuing any goal *in* mindfulness it is not necessary or wise to leave the present. You stay in the here and now. *In* the attitude of mindfulness you are not pursuing any goals, yet *with* mindfulness you might be under certain circumstances.

Why is this simple presence beyond idleness and activity an art? Because our habits and the habits of society make mindfulness difficult. We are used and often forced to want to accomplish something: fun, rest, relaxation, property, recognition, awareness, self-optimization etc. The proposal is: let all these wishes, intentions, and impulses be. Opt for not getting caught up in, "signing", holding on to, and reinforcing them. Stick to observing what is currently happening and open yourself to further experiences. The and-exercises will help you with that (see chapter 4, p.

71).

Thus, mindfulness is:

- conscious
- unintentional
- present
- open and experimental
- accepting (letting things happen)

Let us regard these individual attributes more closely.

Conscious

"Conscious" initially means that we consciously take the attitude of mindfulness, at least until it has not become a habit of its own. We wish to be mindful and to refer to something mindfully by being mindful. We dedicate ourselves as much as possible to the subject of mindfulness. When we begin with this practice we should usually contemplate the special features of this attitude, especially the unfamiliar aspects of being in the present and without intentions.

In order to be able to consciously take in and maintain the attitude of mindfulness, as well as observe the present in a differentiated way, it is necessary to be "awake". Therefore "conscious" also means "awake". Your body tension should be sufficient to stay awake. However, more tension is not needed. This alertness differentiates mindfulness from relaxation exercises, where a blurred conscious is welcome as long as it leads to relaxation. In contrast, being mindful means to perceive and feel in a more differentiated way. A state of trance, which can be helpful for dreams and fantasies, is also unsuitable for mindfulness. This differentiates the practice of mindfulness from the practice of imagination exercises and imagery programs. When in the attitude of mindfulness only what is and not what could be, or could be imagined, is of interest. Mindfulness should be as close to everyday life as possible. A normal degree of alertness is optimal for this reason as well.

Unintentional

This is an aspect of mindfulness that sometimes causes problems. Those who practice mindfulness do not wish to accomplish anything while *in* this attitude (first-person perspective), not relaxation, comfort, self-understanding, wisdom, or spiritual experience. Mindfulness is also not interested in analyses – neither of the environment or of oneself -, as this would also be a purposeful and strenuous activity. Such goals can certainly be connected with mindfulness (third-person perspective). However, mindfulness does not reach such goals directly. Instead, they are reached through the detour of being without intentions. So, before an exercise, we can definitely make it clear to ourselves why we begin with this practice – and insofar there is an intention in regard to mindfulness -, but when we practice it we should treat these goals like every other thought that leads us out of the present. We are aware of it and return to what is currently happening with an "and", for example the wind that we feel on our skin or walking. This is not unusual, because when we, for example, drive our car we are not focused on the destination the entire time and instead look at the landscape, have a conversation etc.

But mindfulness alone would, as every attitude, be left hanging in the air if it was not grounded in a situation or activity. It brings its own perspectives, concerns, and emotions into our life, but is reliant on practices to update itself.[9] But how should it remain unintentional if we engage in such activities? Of course there are intentions behind exploring, forming, and even sensual feeling, for example when we look what is underneath a stone, lay stones on top of each other, or close our eyes in order to be able to hear better. Heinrich Jacoby already described the charged relationship between

9. It is no different with courage, a sense of justice, or aesthetic attitudes (MacIntyre 1987).

effort and "relaxed readiness to receive" (Jacoby 2004 [1945], p. 54), which is his term for mindfulness:

"The short-sighted eye and the hard of hearing ear are only receiving organs so that in such cases "antenna-like" behavior remains the only appropriate one. (…) Gradually they will notice how inappropriately the civilized person behaves when using his sensory organs. He smells flowers, for example, as if their smell did not rise to the nose on its own! (…) [Sister W.:] Is it not so that when someone says something smells good that we direct our attention toward it and feel more? [H. Jacoby:] It would need to be examined what is meant by attention, what thereby happens in us, and how this guiding can occur in the most expedient way. We also usually exert ourselves in order to be attentive. What would happen if someone made us attentive: 'Do you smell how wonderful the lilac smells?' In any case, one would not have to do anything; one would only have to try to be me more present and quiet, meaning letting things that occupy oneself to subside and withdraw into the background. We must act in a way that that which has already struck us can become consciously feelable." (Jacoby 2004 [1945], p. 40-41, own translation, GZ)

In this citation, Jacoby certainly neglects the active side of perception, but he makes us aware that through to much activity and intentionality we miss and weaken the essential aspect of perceiving and feeling: receptivity. When working with mindfulness it is helpful to differentiate between doing something intentionally, which does not require effort and rescinds into the background quickly, and intentionality, which remains in the foreground or always pushes its way to the front. In these cases mindfulness is a balancing act. A good guiding question is: "Is the intentionality of an action still in the service of mindfulness or is it becoming independent from it?"

Present

If we are aimless then there is no reason to leave the present. Intentions lead us into the future or the past (when we learn something from past experiences, compare new experiences, wish to amend something etc.). But what is the present? Usually, a lapse of approximately 3 seconds is felt as present and the spontaneous attention span lasts 8-10 seconds. However, the present in terms of mindfulness does not consist of these short moments. It is not sensible to break an activity, a conversation, a melody, or a movement of clouds in the sky into moments and to move from moment to moment. We could not experience a sunrise this way.

Mindfulness means giving things, people, and yourself time. Time is in things, nature, music, other people, our feelings, and our body. It all consists of processes, rhythms, stability, repetitions, and breaks. A sunrise has its time, a look, a life, sadness, anger, and happiness have their time. Every person moves and feels in their own time. We have our individuality through the time that we are. Time is in the world, in us, and our relationship to the world. If we leave it there it cannot be lost and we cannot lose any time. So it is not about pulverizing time, fighting against the past and future, or lingering in an abstract moment or section of time, but switching to an experience of time that is not about planning, using, and calculating time. It is about being open for the next situation, presence, and willingness, not about worry. The "here and now" is a conscious experience of a different, a qualitative time, not an escape from the time in the moment.[10] The own temporality of mindfulness exists in the constant opening towards the qualitative experience of time. In its consistency of continuous new beginnings lies an experience of *timelessness* and peace. The own temporality and sensuality of the environment are most impressively encountered in nature. Mindfulness entails that sensual processes are favored above symbolic processes (language, pictures, etc.). The use of symbols easily lures us to leave the present; they are a stepping stone to the past or present that must be represented in order to be alert in the present. This does not mean that mindfulness is not compatible with thinking or communicating. Instead, thinking and talking should refer to and enrich the present, not lead away from it. It can be very mindful to observe, speak about, point out things to one another, and to talk about one's own feelings together in nature.

---

10. For the time structure of worry see Heidegger 1979 [1927], for alternatives: Minkovski 1971/72 [1933], Binswanger 1953, Bollnow 1995 [1956], Han 2009, Huppertz 2009, 2013b

Open and Experimental

The present is diverse and always changing. It has many aspects and we can perceive it from different perspectives. It affects people and us differently at various times.

Therefore, we should not hold on to our interpretation of a situation, but be open to it changing. This is known as "deconstruction" (or "defusion") in the practice of mindfulness: our picture of the environment and of ourselves is always an individual and social construction. Nature has a lot to say about this construction though, as it affects us and provides reality. We can question our constructive contribution to what reality is to us at the moment at any time and make ourselves conscious of the fact that it is only a construction with temporary validity. The attitude of mindfulness leads this consciousness to a fundamental tolerance towards other interpretations. We do not wish to be proved right. The openness of mindfulness rules out that we consider some realization – be it our own or alien – as absolute and timeless truth. We can always make new experiences, learn, and develop new interpretations.

The openness of mindfulness invites us to experiment and play with the present situation. It is already an experiment if we just stand still, close our eyes, pick up a stone, and regard it more closely. If we lie on the ground and look at the clouds or crush a herb and smell it. We cannot *do nothing* and therefore it is appropriate in mindfulness to take a look around during a situation and to explore it in various ways. We only drop out of it when we acquire knowledge or wish to change the environment permanently.

Accepting (Letting Things Happen)

If we want, should, or could change something then we should do it. In that case mindfulness is not necessary as an attitude in the foreground, although it may continue its affect in the background. If we do not wish or are not supposed to change something, then acceptance is called for. Acceptance or letting things happen is an essential part of mindfulness. "Acceptance" or "accept" unfortunately has a meaning of benevolent taking in the direct sense of the word and therefore also of at least temporary holding on, and sounds a little too positive. But it has become popular. Acceptance is difficult for many people who are striving for mindfulness. They are struggling with the past or the present, without being able to change it, or are looking for a positive experience through the practice of mindfulness. They want to feel better, have gained insight, changed, improved, and optimized after an exercise. All this and much more leads to exertion and contradicts the aimlessness that is central to the practice of mindfulness. In acceptance we simply answer the present with: "That is how it is."

Of course it is nice if we enjoy ourselves during mindfulness and pleasant exercises are a good introduction. They motivate to practice. The actual challenge and benefit of mindfulness is that it can continue to exist through difficult times. If we are in a crisis, are sad, or angry. When a situation troubles us or is stressful, but we cannot avoid it. When we are confronted by difficult existential experiences such as loneliness, transience, or the fear of death. Especially in such situations, mindfulness can take effect. We do not react with reinforcement, fixation, holding on, tunnel vision, or an exhausting fight against the unchangeable. Instead, we react with a broadening of the horizon, relaxation, and calmness. We regain the freedom to direct our attention, observe a situation more completely, and to feel ourselves extensively.

We return to the present, as many of our problems are related to the past or the future, while the present mostly is harmless, safe, and trustworthy. Mindfulness quasi reinstates the firstborn rights of the present and therefore leads to relativization of problems, to a certain easiness, flexibility, and happiness despite all foreseeable problems. Thereby, problems receive a different frame. Thus, if they are purely of a subjective nature they can therefore disappear. If they do not, we might possibly be reaching the limits of mindfulness.

Acceptance is often connected a demand of "non-judgment". Our experience has shown that this is a delicate point that leads to many misunderstandings and rejections of the concept. We suggest the following perspective: judgments occur spontaneously, are unavoidable, and absolutely fine if they do not cost contact, or precise observation and description. They are important for our priorities, values, and choices of action, thus for our practical and moral orientation in situations (see chapter 12). Many of our emotions such as love, hope, and sadness are not possible without judgment and it is an essential part of these feelings.[11] The attitude of mindfulness is not about observing people and natural phenomena as neutral, elementary, or abstract as possible, and also not about becoming emotionless or unconcerned. We are neither actively changing anything in the attitude of mindfulness, nor anything about our judgment and emotions. We just learn and practice something new, something additional – just like the way we learn a new language. And we assume that this new practice will change our life. When we learn a new language we do not have to forget an old language, but the new language will broaden our horizon. Mindfulness will also reframe our emotions and color them with calmness and rest. It a new attitude towards life with it and thereby leads to a changed resonance and sympathy, but not to neutralization and simplification.

Judgments are problematic, as they can lead to an increased or decreased attention to the assessed, and measure human and non-human by criteria that impair the observation of that which is. I (V.S.) experienced this especially clearly in the ornithologist scene, when we were "hunting" rare species. As often, you could hear: "Oh, that's just a blackbird, sparrow, great tit, or mallard." We quickly continued on and took our attention off this bird that we titled an "everyday bird" and "nothing special". This is why we recommend recognizing judgments and returning to observation or description. The aim of mindfulness is that we do not apply any criteria (or ideals) to people, objects, or ourselves in a situation, and that we do not compare them and instead observe them for what they are right now. Of course things have a function that they fulfill more or less well – for us or

---

11. This is true for all intentional emotions, meaning emotions that refer to an object. Physical sensations and moods can of course also be judged, but they are not intentional in themselves or directed toward objects, and instead are receptive, or rather atmospheric, and therefore not dependent on judgment. See Großheim 1999, Nussbaum 2001, Huppertz 2000, 2009.

among one another. Of course people try to do something the best they can. However, mindfulness parts from these functionalizations and criteria and takes another look. The attitude of mindfulness therefore also directs attention towards that which we would normally reject, despise, or overlook, creating openness for a change to spontaneous contact. These various perceptions can then lead to new judgments and so forth – an endless process. In this way, mindfulness can lead to the observation of intrinsic values. Next to functional values we also know intrinsic values. Something that has an intrinsic value is not precious because it is good for something, meaning it fulfills a function, but because it is what it is. Chapter 12 deals with the ethical significance of mindfulness.

1.2. Dimensions of Mindfulness

The following differentiations have proven themselves in practice. We will repeatedly use them in the commentaries to the exercises. Familiarizing oneself with these terms makes the exercises easier.[12] However, they are especially important for professionals who are contemplating which exercises are appropriate for whom and to whom they might even be harmful. There is a continuum between each of these poles and they are not mutually exclusive.

Focused – Wide Mindfulness in Nature

Focused mindfulness refers to a certain object (natural phenomena, landscapes, creatures, thoughts and emotions caused by nature etc.). In wide mindfulness you observe everything that currently is and what is happening: objects, creatures, thoughts, associations, physical emotions. Wide mindfulness takes in everything that is part of a current situation and does not hold on to anything. Focused mindfulness always requires a certain amount of concentration and can tire more quickly than wide mind-fulness. In wide mindfulness we move like fish in the sea in the present. It is sometimes also called "awareness". An attitude in which one is attentive to all aspects of a situation in nature, but with a certain tension and exertion

---

12. At length hereto Huppertz 2009, 35 et seq.

to be able to observe and react to everything, is closely related to wide mindfulness. It is essential to nature pedagogy and is fittingly called "watchfulness" (Young et al. 2010, passim). Wide mindfulness differs from watchfulness in that it is more receptive and therefore more relaxed. Watchfulness demands the perfection of observation, in order to not overlook distinctive features and changes. It is important in the wilderness and wilderness pedagogy, because there it is important to be able to adequately react in case of an emergency.

The "and-techniques" that we illustrate at the beginning of part 2 are based on the differentiation between focused and wide mindfulness. They are essential to the practice of mindfulness, as they make it possible to remain in the present more easily.

Inner-Relational-Outer Mindfulness in Nature

Outer mindfulness refers to the environment and contemporaries. Inner mindfulness refers to mental incidences (thoughts, inner pictures) or physical sensations. And relational mindfulness refers to the manner in which we interact and are connected to nature and contemporaries.

In nature one can linger, delve into, immerse, and forget oneself in outer mindfulness for a long and ample amount of time. Every passionate naturalist will have likely already experienced this intensely. The own ego and perspective can fade into the background in a wonderfully relaxing way in nature, allowing us to relativize ourselves and our problems. Outer mindfulness can easily be practiced in nature if we take a beginner's perspective, meaning we regard an old tree or animal tracks without a specified concept. We look and observe – as if we had never seen it before. We give our complete attention to the natural phenomenon.

With inner mindfulness we focus thoughts, inner pictures, fantasies, memories, and physical sensations. As we have a privileged approach to these aspects of our lives, a metaphor of the "inner" has developed. Despite all empathy it remains impossible for us to feel the exact same thing as someone else, meaning that nuance or "qualia" ("how it feels to be that way") in that moment. That is what constitutes the singularity of ourselves and our individual perspective. Our mental processes and physical sensations are not intra-subjectively available and measurable in the same was as a tree for example that we refer to together from different perspectives.

In groups and workshops we often meet the following interpretations of mindfulness: "I accomplished being mindful and was completely with myself." "Through these exercises I can reconnect with myself." Or also: "I am in the outer too much. I just can't manage to stay with myself." (Own translation, GZ) Mindfulness clearly reacts to distress. Many people act and react undeviatingly in their everyday life, be it for necessity or out of habit. They do not receive or take the time to let the occurrences affect them, turn inner circles, and then make a decision on whether they wish to react or not. They have the feeling that life is rushing past them, fleeting, meaningless, alien, and weak in its resonance. But obviously, mindfulness brings you closer to yourself, as one takes the time to consciously feel oneself and to notice one's own physical sensations, emotions, moods, and needs. "Being with Yourself" and "Staying with Yourself" is an important part of mindfulness. It is a key to a more conscious life and plays an important role in the prevention and therapy of psychological illnesses. A too strong focusing of oneself however can mean that nature only serves as a backdrop for self-experience, self-discovery, or self-optimization.[13]

Inner mindfulness is always needed so that the participants turn nature and the practice of mindfulness into something of their own, meaning

- they experience the vibrancy and atmospheric aspects of nature
- they realize what a specific nature experience means to them (personally, existentially, spiritually)

---

13. Goldstein 2013.

- they feel alive and committed

- they are able to experience if they are mindful and how it feels

- they are able to take responsibility for the exercise (Is is hurting me? Is it helping me?)

We are *not only* the emotions and the thoughts that are currently predominate. We are also the ones that consciously experience that emotion and are always more than our consciousness currently registers. But without our body and our emotions we are not who we are. It is important that we differentiate between our thoughts and emotions and those of other people, or animals also. Mindfulness is not compatible with the idea of the dissolution oneself into a greater whole (for how it can transpire in trance experiences and meditative practices, see chapter 13). Instead, it aims at a differentiated observation of ourselves and the environment, as well as the connection and difference to our environment and contemporaries. The disregard, renunciation, or dissolution of oneself in favor of a greater whole is therapeutically, morally, and politically dangerous.[14] Only if we feel and experience ourselves (our emotions, needs, resonances to events, thoughts, fantasies etc.) and differ from the environment can we take care of ourselves, as well as take responsibility for ourselves and others. As nice as it is to temporarily lose yourself in nature, a permanent self-forgetfulness in nature makes it impossible to understand its meaning for our life.

Inner mindfulness often offers a good introduction to mindfulness in nature. After all, the participants bring a certain constitution, experience, expectation etc. with them into nature. It is helpful to notice these preconceptions that we approach nature with. But it could also be that case that it is easier to begin with outer mindfulness, so the experience of nature, and to feel oneself in that way. Usually, and especially when we are in nature, the feeling of oneself in contact with the other occurs, with something that we are not and differs from us in essential characteristics. Something that does not think, speak, or talk. Therefore, mindfulness in nature especially means to feel and observe oneself in contact and resonance with this other.

14. Victoria 1997, Huppertz 2009, 2013a, Manstetten 2013, also see chapter 13.

At the same time Mindfulness can also apply to the interactive happening itself. We call this *relational mindfulness.*[15]

Perceptions, thoughts, communication, behavior, and actions are firstly ways to interact with the environment. Emotions have many interactive and intra-subjective aspects and follow complex scenarios that are comprised of typical triggering situations, gestures, facial expressions, as well as physical orientation and behavior. But they are also comprised of interpretations of situations, memories, associations, and physical sensations. Biographically as well as in every current life situation we are initially in contact with our environment and contemporaries. We breath, lie, sit, communicate, hear sounds, experiment with objects etc. This does not change when we close our eyes, think, or dream. On the one hand, fundamental contact with our

15. The terms "relational mindfulness" etc. are shortened, as it must actually be termed "inward mindfulness", "outward mindfulness", and "mindfulness to the relation". But they are common and easy to understand. That is why we kept them. In any case, they only have a pragmatic sense, as this spatial imagery is not too long ranged, see annotation 74. The term "relational mindfulness" can already be found in a different sense in J.I. Surrey (2005).

physical position in a space, temperature sensitivity, breathing etc. remains, and on the other hand the material with which we fantasize, dream, think, and make plans is taken from the contacts that we live and have lived.

We are often not conscious to the fact that we have always been interacting with our environment and fellow humans, because we like to ascribe interactions to a subject in our everyday orientation. In order to clarify room to maneuver, goals, values, and responsibilities it is necessary to perform subject-object separations.[16] But this strict separation partially obstructs the perception of systematic connections as well.[17] In everyday life we often do not take the time to pay attention to many interactions that make our conscious actions possible in the first place: the atmosphere that we create together with our environment and contemporaries that influence our mood, as well as the fine time coordinations that make a conversation or cooperation possible. Mindfulness can lead us to consciously observe these processes and thereby trace the trust that we have always lived.

Mindfulness tends to connect inner, outer, and relational mindfulness. Ideally, it brings inner and outer mindfulness together on the basis of the consciousness of the interactivity of our immediate existence.

16. "Hegel speaks of the power of being able to part and to separate between things and referred to it as 'the negative power of the mind' - a fitting term. Hegel saw the most miraculous strength in the negative power of the mind, the thing that distinguishes humans from all other creatures. The recently popular grievance over the so-called subject-object separation is sentimental and silly, as humans only become humans by being able to face the world that they are a part of" (Löwith 1960, p. 237, own translation, GZ).
17. For aspects of action theory see Jullien 2009.

2. | Mindful Approaches to Nature

2.1. Nature and Approaches to Nature

"What do you understand under the term nature?" "Nature is that which is not created, essentially formed, or influenced by humans." Most of our friends and acquaintances answered in this or a similar way when we asked them about their understanding of nature.[18] However, in its application to reality this understanding of nature becomes very fuzzy. We never encounter nature as something uninfluenced by humans. If we think of the consequences of human actions for the atmosphere and those of the atmospheric change for the entire planet, than nature is never pure wilderness. What we usually call nature in everyday life is a visible part of civilization: timber, meadows, parks, pets, and Antarctica as well. On the other hand, culture and technology are natural to a certain degree – sources of energy or resources of any kind in bridges, oil paintings, semiconductors etc. Therefore, it cannot be claimed that something exists that is completely natural or that everything can be divided into natural and unnatural, even if this misunderstanding is suggested by the noun "nature". But this line of argumentation does not exclude that something can be more or less natural and that we can define this quality. In order to preserve this idea of nature untouched by civilization, the term "wilderness" has been vernacularized. "The term 'wilderness' builds on this foundation of an unclear dif-ferentiation between cultural and natural phenomena. It makes a further differentiation possible by discerning between controlled and changed, as well as untouched nature" (Niebrügge 2007, p. 3, own translation, GZ). The author suggests (on the basis of R.F. Nash) a relative term of wilderness that "can be placed on a bipolar spectrum between imagined pure wilderness on the one side, and that of pure civilization on the other." (Niebrügge 2007, p. 22). But if we proceed in this manner the terms "nature" and "wilderness" primarily live on their differentiation from human culture. We do not seem to reach autonomous terms for nature and wilderness this way. How nature

---

18. We received this answer when we insisted that no examples, and instead an actual definition of the term, be given. Without this limitation the answers were more descriptive and directed toward living nature. Children also answered with examples and descriptions, and favored mentioning creatures.

can more precisely be determined is evidently reliant on how it appears to us and how we approach it, as well as what we want or do not want from it, and how we deal with it. In the course of history numerous relationships with nature were developed by various cultures, in which these cultures were just as involved as nature itself. Humans wish to conquer, control, conjure up, use, research, preserve, admire, observe, and love nature. They also wish to melt together with, return to, find themselves in, measure themselves with, and test their own boundaries with the help of nature. Equally, nature reveals itself in the past and the present as nourishing, promising, conniving, menacing, charming, impressive, playful, creative, objective, law-abiding, disinterested, helpful, calming, challenging, secretive, inspiring, lofty, beautiful, harmonious etc. We wish to deal with a single one of the many possible approaches to nature: growing, aimless, present oriented, open, playful being in nature, meaning the mindful approach to nature.

2.2. The Mindful Approach to Nature

Mindful approaches to nature are so diverse that we created a breakdown, which we will also use for the presentation of the exercises in chapters 4 to 9. This breakdown results from mindfulness only being the *attitude* that we have in nature: sitting on the forest floor, walking in the area, lying in the grass, listening to animal voices, breathing into the far, looking at clouds, touching leaves, or molding moss. Since in our opinion mndfulness towards nature itself should play the central role in mindful approaches to nature, we only considered approaches with *direct interactions with nature* in their foreground. We found six forms of mindful approaches to nature this way:[19]

1.   Receptivity

2.   Exploration

---

19. Other compositions of approaches to nature that especially play a role in nature pedagogy can be found in Bögeholz (1999), Kellert (2002), Pohl (2006). Mayer (2005) speaks of "dimensions of the relationship nature" (p. 243, own translation, GZ). Although this is actually the nicer and more fitting expression for that which we mean, we have decided to use "approaches to nature". In the context of a practice-oriented workbook it seems reasonable to emphasize the space of the subject.

3. Empathy

4. Play

5. Shaping

6. Contemplation

2.3 Forms of Mindful Approaches to Nature

Receptivity

How much of my environment, contemporaries, and nature do I observe? How do phenomena make me feel? How do I feel myself in nature? Nature is the root of many diverse sensual experiences.   First, we can focus on individual sensory channels. With our eyes we, for example, comprehend variations of the color green, the blue or gray of the sky, the morning light, the dark of the night, the movement of leaves or waves, and the shimmering of the moon or sun in the water. Our ears hear the songs and call of the birds, the chirping of crickets and grasshoppers, the rustling of leaves under our feet, or the murmuring of creeks. Our skin is touched by grass, twigs, or even just by wind, and we feel the soft and wet moss. Our feet sense the firm, uneven ground. The smell of wild garlic or pine fill our nostrils, depending on the seasons.

Physical sensations go hand in hand with heat, cold, wind, or rain. Our body does not have less to offer: joy and pleasure, liveliness, the feeling of breathing, the observation of body movements while underway, the beating of the heart and vessels, sweating, tiredness or strength, aching limbs, heaviness and lightness, touching and being touched. But being in nature also means moving in diverse and partially intense atmospheres. Atmospheres are based on synaesthetic experiences that include physical feelings.[20] "Synaesthetic" means that an experience covers different sensual experiences in a consistent, holistic manner. People experience their environment "crossmodal" from birth, which means they do not differen-

---

20. G. Böhme 1995, 1998, Hauskeller 1995, Huppertz, 2000, 2007.

tiate between sensory channels at first. This differentiation is acquired over time and requires more precise self-observation. In order to experience atmospheres, one must engage oneself in, sense, and feel them. We do not just experience atmospheres, we also create them – we create landscapes, gardens, parks, as well as apartments and other cultural spaces.

In nature we can use our senses in a focused manner and pursue our "search picture" when observing birds, flowers, and mushrooms. Nature pedagogy works with such sensual focusing (see chapter 10). But we can also let our senses wander and open ourselves.

The attitude of mindfulness is lost during sensual observations, when we hold on to pleasant sensations and wish to multiply or intensify them, or when we try to have especially intense sensual experiences. We also lose this attitude when we hold on to judgments of sensual experiences, for example "bad weather": "too muddy", "too wet", "too cold", "too windy". This judging applies a standard of how things should be and prevents new experiences.

Exploration

Nature does not reveal itself in its diversity and complexity at first glance. First, we must and wish to explore many things – with our hands, eyes, ears, nose, and taste. We roam the landscape, follow paths and roads, and explore places and spaces in order to see where they lead. We orient ourselves through markings in the landscape such as hills, trees, hedges, bushes, viewpoints, rivers, lakes, and springs. We notice the insects at our place of rest, pay attention to the form and patterns of waves on the lake, and differentiate between the various smells that the water causes through contact with the subsurface. We do not ask ourselves the question: "What is there around me?", but also: "Where am I here anyway and who else is here?" We make discoveries in passing, while we are exploring the area, strolling around, walking unusual paths, as well as recognizing and following our curiosity.

We do not only explore things and spaces, but also effects that our presence in nature causes. So when we explore we must also sometimes experiment a little with natural things or creatures. Here, experimenting is not meant as a review of a hypothesis, but something much easier instead: handling an object in a manner that allows more holistic observation. We turn a stone around and look what is underneath it, creep up to a bird and find out how long his escape distance is, take an apple apart, or lay in the grass. The exploratory approach in the context mindfulness is about a very personal or group approach in this special situation – without the claim to universal knowledge.

The social aspect of the exploratory approach must not be under-estimated. More is observed in groups and one's own experiences are expanded through imitation as well. We are able to perceive what others perceive and can interpret the exploratory behavior of the others. The attitude of mindfulness can be lost through exploratory behavior, if we exert ourselves too much in order to find out something or make new experiences in a goal-oriented manner.

Empathy

Empathy is the recognition of the experience of another subject and – insofar we are dealing with an approach to nature – that of a non-human subject. This approach to nature is not easily determined, as its boundaries are difficult to measure. Arguably, only creatures can be considered as candidates for empathy, because there is no reason based on experience to ascribe subjectivity to inanimate nature (stones, water etc.). Reasonable empathy with other creatures is clearly reliant on two things: the first being that we can justifiably ascribe a form of subjective experience to them, the second being that we understand this experience in some way. Even if some people speak to their plants and children sometimes consider plants, trees, and animals to be emotionally equal, it is unlikely that plants have any form of self-awareness in the sense of "how it is to experience some-thing, to do, to be". In contrast, there are clear indications that animals have physical and emotional feelings, so elementary forms of self-experience.

Clearly, we can communicate with some animals, for example with mammals, but it is difficult to communicate with others, for example with insects. The communication and expressions of great apes, but also of dogs, cats, or horses, through which we can access their experiences, are much more plausible to us then for example those of a fish, even though there is much evidence that fish also experience pain or breathlessness. Even if we cannot easily understand many animals, they do appeal to us and spark assumptions and emotions in us. We answer them in our language so to speak.

However, the foundation of relation causes a different problem. Do we really understand animals or do we just anthropomorphize them, and fall victim to conclusion by analogy? Do chimpanzees "rape" their females? Or does it just look that way? What do the females experience? What do the males experience? Are such human categories even sensible in the animal kingdom?

But even if there are limits to an empathetic approach to other creatures: we understand our pets and productive livestock relatively well and we can adjust to them. They also, to a certain degree, comprehend how we are doing and adjust to us. We can open ourselves for this mutual experience and also change with it. Animal encounters can support the change of one's own perspective – a possible foundation for the transfer of this ability to interpersonal relationships. An emphatic approach to and handling of animals can therefore primarily be found in animal based therapy (see chapter 11), in the handling of pets, in the research of wild animals, and in dealing with wild animals (for example in the distance that we show towards fawns – do not touch! - or the needs of wild animals, or by not entering tree nurseries or the breeding grounds of birds). As our exercises are invested in simplicity, we have only illustrated a few that can be performed everywhere and spontaneously with small animals.

Play

The playful approach is mainly about motor interactions and the experience of nature as animating, challenging, and resistant. A tree shows itself from a different side when we climb it, as does a cliff when we slide or role down it, or a creek if we cross it on stones or jump over it, as well as the night if we take a night walk, rather than looking into it from the balcony.

We can playfully experience ourselves intensely – as active, alive, challenged, skilled or unskilled. We get to know boundaries and resources, as well as emotions like fear or pride. We are not interested in the performance, but the experience which is possible with little effort and is close to everyday life. So we do not *climb* a hardly accessible tree and do not try to climb as high as possible. We do not climb anything in the conventional sense, because we are not interested in having "climbed" something, but the climb itself.

If we overstep the playful attitude in the direction of an achievement-oriented attitude (improving or maintaining performance) or self-improvement in the broadest sense, we enter the realm of sports. We meet joggers and mountain bikers in the forest, paragliders circle in the sky, and on former fields golfers pick up balls. We meet windsurfers at rivers, lakes, and the ocean, as well jet skiers, canoeists, and sailors. Of course some of these sports activities can be combined well with mindfulness. Many people access an attitude of Mindfulness during sports. Jogging is a sport which participants often refer to as an opportunity for informal mindfulness. The relative lightness of doing, the uniformness, and alertness all promote the attitude of mindfulness. The same of course also applies to hiking, sailing, and many other sports. The requirement for a mindful experience is that the sport is performed in a largely practiced and implicit manner. Whoever does sports in nature this way is not following a specific goal there and is not mainly coping with difficulties and challenges, but instead can observe the environment, its activities, its interaction with nature, as well as its properties and resistance etc.

If the expected performance is marginal and the attention is focused entirely on its success, mindfulness becomes difficult. A so called flow (Csíkszentmihályi) can also occur, a sort of alert-trance stance in which everything is faded out that does not contribute to the success of the activity. A state of flow is the maximum concentration on a goal and the connected goal-oriented activity. There may be much concentration needed for that, but less of the relevant to the present day, receptive, relaxed, and open attitude of mindfulness.

Shaping

When we change or shape something in nature we usually follow a certain purpose or intention, such as protection, food, beautification etc. The mindful shaping approach to nature is about the creative process and not the result. Many people enjoy to shape nature, to play with its forms and colors, to experiment how they fit together, and which patterns and contrasts are the result. In different combinations and backgrounds natural objects have entirely different properties. Stones look differently in water than when they are dry and a piece of wood, a mushroom, or something similar under a bush looks different than if you lay it in a field of snow, on a white cloth, or on moss.

Humans also enjoy creating patterns in nature. They carve on trees, draw in the sand, build sandcastles, create ponds, and arrange stones or muscles. They adorn themselves with feathers and shell necklaces, dress their hair in different ways, or get tattoos.

But the shaping game is not just a matter of sight. We can also shape sounds or atmospheres (places of assembly, tents made of branches, small igloos etc.). In this way we reveal the acoustic, haptic, olfactory, and atmospheric possibilities of nature.

> "With each of my works I concentrate on a certain property of the respective material or place. The blade of grass is hard, brittle, hollow inside, and breaks when it is bent. Its ear panicle is flexible, thin, strong, and smooth. It took many works before I understood the blade of grass – let alone grass as a whole – properly. This learning process never ends." (Goldworthy 1991, p. 2, own translation, GZ)

In the mindful shaping approach to nature it is important what happens to us:

> "I often need days of pure working with the senses to finally pass over
> to shaping. If I have made the connection to my environment every-
> thing becomes shaping. Every everyday action such as searching for
> wood, making a fire, cooking, cutting dry grass for a sleeping base, or
> reacting to the weather are demanding on my senses. I am shaped and
> influenced by experiences. Experiencing is part of the process of
> shaping in the end. The more knowledge and experiences I have
> collected through my senses, the richer and more intense the process
> of shaping and the relationship to the experienced landscape
> becomes." (Joller 2008, p. 10, own translation, GZ)

The transition to aesthetic in the narrow sense, so artistic shaping with natural materials, to Land art, is fluid. The stronger complex ideas or explicit aesthetic criteria are followed while shaping, the more sensible it is to speak of an aesthetic approach, for example during the shaping of gardens, parks, ikebana, program music, Land Art, or landscape painting. The attitude of mindfulness is thereby easily lost when aesthetic criteria or a more challenging idea of how something should be guide the process of shaping. The mindful shaping approach should not carry a special challenge or aesthetic goal with it. Insecurities, inhibitions, and pressure to perform can be avoided this way. The mindful shaping approach is only convincing if activities and shaping tasks really are not a challenge; suggestions concerning this should be technically easy.

Contemplation

The small cottage in Rydal Hall in England's Lake District was built in 1669, in order to be able to observe the Rydal-Beck waterfall. To us authors it expresses in a wonderful and atmospheric way how the contemplative approach to nature can be cultivated.

The contemplative approach distinguishes itself in that we can calmly concentrate on one theme, which results from contemplation, in our approach to nature. Nature is a good place to come to peace and contemplate. But a corresponding attitude is needed.

A mindful contemplation is not classic "thinking". When we mindfully contemplate something we do not wish to achieve a goal. Instead, we just want to see what comes to mind in regard to a natural phenomenon and a related issue. It becomes the center of thoughts, fantasies, memories, and emotions in the sense of brainstorming. Of course one can come to durable insight this way, but we suggest to not hold on to them and to instead let oneself be inspired over and over again. Nature possibly has a strong impression, but what an impression is to me and which effect it has is reliant on my resonance, which I trace and give room to in my con-templation. Contemplations in nature usually last 20 to 45 minutes for us.[21] During contemplation one's own priorities can be put in order, important things can be sorted from the unimportant, one's horizon can be broadened, and new associations, pictures, ideas, and emotions on individual, existential, or spiritual themes can develop.

---

21. So called vision quests, which follow Indian traditions, combine contemplation in nature with ascetic practices and intensely prepare and follow up on them in conversation, often taking a few days for such processes.

A contemplative process in nature can originate in different ways. We describe this in the corresponding section of the exercises, especially in exercise number 76.

But we wish to discuss one possibility with you at this point, because it causes many questions. It is possible that a natural phenomenon or a certain situation causes powerful processes in us. We have spontaneous nature experiences that can have special meaning to us when we take a morning walk and experience sunlight suddenly breaking through the fog, when our gaze falls on an accumulation of fly agaric, or when we hear a Mockingbird or grasshopper close to us. In this case, we speak of *experiences in nature.*

We can consciously look for such natural scenarios. There are natural objects and situations which are similarly impressive to people of a similar cultural background: sunrises, sunsets, the night, special views, storms, the ocean, the desert, cliffs etc. Also clearly hybrid – meaning practically staged with human participation – nature experiences such as a bonfire, garden, lighting etc. can be impressive in a partially expectable and planned manner, and can initiate themes, associations, emotions, and thoughts. The experience-oriented approach plays a big role in our society, as does the exercise approach, and both are not seldom connected to each other. At the same time, mindfulness is not self-evident. The harder we (must) search, the more pronounced the feature ("eventlike") in the foreground, the less we thereby interest ourselves in nature itself, and the less time we take to trace the meaning that a situation has to us in the moment and not conventionally, the more we distance ourselves from the attitude of mindfulness. Situations which can easily be found are especially suited for an experience-oriented contemplative practice of mindfulness. A sunrise, just as like a walk at night, is unquestionably a special experience for many people, although the sun rises daily and nature is shrouded in darkness for many hours of every day.

The themes which we contemplate in nature can be of a *personal, existential, or spiritual* nature. In the first case, the resonance and therefore the meaning that we give to an event, object, or situation is very much shaped by our individual history: a certain flower, landscape, lighting, a smell, or an atmosphere which is only experienced as something special by ourselves. It could be that we do not know precisely what touches us so much momentarily, but it could also be the case that we immediately have scenes or stories in our mind. When I (M.H.) for example walk past a small sandstone formation in the forest that offers a view, I immediately think of the hours I spent on such rock formations as a young man. The smell of Swiss pine causes intense moods and memories of summer in the mountains in me (V.S.). Certain places are connected with specific episodes or fateful moments for a lifetime. Sometimes, strong preferences, dislikes, fantasies, associations, wishes, and dreams arise. A fox roams the forest alone and, depending on our personal situation, brings our own loneliness or happiness to mind in regard to being alone. Our personal associations are dependent on our history and momentary life situation.

Existential experiences touch on themes that belong to the foundations of human life in a specific society (and sometimes beyond that). Such themes are, for example, belonging to a social community or relationship (closeness, safety), loneliness (distance, separation), transience, death, sickness, suffering, fear, happiness, unhappiness, guilt, care, recognition, handling of time, autonomy, freedom, and visions for a good life. The responsiveness to such themes is determined by one's personality, present interests, current life situation, the setting of a nature encounter etc. Therefore, it is especially interesting and important to talk about different experiences during contemplation.

When existential themes not only arise, but also undergo a solution-oriented transformation, we speak of spiritual experiences. A spiritual experience can happen at any time in the attitude of mindfulness (see chapter 13), but contemplation is much more likely to cause spiritual experiences than other approaches, because it directly addresses existential experiences, usually lasts a longer amount of time, and therefore make a more intense mindfulness experience possible.

3. | Recommendations for the Practice of Mindfulness in Nature

It has proven itself useful to differentiate between various possibilities of practicing mindfulness:

Formal Exercises: You only do something because you want to practice mindfulness. For example, you close your eyes, are mindful of the wind, and spin in a circle. You let other people feel objects or practice wide mindfulness. Formal exercises have a clear time duration and are clearly distanced from everyday life. They often make mindfulness easier or clarify certain aspects.

Informal Exercises: You practice during everyday activities. You stay mindful to sensations (hearing, smelling, views etc.) or everyday activities that allow for a sufficient amount of aimlessness: normal walking, breathing, sitting, lying, jogging, or whatever you already do in nature. Consciously incorporate the practice of exercises into informal exercises from the beginning as well by envisioning the attitude of mindfulness and ending the exercise consciously. It is helpful to set a certain amount of time (for example: approximately 3 minutes) for oneself to do this.

Pause: Continue to pause from time to time and make yourself aware of the current situation, for example in this sequence: posture (without changing it!) - contact to the ground or bench – breathing – sensations – mood and level of energy. It is good if you only pause for a short moment (approximately 30 seconds for everything!), as you are then more likely to repeat it often. Pausing is also a good possibility to always remind oneself of the attitude of mindfulness. If you are thinking of mindfulness and it is somehow possible pause for 30 seconds, instead of saying to yourself: "I should practice again. When will I do it? Oh yes, later when...."

Mindfulness as a New Habit: You are simply mindful, for example as soon as you are in nature or in another suitable situation, and you notice if this attitude is lost.

3.1. General Recommendations

1. Begin all exercises by first *arriving* in the situation. Which posture do I have at the moment? Do not change it or take an exercise stance right away! How is my breathing, my energy level, and my mood? This is also a recommendation for group leaders.

2. *Make Yourself Aware of the Attitude of Mindfulness Repeatedly*: Take your time to think about and discuss yourself. Visualize the attitude of mindfulness before the practice of each exercise (formal and informal) and make a conscious decision to take on this attitude and to place it in the foreground for a certain amount of time. Do not exert yourself too much but maintain enough tension in the body in order to not fall asleep. If such a medium amount of bodily tension is difficult for you, then stay the way you are for a moment and see what changes on its own. When you finish this exercise it certainly does not mean that you abandon this attitude immediately but it will realisticaly move to the background.

3. It is pleasant when exercises are easy to repeat and can be incorporated into your everyday life. That is why the exercises should definitely *not be technically difficult*. Sometimes looking into the clouds above you is sufficient. The technique should not push itself into the foreground, neither should the length of the exercise, its uncomfortability, pain, or excessive bodily challenges. You should invest in this attitude, not in procedure of exercises.

4. Mindfulness exercises can help when things are uncomfortable, but they cannot when *danger* is looming. In that case, it is not mindfulness that is needed as much as smart decisions, for example if a storm is approaching. It is just as important to recognize personal *boundaries* and to allow oneself to be helped (on slippery roads, backpacks etc.). Proper equipment is therefore crucial. Be aware of the dangers and learn to assess them.

5. There are many outer *obstacles* for mindfulness, but in our experience there are mainly three central personal obstacles:

- *Lack of Motivation*. Motivate yourself through your goals, pleasant exercises and surroundings, fascinating natural phenomena, short exercises, planned breaks, conversations with other interested people or participation in a group, or being helped by a person experienced in mindfulness. In the end, motivation is in your own hands so take responsibility! Always make new decisions. Do not blame yourself for not practicing, as it is a waste of time. Instead: Recognize blame – "and" – pause and practice.

- *Impatience*. Make yourself aware that mindfulness is only enduring if it is incorporated into your everyday life. In order to achieve this, the practice of exercises – in whatever form – must become a habit. In our experience, 10 minutes of practice (does not have to be in one session!) are a realistic and helpful goal for most people. Even if you are not in nature more often for longer periods of time, 10 minutes of mindfulness is not bad. It is difficult to say when you develop a feeling for mindfulness or notice its effects, but 4 to 6 weeks is a realistic estimate with this approach.

- *Exertion.* Since you are following no particular aim while in the attitude of mindfulness, besides being mindful, there is no reason for exertion. Let us assume you wish to focus on something (e.g. listening to a stream) and thoughts of events during the day come to your mind, in which case you stay with those thoughts! Then you have to make a small decision: ending the exercise or turning your focus back to the mindfulness exercise with an "and". There are no "distractions" or "disturbances" with mindfulness. Being mindful means recognizing and to accept that which is. That is why "being mindful" should not be called "not thinking". That would mean placing the exercise above the attitude. The remaining challenge is to notice that you have lost your focus and are thinking of something else. As already stated, self-criticism or harshness with oneself is not necessary. Maintain an experimental basic attitude in the practice of mindfulness. Everyone can and should diversify their exercises. It can be very sensible to occupy oneself with the original suggestion first. But if it becomes clear to you that this exercise does not help you to become more mindful, then choose another. There are enough exercises. But: do not end or vary an exercise because it is uncomfortable for you. Then you will perhaps never learn to mindfully deal with uncomfortable experiences. End or vary an exercise if you notice it is not helping you on your path to mindfulness or if you think that it could harm you.

3.2. Recommendations for Group Leaders

1. Make each group aware of a few basic rules:

- There is an obligation to secrecy. What participants share with the group stays in the group. This is also sensible in non-therapeutic groups, as you can never foresee if personal experiences might come up for discussion.

- No one has to speak in the group. If you, as a group leader, want to know how a participant is feeling, thinking etc. you can of course ask them in confidence. This rule takes a burden off of many people who feel anxious in groups and cannot find a way to mindfulness.[22]

- Everyone can vary or end each exercise at any time, but should not leave the group without letting the group leader know.

2. When you are instructing a group always quickly repeat the attitude of mindfulness. Sometimes it is enough to just point out one or two aspects or to just ask the participants, if they are familiar with the concept, to take in the attitude of mindfulness.

3. Speak with a normal voice when instructing and avoid speaking in a trance inducing manner!

4. If you are combining mindfulness exercises with, for example, guided imagery programs, make a clear distinction! That way you avoid irritation and confusion among the participants and guarantee a clear concept of mindfulness.

5. Conversations and discussions on the sense of exercises and Mindfulness itself are useful time and time again, because it makes the attitude of mindfulness clearer, allows for misunderstandings and difficulties to be addressed, and addresses its application in practice. You also clarify that mindfulness is not esoteric, but justifiable and criticizable knowledge and practice. Finally, you learn a great deal yourself as a group leader about the effect of mindfulness through this process.

6. Do not take the experience away beforehand that exercises make possible or suggest. Do not say "what they are good for" or what you usually experience during them. This restraint is a possibility to minimize the unavoidable suggestive portion. The practice of

22. We took this suggestion from Paul Chadwick (2006). It has proven itself very useful.

mindfulness is also experimental in the sense that we do not know what a certain exercise is "good for". Equally we cannot and should not take away from what the practice of mindfulness effects in certain people as a whole. The individual experience is central.

7. In our general experience formal group sizes (registered persons) should not be above 14 participants. In the case of continuous groups over a longer period of time this usually means an attendance of 10-12 participants. You can still keep an eye on a group of this size in nature and it gives the participants time and space to contribute. If possible, you instruct such groups with two people. This gives you the possibility of intervision, as well as to assist individual participants, and offers aid in the case of disputes with or in the group.

8. In psychotherapeutic groups you should have sufficient therapeutic experience with the disorder that you are treating. You should conduct preliminary talks and supervise the group in a team of 2 or, if that is not possible, admit less people into the group.

9. It is indispensable to visit the place where the group is supposed to take place beforehand. The path through nature will inspire you to certain forms of practicing mindfulness and you can have a look at the place's possibilities.

10. It is generally sensible to announce the duration of an exercise beforehand. This encourages participants to stay with an exercise that is uncomfortable or difficult for them. It also guarantees that participants come together on time if they spread out during an exercise and someone does not hear your acoustic signal.

11. Concerning the duration of groups in nature, longer meetings (4 to 6 hours) have great advantages, as they allow sufficient time to arrive in nature, make longer exercises and conversations possible, and more easily convey the atmosphere of being in nature. Shorter settings have

the advantage of closeness to everyday life, as many people spend shorter periods of time in nature, go to the park, take a walk etc. It is certainly also possible to only perform individual exercises in nature during a consultation or therapy.

12. We adamantly request the participants to only speak of what is happening at the moment, so that which has to do with the practice of mindfulness, during their time in the group – or to be silent. The participants greatly enjoy this. It unburdens them from all distractions and small talk, unwanted questions etc. We consider breaks to be breaks. There are no special rules for those periods so that the participants have a chance to get to know one another through conversation during breaks. Being in nature also has a strong communicative and social meaning. For many participants it is a possibility to get to know like-minded people and to do something as a group that they would never do on their own. Most women would not walk alone at night through the woods or distant places. The joint activity, the shared interest, as well as everything that is expressed during sharings and meetings on exercises brings people together.

13. The participants should be equipped for every relatively normal weather condition and the chosen area. It is good to repeat this in every invitation and remind them to bring insect repellent, notepads, or flashlights if needed. Aluminum coated sitting areas are very helpful as they keep the cold of the ground away. They are inexpensive and we purchase them for everyone at the beginning of a group. Coldness should not be a problem. It simply requires proper clothing and activity, which also applies to light rain in our experience. These are all opportunities for special exercises. Strong rain and storms are a different matter. If the participants are dripping wet it becomes difficult and in case of a storm you have a special responsibility as group leader. A timely termination and a plan B for a sheltered space are recommended.

3.3. Recommendations for the Practice of Mindfulness with Children

The ability to be in the present is a gift of childhood which we can maintain to an old age (Altner 2009, p. 13). Children show us ways into the present, refresh our awareness again and again with their happiness to explore, creativity, and their wonder in regard to the world. Being in the present is a central element of mindfulness. To conclude that children are born with the ability for mindfulness however (Renz-Polster&Hüther 2013, p. 225-226) is going to far.

Central aspects of mindfulness are exceptionally difficult, if not impossible, for children: aimlessness, non-activity, relativizing judgments and modes of interpretation, wide Mindfulness, deceleration, empathy, distance, and looseness. Such elements and configurations of mindfulness are virtually evidence of a person maturing. These are competences that a person can acquire, more or less, but does not have to. This learning can occur intuitively, but it is usually helpful if the attitude can consciously be learned. For this it must be taught and understood transparently. The concept itself is relatively abstract and therefore requires a certain ability of abstraction that is only developed at a certain age (approximately 12 years of age). This is without speaking of qualities such as patience and a tolerance for frustration in the practice of exercises.

But how can we lead children to the attitude of mindfulness? Which steps are easy for them? Which activities can motivate them? In other words: which approaches to mindfulness are appropriate for children? Here are some suggestions to answer this question:

1. Children love places they know and that give them a feeling of security and protection. Spend time with them in a familiar, diverse, and safe place with many natural materials that activate the senses. Make sure that the children can do something there and can go exploring. For children under the age of 6 places nearby are optimal and slightly longer trips can be undertaken with children of school age.

2. The ability to be fully in the moment is considered typical for children. Many children leap from one activity to the other though and have difficulty concentrating or paying attention: "I'm done already, what can I do now?" The urge to go back into interior rooms can be astounding in children that live disconnected from nature. Give the children time to arrive. In our experience most children, for example, are open for exploratory and creative activity if you give them enough time. Make it possible for the children to have time and free space to linger that they otherwise do not have in their organized everyday lives. In my experience (V.S.) this makes it possible to familiarize children with a plurality of sensory experiences, to motivate them to dwell on things, and in doing so bring them into the present. See the exercises as offers only, if the children turn it into something else that is completely fine.

3. There are activities and interests in nature that fascinate children and where they participate with their heart and soul: the fondness for the life of big animals, the free exploration of secrets, building and forming in general, especially of huts and meeting places, playing with sticks, climbing, and games of skill in nature.

4. Begin your time in nature by, for example, building a meeting place that becomes a point of reference for the entire occasion. It should be taken down at the end of the meeting. It is nice to make a pile of branches for animals to hide under out of it (see chapter 4).

5. Offer the children a change in perspective if your goal is to be aware of and explore the surroundings with all your senses. Many children love to take on different roles. You can show the sense of an awareness exercise much more easily to children, if they approach it from the perspective of an animal or recognize the necessity of this perception from the perspective of animals. In the role of a fox or a squirrel children delve into slightly unknown sensory exercises for themselves and playfully train their ability for empathy. Pre-school children can, for example, be enchanted to be an animal and with approximately 6

years of age children like to jump into the skin of mystery animals. Children are especially open to new sensory experiences and a change of perspective if they are dealing with young animals that have to learn to train their senses in order to survive in nature. Talk to the children after the activity about how it was to feel something, to be blind etc. How was it to change perspectives? How is it with us humans? Do we all feel the same way? With older children an introduction with role play in an entirely different life situation can be suggested (nature filmmakers or photographers, researchers, hunters, collectors, Indians, forest people, hermits etc.) in order to learn the ability to recognize nature with all your senses, and to be present, attentive, and watchful. Good and thoughtful introductions can make participation in silent group exercises possible.

6. Try to lighten the strong judgments and dislikes ("I like or dislike this") of the children, for example, through small dares and "crossing boundaries". Let the other children say which likes or dislikes they have. This already relativizes a lot for the children. Think about your own judgments: you can also take the group for a walk in the mud or let them get wet in the rain.

7. Do not avoid every small danger. This is the only way real danger can be recognized and assessed later. Place some trust in the children. Let them, for example, climb a tree only to the point that they feel comfortable and can get down on their own. If something does not work out right away have the child repeat it, practice it, and pay attention to what changes with the repetitions. Children usually find the boundary between safety and (small) dangers very attractive. Unfamiliar situations such as storms, darkness, and confusing terrain often make children scared. Take small steps towards such challenges.

8. Calm mindful exercises become easier if they are practiced regularly. If you go outside more often with children it is sensible to conduct certain exercises at the same place and thereby create rituals and routines.

9. The beauty of a landscape is seldom recognized by young children. Often singular, not especially pretty objects bind their attention and are regarded as small wonders. The most unspectacular can be spectacular for small children. Look at the small, self-evident things at the edge of the forest, collect them, listen, touch them, and take a lot of time for the next 30 feet.

10. Also let the children take home natural materials. This makes it clear that the outer world has to do with their own lives. Especially in early childhood, between 3 and 6 years old, stones, cones, and leaves are taken into possession and belong to the children with a surprising self-evidence. As long as animals are not involved you can support this wish and bring containers for collecting and transporting along.

11. The world becomes larger and more exciting in the middle of childhood. Nature no longer consists of many small wonders and is instead explored and researched. Children of this age do not always need grown-ups by their side in order to understand nature. Always create "grown-up free" zones, allow for own adventures, and give them moments of freedom.

12. Be aware of the fact that interest in playful, sensory-oriented activities in nature deteriorates starting at age 12 or 13.

13. Nature is "secondary" for many youths, there is a "Nature Time Out" for some (Kaplan&Kaplan 2002, p. 227-253). Positive experiences in nature should not become an obligation and nature can wait. Youths now test personal and social boundaries and new questions of identity are raised: who am I, what do I want, in which relation do I stand in regard to other people, which role do I have in the group? All of these questions are often more important in this phase. The danger of making plans not corresponding to needs is especially high in this phase of life. Settings are helpful that the youths come to on their own or occasions that last a certain amount of time, for example, camping in the forest.

Outer nature can play a big role, as wilderness retreats for several days with youths has shown over and over again. A jointly built or renovated meeting place to exchange experiences is recommended. New experiences can be analyzed and reflected on together. Here, the fact that we can explain the attitude of mindfulness helps us.

14. Remember that thinking in larger time and space dimensions, as well as in abstract   contexts, only develops around 12 years of age. Ecosystems, landscape, evolution, processes, and natural occurrences that cannot be visualized, but important for the contextualization of humans in natural processes. That does not speak against the practice of mindfulness in childhood, but against the expectation to be able to communicate mindfulness as an explicit attitude easily. The problem can be named, but it naturally depends a lot on the individual child. We also need to collect more experience. But you will see that we did not – unlike with the grown-ups – strictly discern between mindfulness exercises and fantasies. Fantasies like, for example, "how would a squirrel experience this place?" lead children into mindful perception and exploration, and as long as they do this we will use them.

15. At around 12 years of age likes and dislikes that nature causes in us can be incorporated into a general value system more and more. The values move from personal, egocentric experiences to social attitudes and to the interests of others, as well as to the natural environment. A sometimes very quick development of conceptual thinking, morals, and spiritual feeling begins.

Part 2 | The Exercises

The following 84 exercises can be utilized easily alone or in groups. We wanted to offer a collection of exercises that could be implemented easily.

There are multiple exercises that are repeated in all groups, or rather provide the framework for mindfulness in nature. Some of them are common knowledge, not specific to Mindfulness in nature, and are used in many seminars and groups. However, as this book is also written for readers who are not familiar with teamwork practices we want to introduce them first.

A number of other exercises, which are not only practicable in nature, have been listed by us nonetheless. These are either basic exercises of mindfulness, which should also be practiced in nature and are very doable there, or exercises that have a special appeal and their own character in nature. Sometimes a nature specific version is possible for these exercises.

We tried to cite a source for the exercise wherever possible. In these cases we cannot guarantee that these are the oldest sources, but they are the oldest we could find and that we use, meaning we have at least been inspired by them. If we have not cited any sources, it means that these exercises are a form of common property and are described in various places or that we have developed them ourselves.

Many exercises have variations. We summarized as many exercises as possible in order to offer a clear collection. The variations may differ greatly in their execution, but in our opinion they make similar experiences possible. By the same token we listed some exercises that are similar in their execution separately, if they they make different experiences probable in our opinion. Finally, we wish to encourage readers to think of new variations and exercises. We would be happy if you shared them with us and will try to include them in our next edition.

Flashlight

Instruction

During a flashlight, participants briefly trace their current feelings. As a group leader, allow for some time beforehand and ask everyone in turn to find a word or sentence for their *current* feelings. It can also be a metaphor, a color, or a weather report. Make sure that the participants speak in the moment, so not about what has happened in the last few days or previously that day, what they *have* experienced or in which phase they are now. Feeling and expressing what currently is makes this exercise a mindfulness exercise as well. Also, if participants only voice a judgment ("I feel good"): what do they feel exactly, what do they mean? Keep our recommendation in mind to allow everyone to remain silent temporarily or for the entire time. In that case, just proceed to the next participant.

Comment

A flashlight is usually conducted at the beginning and end of a meeting. It helps the participants arrive in the moment and group leaders get an impression of the individuals and the group. This can lead to the planned program being modified a little, for example that you begin with a more dynamic exercise if many participants are tired, or a less intense exercise if the mood is very dark or instable, etc. Likewise, group leaders find out how the participants are feeling when they go home at the end of the meeting. The flashlight should not lead to a feedback, which occurs time and time again. It can be useful, but then it would be a round of feedback and not a flashlight anymore (which always includes a feedback in its own way).

Sharing

Instruction

Sharing is an exchange on the subjective experience of an exercise and requires at least two people. Typical introductory questions are: "What did you experience during the exercise?", "Was something interesting or surprising to you during the exercise?", "How did you feel during the exercise?", etc. Exchanges are not commented on, but clarifying questions can be helpful. No one is forced to speak here as well and the round is open, meaning we do not proceed in a specific order and anyone can contribute as soon as their predecessor has finished.

Comment

Sharings are usually very useful: They allow the participants to again trace and define their experience more precisely. It usually becomes clear that the same exercise is experienced differently. This multitude of perspectives is an important consequence of mindfulness. Additionally, group leaders gain experience with the exercises by learning what they effect. The participants get to know each other and get into better contact with one another. They can address their problems in connection with the exercises. The group leaders get a feeling for the participants and the group and can more effectively intervene, continue, and answer questions. Sharings are especially important in therapeutic groups.

During a Sharing group leaders can pick out questions or problems that they can answer or clarify afterwards. A second open round can be of use that is reserved for questions, criticism, and discussions. It often revolves around how these exercises relate to mindfulness and if they are practical for everyday life. This discussion phase does not have to take place though, if there are no open questions and difficulties in the room. If we are pressed for time, we sometimes mix both phases, meaning the group leaders already confer with one another during the Sharing.

And-Techniques

Instruction 1

If you wish to focus your mindfulness (for example on walking in a natural landscape, light and wind, water) and notice you are thinking of something else, then please accept this calmly. Give your thoughts some time and then return to your focus with an "and" or open yourself in wide mindfulness to new experiences in the present.

Instruction 2

If a focus forces itself on you again and again (a specific problem, fear, mulling things over, pain, obsessive thoughts, etc.) and you wish to observe the situation more comprehensively, then this is possible with an "and" as well ("And what else is happening at the moment?"). You can expand your experience in the present this way.

Comment

And-Techniques help you to remain in the present. They are not to be confused with distractions. They are actually the exact opposite. While you mull things over or think of something else you are distracted from natural phenomena and the present. With these simple techniques you end the things that are distracting you from the wind on your skin, the light, the ground under your feet, etc., and can return to the present and widen your experience of it. To deal with distractions we create a powerful new focus with which we can combat these involuntary focuses. This is exhausting in the long run, wears you down, and has nothing to do with mindfulness.

It is completely normal that you observe something different every time or think of something that leads you away from the present, at least if you practice mindfulness in everyday life. But please do not attempt to *not* think. That is much too intentional during the practice of exercises. And you also then attempt to fight thoughts with thoughts and fighting is a form of intense contact. Accept them and exit the contact light-footed!

Which Nature Type are You? - Round of Introductions

Instruction

First, quietly think alone about as what and as who you actually enter nature usually in everyday life. Which role do you like to take? That of the person searching for relaxation? Of a nature enthusiast? Of a gatherer? Do you always have the same role? Is it different if you are in the forest or at the ocean? What do you enjoy doing in nature? Sport, taking a walk, sitting on a bench and just enjoying the view?

Then choose a conversation partner and ask about their roles, or rather their personal approach to nature. How important is nature in everyday life for my partner? After the conversation, we introduce each other in an introductory round.

A questionnaire can also be submitted at the beginning, for example: "Find one person, who had a tree house or liked to climb trees, who has overnighted in a tent alone in the woods before, who prefers to be in a mall than alone in nature, who has been to a rainforest, who is knowledgeable on constellations, who feels very uneasy in the wilderness, who had a favorite place in nature as a child", etc. Find a person who has experienced these descriptions for each aspect. Write the name of the person fitting the description behind every question.

Comment

This exercise is a good introductory exercise for a group. These questions regarding one's own experiences in nature are generally answered very gladly, even to a stranger. They are private, but not too private. It has proven itself useful to walk during this exercise. In order to bring a group together that does not know each other and will stay together for a longer period, questionnaires have shown to be a nice possibility to learn of aspects of the participants that they would otherwise not share so quickly.

One's Own Place

Instruction

Walk around and look around. Observe how different places in your close environment affect you. When you have found a place that is inviting to you for a stay then do it. Continue to feel how the place affects you while you are there and how you perceive the natural space around you as a whole. Then continue to move around and look for another place. Experiment with places that you do not find inviting at all if you wish. This can loosen your stance and make it easier for you to find the fitting place. When you have arrived at a place where you wish to stay then remain there and mark your place with natural materials. That way you will always be able to find it again for the duration of your stay in nature.

Variation over a Longer Period of Time

If you are in nature regularly, create your own place that you can always visit: during different weather, times of day, times of year, and phases of life. Do not just choose one place to sit, but perhaps even multiple that you can visit for longer or shorter periods on your walks, bicycle tours, etc. We recommend one place to sit near your residence, one in your community, and one on your walks in nature.

Variation for Groups

It can be a useful addition to take in the sitting places of others and to observe nature from there when you are in a group. Can we understand why someone else has chosen this place? How does it feel? This extension must be introduced carefully, as one's own place enjoys an almost private character for many. If there are two group leaders underway with a group they can also place participants in random places, so they cannot see each other. After 10-20 minutes the participants are called together again or "collected". Which experiences did the individuals have at their place?

Comment

Becoming accustomed with your own place is an introductory exercise for further mindfulness exercises, but also connects you with nature. One's own place can be visited time and time again. When larger distances have to be covered or we are in nature reserves, the variation of distributing places to sit along a larger path has proven itself.

One's own sitting place is a useful instrument to come into contact with animals in nature. Especially birds approach you relatively quickly. Through repeatedly visiting these places they become more and more familiar.

Meeting Place

Instruction

All members of the group gather branches of wood or tree trunks together and create a comfortable place for meetings, relaxation, and discussions to which we can return after every exercise.

Comment

Creating a meeting place that you always return to together as a group creates orientation and familiarity. For singular occasions we suggest to return the dead wood back to the forest at the end of it.

4. Receptive Exercises

1. Calling out Ideas

Material: none

Location: any

Duration: up to 15 minutes

Setting: partner or group exercise

Age: everyone

Instruction

Pay attention to different observation focuses one after the other along a stretch of your journey. The participants call out different focuses in a random sequence every 30 to 60 seconds for the group that everyone then turns their attention to, for example: sky, trees, green, lines, sounds (or specific sounds caused by walking), mosquitoes, wind, light, shadow, etc., but also breathing, feeling movement, thoughts, etc. Anyone can suggest something and gladly more than once, just not in close repetition. If two participants call out something at the same time, the group leader decides. The exercise can be performed in pairs and also together as a group.

Strictly Acoustic Version

The rustling of leaves, breathing, footsteps, traffic (cars, planes), conversations, animal voices (birds, insects), wind, water, lapping water, crackling sand, silence.

Comment

A basic exercise for our groups that can be repeated often and with which stretches of a journey can be filled. Sometimes there are astonishing ideas. But nothing special must be identified. Sometimes the most obvious is also the most remote. A participant once called out "white" to the group while it was snowing, which led to amusement and possibly insight. This exercise is well suited for nature reserves with path restrictions. The greatest part of this exercise is that it is not the group leaders determining observation suggestions, but the participants calling out to one another.

2. 90-Degree Turn

Material: none

Location: any, but preferably with some wind and perhaps sun

Duration: approximately 10 minutes

Setting: individual or group exercise

Age: everyone

Instruction

As a group exercise: please gather in a circle and close your eyes. Now please only concentrate on sounds and the feeling of your skin (face, arms, hands). Please remain standing like this for approximately one minute. Orient yourself according to your own sense of time, as precision is not important. (When leading a group you can also mark the phases with a cymbal.) What changes? After approximately one minute, please turn 90° to your right and repeat this movement until you have completed a full circle. (As a group leader you can also tell the participants when they should return to their initial position.)

After this round, the group dwells a little with closed eyes and then continues: now please open your eyes and repeat the same round at about the same pace. Pay attention to changes in your perception.

Variation

You can also suggest long continuous turning. Then you are missing a pause, but the timing is easier.

Comment

An easy, but impressive introductory and basic exercise, because it makes
the multi-faceted influences of the senses clear. The exercise can also be
found in Joller (2008, p. 33).

3. Hearing a Place

Material: none

Location: possibly impressive background noise, for variation use pencil and paper

Duration: approximately 5-10 minutes

Age: everyone, with variations for children

Instruction

You can sit or stand. Please observe all sounds that you notice around you...now concentrate on the sounds that are typical for the place where you are. Differentiate sounds that will sound similar in an hour, day, month, or year. Which sounds can be heard as of late and which can already be heard for a long time?

Variation 1: Hearing Silence

Pause and focus on the silent space around you. How far is the next sound, the next noise, away? How far does the silence around you reach?

You can also spread out around the area and let everyone listen to silence in their own place.

Pay attention to the gaps between the sounds and noises. How long do you hear nothing?

Variation 2: Sound Map

Put your mark in the middle of a blank piece of paper. Then you put down simple symbols for every sound that you can hear around you. Choose simple symbols – for example you depict the wind with two wavy lines or a song bird with a note sign. You should spend less time drawing and more time listening in this variation. The symbols should be arranged in a manner that also makes time between hearing sounds and the direction from which they were heard clear. This way, a sound map is created from a bird's eye perspective.

Variation 3: Sound Space

Pay attention to the three-dimensional sound space around you. Keep your eyes closed. Which sounds come from the left? Which from the right? Which from the front and which from behind, top, or bottom? Does ability of perception vary depending on the direction? Can you listen past a loud sound and focus on a quiet one? Which noises and sounds are loud or quiet, which is closest or furthest?

Variation for Children

Hearing silence: you can lay on the ground with children, close your eyes, stretch out your hands, and clench your fists – raising a finger when each phase of silence occurs.

Sound space: Collect 15 to 20 small natural objects as preparation, for example, grass, stones, pine cones, acorns, etc. Now look for a place of your own in the immediate area where you can hear different sounds and noises. If you are underway as a group, you should also be able to hear the acoustical signals of the group leader, for example a cymbal, a whistle, or clapping. Please focus on the sounds in your environment completely. Lay a noticeable symbol made of natural materials in the middle of a 20" x 20" area. Place a corresponding object in it for each sound, as if you wanted to mark the place of the sound on a map. Do not spend as much time with discerning the direction and distance of the sound, and instead focus on really listening. Now make a symbol in the area out of natural materials for each sound that you hear. Are there rhythms that repeat themselves?

The intensity of the exercise can be improved for children if they exchange their ideas on their sound picture in groups of two.

Comment

Some places in nature are influenced by specific natural sounds and have their own sound quality. Examples are places near a creek or a river, a waterfall, the surge of waves by the ocean, etc. The sounds and noises belong to the place in a certain sense and result from landscape formations, the presence of water, stones, etc. They are constant, but change daily in their quality and intensity, depending on the time of day, weather conditions, etc. Some places are so exposed to wind that we always hear the wind rustle. If we have the possibility to visit these places repeatedly, we will be able to notice these differences.

The exercise with paper and pencil can be found in Cornell (1991, p. 74). It can be performed well on nature pedagogical excursions in order to, for example, attune to an early morning bird concert and notice the diversity of sounds.

The child variation to hearing silence can also be found in Cornell (1991c, p. 29). There is *also* silence everywhere, even if it is only 1' around us.

4. Perceiving Outer and Inner Pictures

Material: none

Location: anywhere

Duration: approximately 5-10 minutes

Age: everyone

Instruction

Regard a certain object of nature such as a tree, flower, piece of forest ground, or landscape. Now close your eyes and allow an inner picture of the viewed image to emerge. This can be a general impression, individual objects, or forms, colors, and spaces as well. Perceive that which arises in your inner eye. Now open your eyes again for a few seconds, memorize new details, and complement your inner picture with them. Look as often as you like and compare the inner and outer picture constantly. Trace which details arouse your attention and how the perception of an object and perhaps your reaction to the picture change.

Comment

The seeing person is repeatedly motivated to perceive the chosen object of nature more completely and precisely. This can lead to a surprising intensification of perception. Overlooked details of natural objects are perceived for the first time. Do not pressure yourself to perform by striving for completeness. If you feel pressure, recognize it and return to the suggestion of this exercise.

5. Near-Far Exercise

Material: none

Location: extensive panoramic view helpful

Duration: approximately 5 minutes

Age: everyone

Instruction

Look down while standing or sitting, regard the ground along your body. Take a soft look, so relax your eyes and do not observe any details. Then you lift your gaze slowly, increasing your field of vision until you can see your entire field of vision. Pay attention to changes in your breathing, stance, body tension, or mood.

Comment

The exercise is of course especially fitting if you have an extensive panoramic view, for example of a landscape. Similar exercises can be found in Cornell (1991c, p. 40) and Joller (2011, p. 33).

6. Opening the Horizon

Material: none

Location: everywhere in nature

Duration: approximately 5-10 minutes

Age: everyone, with a variation for children

Instruction

Please stand up. Make sure you stand easily and feel the contact with the ground. Leave your eyes open and look straight ahead. Now very slowly move your arms to the front and top, until you have reached eye level. Your outstretched hands should then be about 4" apart, with the palms facing inward. Then please move your arms slowly outward as long as it still feels easy and good, until they are almost stretched laterally. Then you make the same movement back, so that you are imitating the form of a curtain with your arms that opens and closes. Pay attention to your bodily feelings and associations during the different phases of the movement. Also feel the resonance that causes the expanding and narrowing field of vision.

Variation

Imagine that you have a very limited field of vision (for example you are looking through a pipe or are wearing blinders). Move around the area in this "optical stance" for at least one minute. Now broaden your vision and imagine that you have a balloon of 10' to explore, then the size of a gym, and then the entire field of vision, as far as the eye can see. Observe your way of moving, stance, speed, mood, etc.

Variation for Children

Humans and animals have a different breadth in their fields of vision. We differentiate between tunnel vision and "owl vision". Tunnel vision focuses on clarity, meaning we stare at something and blend other things out. For tunnel vision we can look through a tube or through forwardly outstretched arms. Squirrels possess such tunnel vision (45°), with which they can excellently judge the distance of their jumps. The forwardly outstretched arms now slowly move apart in a breast stroke movement. When the children cannot see their fingers anymore and can in a way play with the visible and invisible they can imagine the field of vision of humans. Sight becomes softer and we stare less. The wolf can look over his shoulder (250° field of vision), rabbits and owls almost have "wraparound sight" (360°). The arms now come together again, past the "wolf" and the "human", and stop at the approximately 45° of the squirrel. This sequence can be repeatedly "looked through" in slow movements.

Comment

The exercise can be found in Kaltwasser (2008, p. 136-139). The variation for children is implemented in nature pedagogy, in order to help approximately understand the field of vision of animals. This way, children can be shown how other life forms perceive the world.

The terms "tunnel and owl vision" come from the tradition of Coyote teachings and can be found in Fischer-Rizzi (2007, p. 106). With tunnel vision we blend out and stare. This often occurs when watching birds with binoculars for example, and more generally when we wish to see clearly and focus on details. "Owl vision" as a type of soft angled gaze makes open, soft, and more peripheral sight possible: humans have approximately 180° in horizontal and 120° in vertical sight. Our vision is slightly blurred in this mode of sight.

7. Walking on Uneven Ground

Material: none

Location: anywhere

Duration: approximately 10 minutes

Age: everyone

Instruction

Please walk around slowly and pay attention to your movements, contact with the ground, how you feet and movements adjust to the ground, and how the ground "demands" this. Also look for distinct indentations and elevations! If you lose your focus, which will certainly be the case, remember the "and-techniques".

Variation

Change your walking pace and try a higher speed if you like, while still paying attention to how the uneven ground feels now, as well as how your feet and entire body shape the contact with the ground.

Or walk with greater strength and feel how the ground and contact with it change. How do you feel during this?

Expansion

Do not pay attention to the contact with the ground and instead focus on your breathing and how it changes your experience of the environment.

Comment

Walking slowly is a well-known mindfulness exercise, which is primarily practiced in Zen Buddhism. In nature it requires, or rather it makes, more outer and relational mindfulness possible.

8. 3-2-1 Exercise

Material: none

Location: anywhere

Duration: 10 minutes and more

Age: everyone

Instruction

Please pay attention to three things that you see in front of you, for example the beech tree – the creek – the rock on your way (two to three seconds of observation each). Then do the same with sounds, for example the gurgle of a creek, stepping on leaves, and the singing of a blackbird. Now choose three feeling sensations, for example feet on the ground, cold wind on the cheek, and hands in pockets. Now pay attention to two things that you see, hear, and feel. Choose new phenomena, but if it is easier you can use the same again...now a natural phenomenon that you see...a sound...something you feel...

Comment

This exercise is very popular. It can lead to surprising effects, even with children (see chapter 10.3). It is almost impossible to hold on to everyday thoughts during it. The current sensory perception in nature is usually more powerful. Such exercises can therefore be used to interrupt unproductive thought patterns (musing). A 5-4-3-2-1 variation is also easier in nature with its diverse possibilities of perception, but the 3-2-1 exercise is sufficient for children. The exercise stems from hypnotherapy and is attributed to Betty Erickson.

9. Three Focuses

Material: none

Location: anywhere

Duration: 10 minutes and more

Age: everyone

Instruction

First, please be mindful to the act of walking. Feel your movements and the contact with the ground. After about 3 minutes you add another focus, namely breathing. As a rule that means that you quickly switch between these focuses (to oscillate). After another 3 minutes you add a third focus: sounds. It is very pleasant to connect this with mindfulness in the next phase (see exercise 23).

Of course, many combinations of three focuses are possible, for example walking – smelling – sounds, sounds – smelling – breathing, seeing – hearing – smelling, seeing – moving in nature – movements of the own body, etc.

Comment

More than three focuses at once are generally too many to concentrate on. After three focuses, wide mindfulness, so the abandonment of all focuses, is easier. The experiences of participants are very different in this exercise. Many have the greatest difficulties with one focus, others with three. It is good to always keep reminding participants that it is not sensible to exert oneself. If the exercise is technically too difficult for someone, they should modify it.

10. Two-Trees Exercise

Material: none

Location: with trees, as much wind as possible (variation with less wind)

Duration: approximately 10 minutes

Age: everyone

Instruction

Look for a tree from which you can see another tree within, for example, 30 feet. Lean against the tree with your back. Please regard the tree in front of you and try to observe its form and movements in the wind. Then feel the contact with the tree you are leaning on. Feel if it is moving, how your body reacts, and how you feel during this observation. Even large tree trunks move a little, if the wind is strong. But you only feel it when you lean against it. Please try to observe all this at the same time (or oscillating, so doing it in quick sequence), namely the tree in front of you, the one in your back, and yourself. The theme of this exercise is movement and getting into swing.

Variation

If there is little wind, look for a young small tree that you can lean on. Now bring it into movement yourself and feel how it moves you in return. At the same time, observe the movements of the branches and leaves of "your" tree and other trees.

Comment

The different focuses are foremost in relation to movement, but also stay in contact with yourself. How do the movements that you see and sense make you feel? The exercise is pleasant for most participants and serves as an invitation to associations and inner pictures. Juliane Teuscher was involved in the development of this exercise.

11. Natural Points of Contact

Material: none

Location: anywhere, but preferably with a little wind and sunshine

Duration: approximately 10 minutes

Setting: group exercise

Age: everyone

Instruction

Form two groups. One group takes a seat on the ground. If that is not possible, the group can stand as well. This receptive group closes their eyes. The other participants form the active group and collect natural minerals that feel interesting in the surrounding area (about three different things per participant): plants, flowers, stones, grass, wood, moss. The objects can be dry, wet, angular, etc. They do not have to feel pleasant, but should not be too unpleasant either (thorns, snails, worms, etc.). The active group of course carries responsibility for the receptive group. Now the active participants go to the receptive participants and touch them with the objects on areas where their skin is exposed (arms, face, neck, etc.). They go from one to the other and crisscross however they like. After about 10 minutes, allow the exercise to slowly come to an end. Then the groups switch roles, so the receptive group begins to search for natural materials, etc.

Comment

A sharing and a conversation are recommended after the exercise. It is a very popular group exercise that causes intense feelings, not just tactile, but also on the relational level. For many participants it is very enjoyable to be able to be passive and to be surprised and spoiled, as most of the contact is pleasant. It is also surprising that such tactile sensations are caused with so little effort. The exercise leans on a description by Joller (2008, p. 74).

It can be helpful sometimes to ask, if anyone has an allergy to certain types of grass, and some participants will wish to not be touched in the face. Often others then speak who had not thought that it may be uncomfortable. But since the exercise is harmless and enjoyable it is worth convincing those participants a little. Allergies must of course be respected. The exercise has a distinct relational aspect.

12. Touches of Nature

Material: none

Location: anywhere

Duration: approximately 10 minutes

Age: everyone, with a variation for children

Instruction

Walk slowly (!) through a piece of forest, shrubbery, and underwood and allow yourself to be touched by branches and twigs. Consciously feel and observe the things that you were previously touched by.

Variation for Children

Let the children pretend to be badgers when they go through the underwood. Badgers are known as rummagers when they search for food. In the beginning, I (V.S.) allow the children to cover their eyes with one arm. Since animals do not do this, the children can take their arm away after a while and continue to go forward carefully. In this exercise, especially in the underwood, you do things that you usually avoid. Often you can hear: careful of the branches! It is a game that many have probably played intuitively in their childhood. Afterwards, "3-Stage-Touching" offers itself for example (see exercise 14).

Comment

This exercise clarifies two forms of contact in a pleasant way: we can actively come into contact with objects in nature (touching, feeling) or we are touched without having to do anything: by grass, leaves, wind, sunshine, rain, and snow.

13. Touching in a Circle

Material: various objects

Location: anywhere

Duration: 20 minutes and more

Setting: group exercise (up to 10 people; if there are more, form two groups)

Age: everyone

Instruction

Each participant looks for a natural object in the environment that they find tactilely interesting. Then the group forms a sufficiently close circle, in which the objects can be passed around. Everyone now closes their eyes and passes their object to the left. The new object is explored for approximately one minute with your sense of touch, then the objects are passed to the left. The group leader can determine the rhythm ("please pass the objects" or more pleasantly with natural sounds, for example by hitting wood together). When the objects have reached their original owners, participants open their eyes and pass the objects around one more time.

Variation

Choosable materials can be limited to leaves, stones, etc. Also, only one object can be passed around and each participant names a keyword, for example a perception or association, after feeling it. A further possibility is to pass around objects which additionally smell good and observe the smell.

Comment

The exercise in a circle is used in many variations and is widespread in nature pedagogy. It can be found in Kalff (1994, p. 54), for example. The individual variations have different effects and aspects and we recommend only trying one. The variation with associations to only one object makes the diversity of perspectives and experiences very clear. The variation with only one type of material, for example leaves, becomes incredibly diverse. It can be found in Joller (2008, p. 70-71) and the variation with associations can be found in Cornell (1991, p. 31). It often becomes clear how different and diverse nature is and how natural materials differ from artificial materials.

In larger groups it is not always easy for children to pass things the objects in a circle, and sometimes an unsatisfactory mood develops due to movement mishaps and social incompatibility between the students. For this reason, I (V.S.) now mainly use "3-Stage-Touching" with school classes (see exercise 14).

14. Three Stage Touching

Material: various natural materials, maybe a collection basket

Location: anywhere

Duration: approximately 10 minutes or more

Setting: partner exercise

Age: everyone

Instruction

Collect various similar natural materials and give them to a partner, who has closed eyes, to feel.

Stage 1: Place natural materials in your partner's palm and tell them that they are not allowed to grip it. They should consciously observe the impulse to grip it, but refrain from doing so.

Stage 2: The seeing partner slowly strokes the fingertips of the open palm with the object, then the cheeks, the "mustache area", slowly between the lips (!), across the ears, or something similar. It is important to touch the hand first and then the face.

Stage 3: The material is placed on the palm and the partner with closed eyes can grip and feel it extensively with their fingers.

Extension

The seeing partner shows the "blind" partner an assortment of objects at the end. Which one was it? With which body parts did they receive important hints of what it could be? It is easy to select between moss, sticks, and leaves. Try it with different nuts (hazelnuts, acorns, etc.). It becomes challenging and more interesting with different leaves, for example beech (without teeth and tough), hazel (with teeth and velvety smooth), maple (hand shaped), oak (wavy edge), or elm (raw like sandpaper).

Comment

People mainly feel with their hands and blindly know what they are handling, if they are allowed to grip it. Almost no one will know what it is, if the object is just laying in their palm. No animal can grip the way we can. Observations through the sensory hairs of the skin are very important for the exploratory behavior of animals. This aspect fascinates children again and again. For us humans, observation through the skin without gripping has become nearly meaningless. That makes it all the more fascinating to try different natural materials. The exercise "Waldfee" by Kalff (1998, p. 93) was an inspiration for this exercise.

15. Body Journey with Tree

Material: none

Location: with large trees

Duration: approximately 10 minutes

Age: everyone, with variation for children

Instruction

Choose a tree and touch it gradually and in an arbitrary sequence with your hands, a finger, arms, feet, nose, forehead, back, stomach, etc. Always remain in the respective (gladly moving) contact for approximately 30 seconds. Focus on the feelings in the individual body parts during this exercise, and less on the tree.

Variation for Children

Let the children mark trees like foxes, lynxes, etc. Animals have different secretion glands in their cheeks, anus, armpits, paws, etc., in order to mark their territory. They rub tree trunks for example, in order to show other animals that they where there. We try this ourselves, choose a tree, and rub our own body parts gently against the materials. How does this feel on our skin? How do the materials function? On which materials can we rub ourselves especially well? Animals shed their fur in the spring. It itches and they rub themselves against trees more often (for example deers, stags...).

Comment

This exercise for adults can also be conducted in contact with rocks or hills. A body journey in a sprung unsystematic form has the advantage that attention remains high and the exercise can be conducted for any amount of time.

16. Freezing

Material: none

Location: anywhere, but only possible in the cold

Duration: approximately 2-5 minutes

Age: everyone, with variation for children

Instruction

In this exercise, you imagine that you spontaneously freeze in a situation in nature, at least in your face and hands. Now please observe your freezing. With which body parts do you feel it clearly? How do you react, observe these reactions, your possible strains, impulses, and small movements...your judgments, associations, and thoughts. Please try to let these thoughts and comments go and to just feel. Please remember the "and-techniques" (see p. 71) that might be useful now. Let go of unnecessary tension. There is nothing to do right now but feel. Allow all emotions. How do you change?

Now please come back into movement, pat yourself down, and massage yourself if you want to. Stay with this "defrosting" with your mindfulness

Variation: Other Unpleasant Experiences in Nature

Focus your entire consciousness on something in nature that is unpleasant, difficult, or annoying to you. This could be the biting winter wind, the rain, ants everywhere, the burning and blinding sun, insects like mosquitoes or wasps, noise from campers, music, streets, or planes. Explore your own reaction. Is it a small irritation, physical pain, or something unwanted that does not fit into your concept? Feel within your entire body and pay attention to your bodily feelings, then your thoughts, feelings, etc. Do this as described above; stay with the unpleasant experiences or return to them again and again with an "and".

Variation for Children

Winter is a difficult time for animals. Some hibernate like hedgehogs, bats, dormice, and others are dormant like badgers, squirrels, and bears. Deer, wild boar, and rabbits stay awake and do not have a warm house. They lie on the cold ground to sleep. Feel the cold yourself and stand motionless. Where do you freeze, in which body parts? In which parts do you freeze, but it is not too uncomfortable? Where does it really bother you? Which is the coldest body part? Does the cold turn into pain? Is there also a place that stays warm in your body? Where is it? Now blow warm breath on your palms and observe the difference. How does it feel when the breath of the hand cools down again? Feel the warmth of your mouth with your tongue. Nutrition and movement are our furnaces.

Let the children move as they like afterwards, clapping, trampling, stomping, and rubbing. Trace what has changed. If it is possible, show an animal skin after the exercise.

Comment

In this exercise it is especially good to announce the time duration beforehand (and to stick to it). It becomes easier for the participants to concentrate on the exercise that way. But the exercise also has some surprises to offer. I (M.H.) revived the basic exercise from Karin Brück. Freezing is an especially good example for an unpleasant experience, because it occurs so often and proves itself so flexible. Dealing with unpleasant experiences mindfully is also described by Coleman (2013, p. 118 et seq.).

17. Tasting

Material: collect locally edible things (if you feel safe), cloth

Location: anywhere

Duration: 5 minutes or more

Age: everyone

Instruction

Look for different objects in your environment that you are certain you can eat or at least taste. We are thinking of, depending on the time of year, young bright green spruce sapling (like deer, squirrel), clover (max. of 3), folded and crushed stinging nettle leaves, hazelnuts, blackberries, beech nuts (approx. 5), etc. Trees are usually not poisonous (caution: no yew tree with red berries, red elderberries, or dane weed!!!). You can also collect different objects to taste as a group and place them on a cloth. Now each participant takes a young smooth beech leaf, for example, and examines it closely. Stroke over your skin with it, smell it, and grind it a little. How close must you bring it to your nose in order to smell it? What can you feel in your mouth? On your lips, the interior of your mouth? Put the leaf in your mouth, but do not chew at first. Trace how the leaf feels in your mouth and play with the leaf a little. Now taste the leaf!...What happens to the leaf when you chew it?...How does the taste change?...Its consistency?...How long can you taste the leaf?...Now swallow the leaf and observe the after taste.

Comment

This is an exercise from Sensory Awareness Training (Brooks 1979, p. 144), so far we are just dealing with detailed touching, tasting, etc. If you take things from nature, you should feel safe in the evaluation of its edibility. If you feel insecure because of the fox tapeworm, take leaves or fresh pine from trees outside the range of foxes. Nuts would also be an alternative safe from foxes. This is recommendable especially when you are working with a group.

18. Smelling and Sniffing

Material: fragranted natural objects in the environment

Location: anywhere

Duration: 10 minutes and longer

Setting: single or partner exercise Age: everyone, with variation for children

Instruction

What can you smell? Is there a scent in the air? Sniff a handful of leaves and collect various ground samples from covered areas. Grind leaves, flowers, moss, soft deadwood, spruce resin, etc. and form a sniffing bowl with your hands. Observe unpleasant smells as well. Pay attention to your associations and judgments. Before you switch to the next smell, rub your hands dry or wash them in water quickly if possible.

Now form pairs and head out. Continuously come together again from time to time and let the other partner blindly smell interesting material. You can also let them guess what it is. They will probably do so anyway. Make sure to allow for enough time for smelling. With strong smelling leaves, such as wild garlic leaves, but also with a handful of leaves, the blind partner can observe the smell slowly approaching, when it reaches them, and when it starts fading away. Observe their respective reactions and associations.

Variation

The participants collect objects that have an interesting smell and lay them on a bench, a mossy area, a cloth, etc. Then everyone takes one – like a bar of smells. Take your time with the individual observations of smells.

Variation for Children

Let the children smell and sniff like foxes, with small quick breaths of air through the nose and then with deeper breaths. Show the children how to grind the materials with their fingers or stones. A partner exercise is also possible: one child closes their eyes and has two smells held under their noses. Sequence: smell 1 and smell 2. Then they get smell 1 or smell 2 held under their nose again. Was it smell 1 or 2? Even small differences in well ground tree leaves can be observed that way (maple: slightly lemony, bird cherry: marzipan, beech: leafy smell; how do nut, elder, or ash trees smell?). Writing a list of sniffing assignments is also possible, as it can easily be performed: smell dry and moist moss...smell the bark of a tree and a piece that has fallen on the ground...smell a pine cone and a fir branch (spruce, perhaps pine)...smell some loosened soil at two different places...smell two different mushrooms...smell various ground leaves...smell different ground flowers...smell ground fir needles...smell two different pieces of wood.

Comment

A simple and obvious approach in nature that we usually do not take enough time for. Smells are always judged by us and we discern between pleasant and unpleasant smells. That is why this exercise is well suited for recognizing judgments and then continuing to observe and describe.

19. By the Water

Material: none

Location: spring, creek, lake, river, pond, etc.

Duration: 15 to 60 minutes

Age: everyone

Instruction

Walk along the edge of the water. How does the water interact with the solid ground? Choose a place you would like to stay at for a longer period of time. Observe the diverse manifestations of the water. Where does it move quickly, where is it almost stopped, and where does it swirl? Watch the dynamics and the movements of the water and the changing forms for several minutes. In which direction does the water move? Do you see objects that are transported by the water?

How do they move in the water? Can you see the bottom of the water? Are there reflections in the water? Where do these reflections come from? Perhaps stay with the reflections. When the water is dark the landscape virtually doubles to the bottom, everything is turned upside down, the sky is underneath you and you gaze into an abyss. This can be fascinating. Stay with the optical phenomena, but continually include your associations and thoughts into the exercise.

Instruction 2: "Listening to the Water"

Please close your eyes and listen to the sound landscape of the water. Which tones and sounds do you hear? Change your position and take listening samples from different places. Where does it drip, patter, rush, ripple, and gurgle? Where or when is it loud and where or when is it silent? It is very interesting to follow a creek this way.

Instruction 3: "Coming into Contact with the Water with your Hands and Feet"

Go up closely to the water. Begin with your palms and place them on the surface of the water, so that the back of your hands remains dry. Remain in this position and observe the temperature. Then you slowly pull your hands back. You can repeat this approach a few times, for example with your fingertips, the back of your hands, your upper arms, etc. Only at the end can you submerge your entire arms in the water. You can do the same with your feet and legs in the water and also with your entire body, if possible. Do this before you go swimming in the summer! Do not dry yourself right away either and instead consciously observe the drying process of your skin.

Comment

No comment needed. For the contemplative aspects see exercise 76.

20. Observing Impulses and not Following Them

Material: none

Location: anywhere

Duration: approximately 10 minutes

Age: everyone

Instruction

Choose a stretch of path in nature that you continuously follow during this exercise, for example walking up and down a path, around a hut or a thick tree, walking freely in the forest, etc. Now please observe the impulses that come to your senses, for example you notice that you want to rip off a leaf, enter the hut, scratch yourself, drink something, etc. Many changes in behavior will occur automatically. Observe all impulses, feel how they come, change, go, but do not follow them and continue on your path.

Comment

Mindfulness means only observing what is. Impulses remain impulses. There is no reason to judge them, but they also do not have to be carried out. Mindfulness leads to deceleration, distance to impulses, and a playing ground for adequate behavior in harmony with the environment and one's own values. Many people suffer from their impulsiveness or reactiveness, meaning they react too quickly to outer stimulation and do not take the time to examine the circumstances and what this occasion means to them before making a decision.

21. Observing Yourself – Being in Nature

Material: none

Location: anywhere

Duration: approximately 10 minutes

Age: better suited for adults

Instruction

Close your eyes while standing or sitting and be aware of your thoughts and bodily feelings (breathing). Take at least five minutes time for this experience. Then you slowly and consciously open your eyes and observe nature without losing touch with yourself. This can also mean to rapidly switch between observing nature and inner mindfulness, but the perceptions can also overlap and lead to outer and inner mindfulness simultaneously.

Comment

A good exercise to experience the resonance of nature and yourself in the form of bodily feelings, associations, emotions, etc.

22. Lying on the Ground

Material: appropriate clothing

Location: anywhere

Duration: approximately 5 to 10 minutes

Age: everyone, with variation for children

Instruction

Please lie with your back on the ground, for example on a meadow, forest floor, or at the beach. Now come into contact with the ground and feel into your body, without holding on to judgments and wanting to accomplish something. How do you observe the bottom as a whole? How even or uneven does it feel...how cold or warm...moist or dry is it? Now try to observe your entire stance and close your eyes...How are your feet arranged...your hands and arms...your head and shoulders? Now please observe your breathing...How is your mood? Does your perception change when you lie on your stomach...and on your back again?

Extension

Please open your eyes again and look into the space above you, the sky, the clouds, or the leaf crown of an old beech tree, or....What is your mood? Now observe everything that you can perceive with your sensory organs: the sounds, smells....Please sit up and observe how you do that. What changes in your feelings?

Variation for Children

A child lies flat on their back on the ground. The other children or the adult cover them with leaves and twigs until only eyes, nose, and mouth are not covered. The children imagine they are an inhabitant of the forest. One child after the other is covered until everyone is. On command the first child can "crawl" out again and free the other children from the leaves slowly and carefully. Afterwards they all lie fully outstretched with their stomachs on the ground.

Comment

The "covered" child variation can be found in Cornell (1991a, p. 26).

23. Wide Mindfulness

Material: none

Location: anywhere

Duration: 3 to 30 minutes

Age: better suited for adults

Instruction

Take a stance in which you are not unnecessarily stressed, but also have enough tension to stay awake. Leave your eyes open with a soft (relaxed, receptive) gaze, meaning do not observe the environment and its details, and instead allow for all optical impressions...Then please observe your entire posture...and now your breathing, without actively changing it...And now please give up every focus and be open to all outer impressions, all bodily feelings, emotions, and mental processes (inner pictures, thoughts), without choosing, amplifying, holding on, or rejecting anything. Even if a process occupies you for a longer period of time, do not become active, meaning you do not hold on to it, analyze it, and do not ask any why-questions. Do not push it away. It will go away and be replaced by some-thing else. You can also gently proceed to another experience with an "and" ("And what else is there right now?").

Comment

This exercise is a basic exercise of mindfulness. It is not entirely easy, because it does not have a focus to counter any drifting away. The exercise can be difficult and unsuitable for mentally fragile people, because it is possible that difficult subjects emerge which they cannot handle well, or because confusion occurs. Therefore, remind the participants of the ground rule that they can and should end any exercise, if they have the impression it is harmful for them (not because it is unpleasant). Much rests on the duration of the exercise and the experience of the participants here. Like every practice of mindfulness it is not independent from the environment. If you are not very experienced, you will generally look for a quiet and fitting environment, where there is no danger to be captivated by a special stimulation. Monotony of the environment will invigorate mental processes, while a diverse environment will invigorate outer mindfulness. Therefore, it is not irrelevant if wide mindfulness is practiced in front of a white wall or in nature. Practicing in nature will promote resonance with its impressions and rhythms and an experience of abundance and of being in the world, and this can be an important, moving, continuously valuable experience.

It is possible to repeatedly take on the stance of wide mindfulness for short periods of time, but it can only realize its full potential with sufficient time. A longer duration can be very sensible in nature. One can move a little during this. Sitting still is not necessary and can place the focus too much on the sitting itself. That would unnecessarily push nature and the broadness and diversity of natural appearances into the background.

Wide mindfulness realizes the aimlessness and the openness of mind-fulness as completely as possible, which are always slightly withdrawn in focused exercises (see chapter 1). Therefore, if it is fitting, end focused exercises as often as possible with a few minutes of wide mindfulness.

5.| Exploratory Exercises

24. Panorama Exercise

Material: none

Location: a place where we arrive

Duration: approximately 5 to 10 minutes

Age: everyone

Instruction

In this exercise you dive into the outer world with your sensory organs. Stand at a place you have chosen. If it is sunny, please turn towards the sun. Now slowly turn in a circle and look around. Observe your environment with the "eyes of a beginner", as if you had never seen this place before. Give yourself at least one minute of time for this.

For the second round, change your perspective and look into the sky above you and observe the cloud formations, the movements, colors, and forms. Also take one minute of time for this.

In the third round you observe the ground on which you are standing and also slowly turn around your own axis. Feel the ground while doing so.

Extension

Focus your attention on the place where you are at the moment. Then you focus your attention on the atmosphere of the location. Finally, you observe one thing or object after the other, for example the different barks, herbs, or the things laying on the ground. Also observe the movements of these things, their shadows, the forms and patterns, the singing and calling birds, and the clouds passing over you. When something new appears be open to it. You observe inner processes (thoughts, etc.) and then return to observing the outer world.

Comment

A very good introductory exercise for the beginning of an event or a walk. The extension is an exercise in "off-centerness" (German term: "Dezentrierung" , own translation, G.Z.). Many people who feel connected to nature can establish a powerful connection to it this way, because they comprehensively perceive nature and take the focus off themselves. It is also described by Coleman (2006, p. 162 et seq.).

25. Exploring a Location as an Animal

Material: none

Location: a place where we arrive

Duration: approximately 15 minutes

Age: everyone, especially children

Instruction

Look at your environment extensively and trace the question of where you are. Try to innerly adjust to this piece of nature as if you were going to spend a few days there. Or let the participants take on the role of a deer, fox, squirrel, or mouse and explore the forest from the perspective of these animals. Where could a place for sleeping be, where a good place that is safe during bad weather? Where does it find food, where is a safe place to rest, where can it drink? Sun itself? Where does it meet fellow species and where can the young be raised?

Children can discover their territory as an animal individually or with a partner. They take along several colored ribbons. Each animal has its own color. What is there in this part of the forest, for example? Where would I make my nest as an animal? Is there water? Food? Hiding places? Where do I have a good view? The children mark good places with their ribbons, so that other children can discover these places as well. If there is enough time, these places can be described as well: hiding place, viewpoint, favorite place, place for sunbathing, source of food, water, etc.

Comment

This exercise is well suited for arriving at a new place. It makes exploring easy, especially for children.

26. Change in Scenery

Material: none

Location: a path that leads through different atmospheres of nature

Duration: 15 minutes or longer

Age: everyone

Instruction 1: "Atmospheres of Nature"

Please follow a varied path that offers as many atmospheres as possible. This can, for example, be the path from the meadow, past the edge of the forest, into a conifer forest and a broadleaf forest, or a varied park landscape. Pay attention to how quickly the atmosphere and climate change. Do not focus on specifics, but on the entire aura of the location. Trace your own mood while doing so.

Instruction 2: "Exploring Nature Zones"

Please also follow a varied path. Observe the different atmospheres first and then focus on the specifics. Pay attention to the light, colors, moisture, temperature, sounds and smells, ground, vegetation, etc. Follow your impulses to trace the different stimuli and to observe and feel them.

Comment

We are not used to consciously observe atmospheres. We understand them to be the interaction of different, perhaps all, sensory channels, or rather aspects of situations (see chapter 2). It is especially easy to find impressive atmospheres in nature that strongly influence our mood and sensitivities. This perception is easier in nature due to the stronger contrasts that are offered. A Sharing and a conversation afterwards are sensible in order to make this point more clear. When perceiving specifics we realize how atmospheres are composed, although it is possible that the general impression is pushed into the background. In return we experience many details in greater intensity and in context.

27. Exploring the Weather

Material: none

Location: anywhere, with a view of the sky

Duration: 5 minutes or more

Age: everyone, with variation for children

Instruction

Go outside and just explore the weather with all your senses. Do not choose good weather and also practice this exercise in the rain and cold. Begin with the eyes and explore the signs in the sky with the different clouds, or the intensity of the blue or the grey. Now rest your gaze on the vegetation nearby: do you recognize any weather signs on it? Dew or raindrops on the leaves, or movements of the stems, leaves, twigs and branches in the wind? Include your ears as well: do you hear the weather? Then your nose: can you smell the weather? And at the end, the skin of different body parts such as palms, cheeks, feet, noses: compare the temperature, dryness, and wetness of the different parts.

Variation for Children

Where are the warmest places and where are the coldest? Where is it dry and where is it moist? How do these places feel with your palm, fingertips, arm, or the back of your wrist? Allow the children to first find the sunny or shadowy places and to then lay a heat path with, for example, stones, wood, or plant material.

Comment

An exercise that is close to everyday life. We took the variation with the heat path from Joller (2008, p. 83).

28. Aimless Exploration

Material: none

Location: an area where everyone has enough room to spread out

Duration: 15 minutes or longer

Age: everyone

Instruction

Go on an aimless exploratory tour on your own. Move forward in the beginning, or backwards, without any goal. You have no destination when you embark. Just head out and follow you impulses, such as changing directions. Leave everything up to your body, which reacts to impulses and impressions of the nature surrounding you. Try to not find anything out and to follow every new stimulation right away.

Comment

It sounds funny and is in the beginning. Therefore, allow for enough time to get into the rhythm of the exercise. It is an irritating experience of aimlessness. While we otherwise only observe impulses at first in mindfulness, we follow them in this exercise right away.

29. Time Dimensions

Material: none

Location: anywhere

Duration: approximately 5 to 10 minutes

Age: everyone

Instruction

Please look around: first, for something very old (for example several million years for mountains, rocks) and afterwards for something that is a hundred or several hundred years old, then for something that is one year old, something that is several months, weeks, or days old, and something that might be even younger (a footprint, a bud, an insect, a shadow, etc.). Then return to the present: what can you observe and feel *now*?

Comment

An exercise that makes us aware of our time horizon and of the difference between past and present. Arriving in the purely processional and therefore quasi timeless present can be very intense. This exercise was gladly used by me (V.S.) during my work at the Pro Natura Center in Aletsch, in order to find traces of the past in the landscape, for example the moraine of different glacial stages, a forest that is less than 150 years old, etc. The age structure of the forest, including stones, big trees, seedlings, and herbs, can be clarified this way. The last step back into the present emphasizes the aspect of mindfulness.

30. Blindly Feeling a Tree and Finding it Again

Material: trees, perhaps blindfolds

Location: sufficient similar trees in the area (5 to 10), or else anywhere

Duration: approximately 30 minutes

Setting: partner exercises

Age: everyone

Instruction

Form pairs. One partner closes their eyes. If you are the seeing person, choose a tree in the closer area that has somehow caught your attention. Experiment how you can safely and carefully lead your partner. Watch out for potential ground hindrances and lead your partner to the tree with a short detour. Now let them feel the tree with their hands slowly, its extent, its roots in the ground, and its branching. Of course, not only the bark is interesting, but the branches, moss, immediate surroundings, bulges, crevices, etc. that the unseeing partner can find. After approximately 5 to 10 minutes, you can lead your partner back to the initial place. Now your partner opens their eyes and tries to find the tree you picked for them. This usually works well. Then the partners switch roles.

Comment

As with all exercises where one partner closes their eyes and is lead, tactile experiences and the experience of the relationship play a central role in this moment. Unlike as is usual primarily in the context of nature pedagogy, we are not concerned with the refinding of the tree, but with the exploring itself. It is also interesting how the seen differs from the felt, or not at all. This exercise is the work of Cornell (1991, p. 33).

31. Exploring the Seasons

Material: none

Location: anywhere

Duration: 15 minutes or longer

Age: everyone

Instruction

Explore a specific part of nature or a path for signs of the time of year. Do buds begin to blossom in spring? Is the first green grass already growing? Are birds singing? Are butterflies flying? Are tadpoles swimming? You can observe numerous phenomena of the season in free exploration. As with all exploratory exercises you can observe when you begin to exert yourself and wish to excel at this task. In that case, return to the suggestion to just hold on to this focus and to see what you notice.

Variation for Children

Precede more directly with children and give them guidance at the beginning in form of objects to observe. For example, explore the stage of growth of leaves and pay attention to colors, size, texture, etc. Then switch to the stage of flowers, buds, etc. The time of year can also be explored together with children with the sensory organs: spring can be heard, seen, smelled, tasted, etc. The berries are already there in summer, tree leaves are firmer and nibbled off. Fall can be recognized by the change in color of leaves, leaves on the ground, the amount of worms, etc. With winter approaching, many fresh mouse- and molehills can be found, as well as "renovated" badger's burrows etc.

Comment

This exercise can easily be extended to a contemplation on seasons (see exercise 84).

32. Searching and Gathering

Material: baskets or bags, white cloth, list

Location: a not too barren environment

Duration: approximately 20 minutes

Setting: group exercise

Age: everyone

Introduction

Make a list of things to search for yourself or a group with the following text serving as an example:

- *something pretty*
- something colorful
- something yellow
- something soft
- 17 samples of one thing
- something completely straight
- something sharp
- a leaf that has been nibbled on
- something that reminds you of yourself
- an underside
- something that you have never noticed before
- *a message*
- something symbolic

Distribute a basket or a bag with a list of items to search for that are attuned to the area. Now everyone heads out and collects the objects on the list. It is helpful to lay out white cloth at the end of the search area where the items can be presented. Other possibilities for their presentation are an unstructured natural area or a bench. A separate cloth or area should be chosen for the objects collected during "17 samples of one thing".

It is possible to order the objects according to the individual search objective. White cloths with creases can be helpful, so that individual fields can be marked. One field is marked for pretty things, another for colorful things, etc. After a short discussion it is clear for most participants in which field which items should be layed. A sharing is sensible and exciting after this exercise.

Variation

A gathering exercise for groups: when a special natural object catches the eye of an exercise participant they should take it along. In the end, the natural objects are displayed and observed.

Variation for Children

It has proven itself useful to only make a few suggestions for children, for example as many items of three objects as possible.

Comment

When choosing the items to be gathered it is recommended and extremely appealing to changes categories and add qualities such as "something sharp". It is pleasant to take some time for the display and to start conversations with each other. The idea of the list of objects to search for is from Cornell (1991a, p. 78).

33. Mirror Walk

Material: none

Location: an area with trees

Duration: approximately 10 minutes

Setting: single exercise, variation for groups

Age: everyone

Instruction

With a mirror in front of our nose our eyes are offered an unusual glance into a forest canopy. Hold a mirror in front of your nose and walk freely around the forest with it. Experiment with the angle of the mirror and continually choose a different perspective. Pay attention to different perceptions of space, but also observe your body and how you feel.

Variation

In the form of a caravan: the person in the front without a mirror decides on the direction and the individual group members hold on to the shoulder of the person in front of them. The mirror is held in front of the nose with the other hand so that the forest canopy can be observed while walking. In this manner you walk a path for approximately 300 feet. It is also possible to do this without a mirror: with a handstand for athletes, looking between your legs, lying down, etc.

Comment

This exercise is impressive time and again, especially in the forest cathedral of an old beech tree forest or in a forest with low hanging branches and leaves that are above the head. It is nicest far from paths, but there should not be too many obstacles on the ground. The slower we walk, the more impressive it becomes, and dizziness can be avoided this way. The exercise makes you want to lie on your back in the forest and just gaze into the forest canopy. The mirror becomes a helpful instrument to get into the mindful observation of nature by widening our perception and estranging our perspective. This exercise is widespread in nature pedagogy and is also described in the Waldmeister database.

34. Observing the Surface

Material: none

Location: various types of ground (paths, woods, or meadows for example)

Duration: 5 to 10 minutes

Age: everyone

Instruction

Focus your attention on how you feel the ground that you are standing on. Explore it by moving your feet, kicking, stamping, and perhaps jumping. You can also touch it and feel how elastic it is, etc. After a few minutes, go to a different surface and repeat your exploration. Try to remain in contact with yourself during this exercise and feel how your body reacts, how you are standing, moving, and feeling.

Comment

An easy exercise in order to arrive and to "ground" yourself. It is very fitting for example when, due to a difficult subject or a complex exchange, the sensuality and experience of the surface, as well as steadiness and self-reliance have been lost.

35. Gaps

Material: none

Location: anywhere

Duration: 5 to 10 minutes

Age: everyone, with variation for children

Instruction

Our eyes usually regard objects and movements. This occurs consciously and unconsciously. Please go around and consciously look for gaps and room between objects or parts of objects. Observe the "empty" spaces between branches, leaves, trunks, clouds, blades of grass, pine needles, etc. Of course you will see objects that are left or right or up or down, but please focus your attention on the space in between them. Pay attention on how you feel while doing this.

Extension

You can experience the gaps through your movements as well by moving your fingers, arms, head, or your entire body through them.

Variation for Children

Children like to feel like a deer during the exercise. Or like a bee that is flying through a flowery meadow.

Comment

The exercise can also be conducted indoors, but is especially impressive in nature, because the diversity is very great and it is easier to observe emptiness there. Of course your gaze through the gaps does not reveal a void and a background is discernible, but the background is not a definable object. The exercise liberates perception from modes of perception and interpretation, leads to stunned silence, and can be very intense emotionally. It is very old and was already described in different variations in the Vijnana Bhairava, a text of Kashmir Shaivism from the 6th century A.D. (see Bäumer 2008, especially p. 109 et seq., and we thank Karl Baier for the suggestion).

36. Exploring the Environment with the Body

Material: none

Location: anywhere, but preferably dry and diverse

Duration: approximately 20 minutes

Age: everyone, with variation for children

Instruction

Please take in the attitude of mindfulness. Choose a place and look around. Now make tactile contact with the environment with your entire body (lying down etc.) or as many body parts as possible, with the ground, rocks, trees, or whatever comes to mind. Improvise, move from moment to moment, and observe how you experience nature this way. Then take another look at the place. In a group you call the participants back together with an acoustic signal.

Variation for Children

Children can find a nesting place as an animal of this environment and make themselves comfortable.

Comment

This exercise emphasizes the experimental and spontaneously creative aspect of mindfulness, which is certainly a challenge for many people, and should not be forgotten. You can of course try this exercise on your own during any type of weather, but we recommend dry conditions and a sharing session for groups.

37. Photographer and Camera

Material: pages with holes or firm paper, scissors, cardboard tubes of different thickness for variation 2, pieces of bark for variation 3

Location: anywhere

Duration: 10 to 15 minutes

Setting: partner exercise, with variation for individual exercises

Age: everyone, with variation for children

Instruction

First, decide who will play the role of "photographer" and who will be the "camera" in the beginning. The "camera" has its eyes closed at first. The "photographer" moves slowly and consciously observing through the environment with his "camera". Which motif spontaneously speaks to the "photographer"? The "photographer" focuses the face and the closed eyes of the "camera" on the object and chooses distance and section by slowly moving the partners head. In order to "capture" the picture, gently pull on the ear of your partner, who can then open their eyes for no more than 3 seconds. As soon as the ear is let go the eyes close again. This exercise works especially well when the "camera" places a "lens" in front of their eyes. This can be a hand forming a circle, for example.

The exercises of course also works without touching by simply leading the partner and letting them decide when they want to "take a picture".

As a group leader, you can also give tasks to the group during this exercise and its variations, for example to observe a certain type of tree, something beautiful, something that does not belong in nature, different types of bark, or something typical for this place.

Variation 1: "Photographer and Camera" as an Individual Exercise without any Material

You carefully move forward with your eyes closed and open them for a quick glance in between. Move your head while doing so.

Variation 2: "Photographer and Camera" as an Individual Exercise with Material

Take a piece of paper or a piece of cardboard. Fold the paper and then cut a small (!) window (1") along the crease line with a pair of scissors. Then hold your frame 4" to 12" inches in front of your eye. Now close the other eye and play with the distance of the frame to your eye. Observe different sections of the environment with the "creative eye" and linger – the same way you would observe a painting or photograph. Create your own sections that can certainly estrange the object in the process.

Variation 3: "Photographer and Camera" with Natural Materials

Collect pieces of bark or leaves with holes and observe the environment through this natural lens. As it is rarely possible to collect many pieces of bark with holes in them, it is more realistic for group leaders to bring some along. Leaves that have been nibbled on can usually be found often enough during the summer.

Variation for Children

Choose a cardboard tube from a role of toilet paper or a role of paper towels for different lines of sight. Cardboard tubes intensify the camera impression and allow children to slip into this role more easily. We recommend that each photographer take three pictures before roles are switched.

Comment

This exercise is good for outer mindfulness, but also for relational mindfulness, as it is also about letting yourself be led around blindly and to adopt someone else's perspective. This exercise can also be used to interrupt mulling things over. Patterns of perception are also broken. The exercise is reliant on the relative arbitrariness of the section. Very strange perspectives and sections sometimes develop, which makes it difficult to name what has just transpired. This is certainly desired by the practice of mindfulness. But this effect mostly occurs when the eyes are only opened for a short moment. The original exercise is by Cornell (1991b, p. 104).

38. Claiming Space for Oneself

Material: none

Location: an area in which everyone has enough space to spread out

Duration: approximately 15 minutes

Age: everyone

Instruction

Take in the attitude in mindfulness while standing in a certain place. Pay attention to your bodily feelings and movements in the beginning. Leave your eyes open with a "soft gaze", do not observe anything, and keep your eyes relaxed. Pay attention to all the small movements your body makes in order to remain standing in one place...Then make tiny movements that could not be seen by others...Let the movements grow stronger, but imagine that you are stuck in a tight tube...Now imagine that you slowly receive more and more room and extend your movements. Increasingly move your feet and change your position. Now takes as much room as you want. Conquer the area and observe it. Do not lose contact with yourself in the process.

Make your movements smaller until you reach a "normal" stance, trace something, but remain in the explored area at the same time.

Comment

This exercise is well suited when you arrive in a new place. It is important to take as much time as needed for this exercise. It originates from contact improvisation.

39. Nature as a Place to Breathe

Material: none

Location: small niches and gaps, for example in mountains or trees

Duration: approximately 5 to 10 minutes

Age: everyone

Instruction

Stand close (approximately 1 foot) to a relatively large tree and observe your breathing while you breath out (approximately 1 minute). You can also take small niches and hollow spaces in trees or mountains for this first phase. Now turn around, make more space for yourself, and observe your breathing again as it flows into the landscape.

Pay attention to all phases of breathing, also to the pauses. Do not actively change your breathing, but allow it to change.

Variations

If it is windy, breathe against the wind.

Form a breathing space with your hands and observe your breathing and its warmth.

Bring things into motion with your breathing: the seeds of a dandelion, grass, leaves on a tree, or sand on the beach.

Comment

While breathing you are constantly in a relation to the environment. This exercise makes the influence of the outer space clear. The differences in the way of breathing, perhaps the entire feeling of your body, and your mood may be small, but is therefore a clear case for mindfulness. As with all "breathing exercises" in the practice of mindfulness it is important to not wish to do therapeutic work on your breathing. If you consider working to change your breathing to be important, it is good to discuss the difference to avoid confusion. Purposefully changing your breathing (abdominal breathing, extension of pauses in breathing, etc.) can be very helpful! It can also be sensible to work with such suggestions in the practice of mindfulness, but then it should serve as a clarification of the breathing process or as an experiment, but not as a purposeful permanent change to your breathing. This can then of course also develop.

40. Where does it Come From?

Material: none

Location: forest, especially in the fall

Duration: approximately 5 to 10 minutes

Age: everyone, with variation for children

Instruction

Wander in the area and take in all the natural materials that are lying on the ground in front of you. Get a general impression of the diversity of the materials at first and pay attention to your associations with these materials, all your thoughts as well as your existing and nonexistent knowledge of them. Which things are familiar and which are unfamiliar? Choose 5 common objects like pine cones, small branches, acorns, or different types of leaves and lay them on a small area. This space can also be framed with branches. Now take an object and head out with it in your hand. Where is it from, where is its twin still hanging in its original place for example, such as a leaf on a tree or a nut on a shrub? Explore its origins.

Variation for Children

Let the children collect and sort common objects off the ground on a white piece of cloth. Add your own objects if necessary. Now the children can head out in pairs or groups of three, in order to find the original place of the natural materials and to explore them.

Comment

We do not recognize connections in nature right away. That children search for nuts under a hazel bush, acorns under an oak tree, or pine cones in a place where common spruces grow is anything but self-evident. This exercise is also very suitable for the origins of different leaves in the fall. Emphasize the exploratory character so that no pressure to find these things actually occurs.

41. Being Guided Blindly

Material: none, perhaps blindfolds or scarves

Location: easily accessible area, no cliffs

Duration: approximately 30 minutes

Setting: partner exercise

Age: everyone

Instruction

You must demonstrate this exercise, as words are too abstract in this case. Blindfold one partner. If there are no blindfolds available or it is too much of a challenge for the participants, then simply tell your partner to close their eyes. Now carefully turn your partner around their own axis repeatedly. Then you as a seeing person carefully lead your partner to distinctive places in the area, perhaps with a small detour. See how you can lead your partner well. Lead the partner to interesting and distinctive places such as trees, leaves, rocks, moss, or moisture. You can also put something in your partner's hand. The blindfolded partner touches and smells when they want to. After the area has been explored in this manner, the pair returns to the place they started. The blindfolded partner opens their eyes and the other partner shows them some of the places and objects they have just touched. Possibly the blindfolded partner will wish to find the objects themselves. After that the roles are switched.

Variation

Explore a piece of nature around you on your own with your eyes closed.

Comment

The sense of touch is sensitized and activated, and different surface structures can be observed. We list the exercise under exploratory exercises, but it also contains very emphatic and relationship oriented aspects. For some participants these aspects are more important than exploring natural objects. Questions arise such as: Do I have enough trust in my partner? The seeing partner perhaps thinks: What can be of importance around here for someone who cannot see? What would I like to offer them to touch and explore?

This exercise can also be found in Cornell (1991a, p. 27).

42. Cloth Exercise

Material: colorful cloth that can be seen from a distance

Location: diverse environment

Duration: approximately 15 minutes or more

Setting: group exercise, partner exercise with two or three people

Age: everyone

Instruction

Mark a selection of natural phenomena in the area with colorful cloth for the group (or a part of the group, or a partner), for example a picturesque piece of deadwood, an accumulation of mushrooms, many young trees, frost gaps in trees, or conspicuous animal tracks like droppings, pine cones or nuts that have been nibbled on, etc. Pairs or groups of three are formed. They go from cloth to cloth with one another and try to understand why someone has placed these markings in these places. First, everyone should look for themselves. Then perceptions are shared. Only at the end does the person who has hung these markings reveal why they have done so. Make it clear that it is not necessary to exert yourself to find something special.

Variation for Children

Concentrate on animal tracks, mushrooms, or something concretely tangible. Choose natural phenomena that are fascinating and obvious to children.

Comment

The effect of the cloths slowly moving in the wind is astounding. They have something fairytale-like about them and bring us into the present. The exercise is based on the traditions of the Australian Aborigines and the Berbers of the Sahara, who do not use cloths, but make each other aware of natural phenomena and speak to one another about them (also see exercise 43).

43. Nomad Exercise

Material: none

Location: anywhere

Duration: variable

Setting: partner exercise

Age: everyone

Instruction

You head out into nature together. One partner tells the other that they hear, see, observe, or smell something special. They speak about their nature experience. Then the roles are switched, either after a certain amount of time or you take turns pointing things out.

Variation

In this exercise you look for things in nature that have a personal meaning for you, which could be a symbol or a metaphor and tell a story or create associations in your mind. Trace these meanings. Show this natural object to your partner without speaking. Observe your associations again. Are they the same after you have shared or have they changed? Share the meanings that you associate with this object with one another.

Comment

The basic form is an elementary exercise, with which parts of a journey can be completed as a group. I (V.S.) have experienced the existential meaning of this exercise with nomads in the Sahara dessert. Observations of natural phenomena that stand out are shared with each other. In our everyday life it is astonishing, exhilarating, and relativizing time and time again how similar, but also how different perceptions of the environment can be in one place.

In regard to the variation: Since nature offers us many occasions to give it meaning, it is sometimes difficult to decide on one line of association. This is unnecessary. Follow different paths. It will most likely become clear during the exercise how different associations with nature experiences can be. It can be helpful to articulate them and to try to understand those of others. This way new shared meanings are created.

44. Searching for Opposites in Nature

Material: perhaps paper and markers for the variation

Location: diverse landscape

Duration: 10 minutes or longer

Setting: partner exercises

Age: everyone

Instruction

Explore the environment while focusing on opposite pairs. Choose one and observe your environment in regard to this aspect. When you tire of the topic, change to a different opposite pair. Show your opposites to someone in the group and share your experience with them.

Light	dark
sunny	shady
soft	hard
dry	moist
begin	end
similarities	differences
horizontal	vertical
round	straight

Variation

A creative variation: Mark opposites in the area (for example light – shade) or exemplify opposite pairs creatively.

Comment

The allure is that we develop new perspectives on familiar or unremarkable places.

6. | Emphatic Exercises

45. Listening to Animals in Nature

Material: none

Location: forest or meadow with animal voices such as birds, grasshoppers, or bees

Duration: approximately 10 minutes

Age: everyone

Instruction

Stay in a place where you can listen to animals, a place where animals not only make themselves acoustically noticeable for a short moment...Close your eyes for a short moment and listen to the different voices...From which direction are the voices coming?...Is it many animals or few?...Is the sound far away or is the animal near you?...Which feelings do the voices of the animals arouse in you? Spring fever, longing, uncertainty, sense of life?...Observe your mood...Do the animals have anything to do with you or your life?...Does it interest you what is making itself acoustically notice-able?...Or are you indifferent?...Do you have perceptions and images of these animals?...Observe the tones and the feelings, images, and other associations they arouse in you. What could move the animals to these tones, what could they be feeling?

"Grasshopper Concert" Extension

Some meadows or edges of forests are home to a rich fauna for grass-hoppers, so that we can listen to their courtship displays from the end of July to the beginning of October. Move closer to a chirping grasshopper step by step. Is it an uninterrupted chirping, as for example with a sewing machine..., are they short choppy tones..., does it rise and subside..., how many different ways to chirp can we discern...? Focus on one individually and carefully move towards it...can you approach it without it jumping away?...Can you manage to observe how they create their tones...with their wings...with their legs...observe and listen...is a female approaching...or a rival...? Which thought do you have when you take time to observe these creatures?

Comment

This exercise and its extension are suited as previews to nature expeditions which emphasize mindfulness. In spring you hear birds, frogs, and toads sing. In the early summer the different types of crickets begin to chirp first and the constant begging of young birds can be heard. In midsummer they are succeeded by a multitude of different types of grasshoppers. You hear the warning and contact calls of birds the entire year. Sometimes you hear more if you know more. In order to differentiate various basic forms of bird calls (such as songs, contact calls, different warning calls, or the calls of young birds) see Fischer-Rizzi (2007).

46. Microcosm

Material: magnifying glass, small transparent container, paintbrush

Location: meadow, near a creek, forest floor with small lifeforms

Duration: approximately 10 minutes or more

Age: everyone, with variation for children

Instruction

Sit or lie on the ground with a magnifying glass and a paintbrush and observe the smallest objects and processes that you can find. Where is something moving? Where is something crawling or jumping? Carefully capture a small creature with your paintbrush and observe it (perhaps in the container) through the magnifying glass. What does it actually look like? How many legs, colors, and structures does it have? How do you react to this creature? How does it make you feel? We have to remember where we captured it so that we can release it there again. A sharing is sensible afterwards.

Variation for Children

It makes sense to build on children's "excitement for hunting and gathering" and to spend sufficient time in this phase. Try to make sure the children observe the distinctiveness of the creature in its entirety despite their excitement.

Comment

We usually overlook the world of the smallest beings. So this is a good exercise in mindfulness, in order to observe the world more closely, especially since it does not usually challenge us to act, but appears to us in different ways. Some adults lay their magnifying glass down relatively quickly and observe an oftentimes unknown fascinating world. The extended observation of an alien creature can invite us to empathize, as in exercise 47. Anthropomorphizations are unavoidable and quite helpful, even if we remain skeptical towards our own interpretations (see chapter 13, p. 289).

47. Following an Animal

Material: none

Location: forest, meadow, or garden, especially for variation 2 after rain

Duration: approximately 15 minutes or more

Age: everyone

Instruction 1: "The Path of the Beetle"

Search for an easily observable creature like a beetle or a similar creepy-crawler on the ground or the bark of a tree, for example a spider. This creature has sensory perception, a nervous system, and a life of their own, no matter how small they may be. It perceives the world completely different than we do. This creature has "aims or paths" in a certain sense as well. How does this creature perceive this place? Where does it want to go? Why? How does it find its way? Follow it on its path for a while. Of course you can try to follow a larger animal as well, but that could prove more difficult to accomplish.

Instruction 2: The Slowness of the Snail

Look for a snail. Place the snail in your hand and trace its movements. Focus on its slowness. If you become slower does the opposite occur? What do you feel? Does your feeling change? Are there more feelings? What follows for your perception and feelings after articulating your feelings? If your aversion is or becomes too great, place the snail on a stone, a piece of wood, or the ground and observe it.

Comment

Beetles and insects do reflexively flee when we approach, so that this group is very suitable for extended observation on their journey. The extended (!) observation of an alien creature can lead to very different emotional reactions (of course to rejection, disgust, and boredom as well). It is important to allow this to occur during this exercise, even if many speculations and projections come into play. The basic exercise can also be found in Kalff (1998, p. 29&63). It is easily transferable to other groups of insects that move slowly. I (V.S.) like to use this exercise before a longer input on the topic of these creatures, so that the students, armed with magnifying glasses, can capture and identify them. It is part of a careful introduction to the topic of capturing animals. A third grade student once wrote me the following feedback: "I learned that insects are lifeforms."

You should be open to the idea that disgust and rejection can also not occur or change, especially during the exercise with the snail. The articulation of a feeling may differentiate it, but can also simplify and fixate it.

48. Approaching an Animal

Material: none

Location: lively area

Duration: variable

Age: everyone

Preface

You will encounter animals time and time again in nature, which usually flee from you before you have consciously noticed them. Many animals flee from humans. They fly or run away as soon as they notice us. Our voices, erect posture, and fast breathing reveal us as humans from far away. We inevitably cause reactions in the living environment around us. Birds fly away, deer and foxes run away and hide. Some animals also go their way unimpressed by us, for example, ants, and others look for closeness to humans, for example mosquitoes, flies, or ticks.

Instruction

We divide the following exercise into multiple phases:

Phase 1

First, pay attention to the reactions you cause in animals beforehand by experimenting with your posture (erect or crouched), your voice (loud or silent), your arm movements (moving back and forth or close to your body), and your pace (running or slowly sneaking). At which distance do the animals run away? Do the animals show signs of unrest beforehand? When does the crow fly away? When do jays begin to warn other animals in the forest as if they were the police?

Phase 2

While continuing to walk around the area you flow with the landscape and step slowly onto free spaces. Play with light and shade, stay inconspicuous in your appearance, and look for a quiet place where you know that, for example, birds are near.

Phase 3

Stay crouched or seated in your place. Wait until the animals have calmed down again. You consciously reduce the speed of your movements when getting up and approach, for example, a bird of your choice. Pay attention to the boundaries that the animal sets for you. When does it become restless? When does it calm down again? Does the animal look at you or does it look away? Which movements and postures does the animal show? Please observe these signs and remain still until the animal has calmed down. Move back a few paces or evade, depending on the situation.

Phase 4 (with birds)

When you have approached a bird, please do not look at it directly and instead turn to your side and pretend to be an animal that is eating. Pretend to eat something from the bushes. Pretend to be an animal in the forest and observe the reactions.

Phase 5 (with birds)

Observe what happens when you imitate bird calls. How do birds react to you?

Comment

This exercise is the mindful variation of sneaking up. We do not just want to come closer to the animal, we want to observe how other lifeforms react to our presence. Through our own behavior we can play with the range of boundaries where animals flee. This exercise is especially suited with birds, but also with grasshoppers or wild animals as well. I (V.S.) learned a great deal from the Berber Houcine El Kharassi when we set out to photograph birds in the Sahara desert together. I could not even stand erectly for this, but had to crawl up to them. I (V.S.) use this exercise in its basic aspects with school classes when we observe birds. I discuss beforehand how hunters or animal photographers even manage to approach animals and can almost always be certain of an attentive audience. Leaving out arm brandishing and practicing slow fluid movements beforehand already makes a great impression on the children. Then I send out the children on the hunt together. This way it becomes possible for us nature pedagogues to observe the feeding of young birds with, for example, an entire school class or half of one.

Try this exercise on your own on seldom taken routes. You will notice that many animals come into contact with you. Further advice on this exercise can also be found as rules of the wilderness in Müller (2011, p. 37&84).

7. | Playful Exercises

49. Touch Memory

Material: different natural materials, cloth

Location: anywhere

Duration: approximately 30 minutes

Setting: group exercise

Age: everyone

Instruction

As a group leader you collect approximately 10 different objects, which offer various touching experiences, before the beginning of the exercise. Cover the different natural materials, such as leaves, stones, moss, and wood with a cloth. The participants now touch one object under the cloth and search for a tactile "twin" in the closer environment. Everyone brings their findings back and the group reviews if every object has found a double.

Variation 1

The group leader lifts the cloth up for about 30 seconds, so that all objects are visible. Then the group heads out together and tries to find the same object.

Variation 2

The group leader chooses an object based its their differing smell. The participants grab and pull an object from underneath the cloth and smell it. The touching experience and visualization lead to a first orientation, but the smell is decisive in the end. In this case, it is good, if the tactile experiences are similar.

Comment

As with all recognition exercises it is important to remind everyone that it is not about performance: recognize growing pressure to perform (it belongs to us as well), but do not "sign" and intensify it, and return to the object with an "and" instead. Variation 1 can be found in Cornell (1991a, p. 53).

50. More and Less

Material: many different objects, cloth

Location: even ground

Duration: approximately 20 to 30 minutes

Setting: group exercise

Age: everyone

Instruction

While the group is concentrated on something else, collect a multitude of various smaller objects (20 to 50; gladly more of one sort) such as leaves, stones, wood, flowers, acorns, etc. Then spread them across an unstructured base or cloth and cover them. Then the group joins you and the objects can be uncovered. Everyone looks at the objects for approximately two minutes and then closes their eyes. Take 3 (2 to 5) objects away. The group opens their eyes and is supposed to find out which objects are missing. It is important that everyone can first take their time to look and be silent, so they do not immediately say what they know or believe. Then the group exchanges views. In a second part of the exercise, the group closes their eyes again and the group leader adds 3 (2 to 5) objects, which have been set aside for this purpose. The group opens their eyes again and sees if they can find these new objects. The exercise can be repeated multiple times and vary in its difficulty, depending on how conspicuous or inconspicuous the objects are that are taken away or added and how many objects are used altogether.

Comment

A very entertaining group exercise which can also be conducted indoors and with natural or artificial objects. Concerning the issue of pressure to perform see the comment of the previous exercise. It is especially exciting during this exercise that one believes a new object has been layed out in the second part.

51. Leading with Sounds

Material: scattered natural materials

Location: anywhere

Duration: approximately 20 to 30 minutes

Setting: partner exercise, with variation for groups

Age: everyone, with variation for children

Instruction

Form pairs. One person closes their eyes and the other one searches for natural materials with which different sounds can be produced. Wood, stones, and twigs with leaves are especially suited for this. The "blind" partner is led through the area solely with these sounds. Sometimes this is also possible with the sound of the "leading" partner's steps (stepping firmly, dragging your foot, etc.), especially when the surface they walk on is gravel or snow. In an emergency they can whistle, clap their hands, etc., but they cannot speak. The "blind" partner can even be led over uneven ground. It is exciting to play with the frequencies of the sounds or to be silent (the blind partner will usually stop then). So consciously use pauses as well. Unexpected changes in direction play with the expectations of the "blind" partner. The "leading" partner carries the responsibility of course. Sometimes the "blind" partner will follow someone else in group exercises. Playfully recapture their attention! You give the group a signal (Cymbal, etc.) at the end and the pairs switch roles. Afterwards, a sharing between the pairs and within the group is recommended.

Variation "Leading Backwards with Sounds"

The "blind" partner can also be led backwards through nature. Careful, this is not easy!

Group Variation

Everyone stands in a circle and creates sounds with natural materials. One person moves into the center of the circle. Someone starts making a sound and the person moves towards it blindly. After a while another person makes a sound that the person then moves towards, causing a change in direction. Then the roles are switched within the group and someone else moves to the center of the circle. In large groups it is recommended to form 2 circles.

Variation 1 for Children

Conduct this exercise in groups of three. Let every group pretend to be a bird species. Every group decides on birdcall that is to be produced with natural materials: sticks for the different woodpeckers, stones, or the human voice, of course, etc. (it is enough to recreate the rhythm). The birdcall can also be invented as well. The children are supposed to experiment with different rhythms, speeds, etc.

A "blind" child should now be lured to a partner in the group. It is easier for the children to really make use of the space to its full extent in groups of three, as well as to play with distances, because the "leading" partners can take turns and the inactive partner can secretly choose a new location to lure the "blind" partner to.

Variation 2 for Children

The children play a form of hide-and-seek with sounds in pairs: the pairs decide on a sound in order to recognize each other, for example a cat's meow, the hiss of a snake, or the drumming of a woodpecker. Afterwards, one child hides and lures their partner with the sound they decided on. The roles are then switched. This exercise is especially intense and formative for their attentiveness at dusk or in the dark.

Comment

It is an intense exercise that combines outer, inner, and relational mindfulness and is very focused. It is very easy for the participants to remain in the present for a long period of time during this exercise. One does not only pay very close attention to the sounds, but also feels insecurity while walking, as well as fear, relief, excitement, happiness, trust and distrust. The feelings in the relationship are experienced strongly and alternately. The exercise is more emotional than would be expected.

Variation 1 for children can also be found in a similar form in Kalff (1994, p. 66), and we have borrowed variation 2 from Barbara Gugerli.

52. Sneaking

Material: none

Location: anywhere

Duration: 5 minutes or longer

Age: everyone, especially children

Instruction

We are readily apparent when we move through the forest as a group. It would often be sensible if we could sneak and become as silent as a fox. Wild boar trample through the forest. We test the "wild boar walk" (similar to our everyday style of walking, tread with the entire sole) or the "fox walk". For the "fox walk" we first loosen our stance and slowly shift our weight from one foot to the other. Pay attention to your stance: erect, springy, slightly bent knees, and the arms fall loosely next to the body. Your view is directed straight ahead. Breathe in and out slowly and evenly. Now, first touch down with your heel and then roll to the inner side of your foot via the outer side of your foot. Pay attention to cracking branches, rolling stones, unevenness in the ground, etc. Take some steps this way. Now you can touch down with your toes or the ball of your foot first and observe the ground beneath you.

Move very slowly and silently this way and feel the contact with the ground. Reduce your walking speed to the extend that your movements are nearly impossible to notice. Observe your rhythm of breathing during this.

Comment

The "fox walk" is very well suited for children. An entire school class can silently move through the forest this way. The switching of rolls can be seen as an introduction, for example, sneaking like a fox (beginner) or sneaking like a hunter (advanced). Being allowed to trample like a wild boar in between is perceived as very relaxing. I (V.S.) am surprised time and time again how silent a school class can become this way. Some details of this exercise can also be found in Fischer-Rizzi (2007).

53. Forming a Snake

Material: none

Location: anywhere

Duration: 5 minutes or longer

Setting: group exercise

Instruction

All children hold hands in the beginning in order to explore the surrounding area. The chain should not be interrupted. Move over different types of ground with the children: wade through puddles and muddy areas, jump and climb over tree trunks, or walk through a thicket. Everyone travels alone in the next phase and pretends to be a space explorer searching for new discoveries.

Comment

This exercise is suited for arriving in a new place. The exercise can also be found in the Waldmeister database.

54. Speed Variations

Material: none

Location: clearly uneven ground with slopes

Duration: 10 minutes or more

Age: everyone

Instruction

Choose a part of the path with differing and possibly steep slopes. Engage
the slopes and find your own pace. Let the area, ground, and your body
decide which pace you choose. Observe when your pace changes and notice
the impulses that lead to this change...Does the deceleration come from
physical exertion? Do you slow down because, for example, the moss on
the side of the path interests you? When do you become faster?

Comment

No further comment necessary.

55. Tree Telephone

Material: perhaps Morse code, music box, or something similar

Location: forest

Duration: 15 minutes or longer

Setting: partner exercise

Age: everyone, with variation for children

Instruction

One person knocks and scratches in different strengths and rhythms on the one side of a sawed off tree trunk. On the other side the partner listens to the signals by placing their ear on the cut surface and gives answers, so that nonverbal communication develops. The group can also listen at the tree trunk: someone knocks or makes music with a small music box (or something similar) pressed to the tree trunk.

Variation for Children

One child is the squirrel and listens attentively if an enemy, such as a pine marten, is approaching and giving itself away with scratching noises on the tree trunk...or two woodpeckers communicating with each other...or the children develop their own secret language and send Morse code to one another.

Comment

A Morse code can be downloaded from the Waldmeister database.

56. Climbing a Steep Slope

Material: perhaps a rope

Location: a steep slope (for example 150' long) without a path that can just barely be climbed erectly

Duration: at least 30 minutes, longer is better, several phases

Age: everyone who is sufficiently mobile and strong

Instruction

The exercise consists of several phases that can be marked in the usual way (clapping, sticks, stones, cymbal, etc.). If you are underway with a group you should give all explanations and answer all questions beforehand, as the individuals will be spreading out. Therefore, it is not possible to repeat instructions during the exercise. A complete form of the exercise would look like this:

- stand in front of a slope together, for example in the woods

- recall the attitude of mindfulness into your consciousness or explain it to the group again. Especially consider the playful character and the interaction between inner, outer, and relational mindfulness

- take in the slope and observe which reactions and impulses it causes in you. The impulses are only observed at first and not exchanged with one another or put into action

- very slowly begin to walk or crawl up the slope after approximately 5 minutes. Move however you wish and experiment! Pay attention to how your body adjusts to the slope in order to fulfill this task.

- when you arrive at the top (loosely define in the beginning!) look for a place to stand or sit and view the slope from above. Are there surprises?

Does it seem higher or more steep than you thought? Which feelings does this view from above cause? (approx. 5 minutes)

- now make a slow experimental descent (approx. 10 minutes): climbing, walking, crawling, or sliding.

- return to your starting point and take in the slope. What has changed? (approx. 5 minutes)

- sharing and discussion

Variation

If the slope is very steep and/or the participants are not very mobile, you can attach a rope to a tree at the top that the participants can use for their ascent (approx. 10 minutes). This variation is also suited for children. Also attempt to teach the children how to mindfully ascend and descend after an athletic phase. If there are enough ropes, than all the better.

Comment

This exercise is only sensible when it is conducted slowly and with a sufficient amount of time. Intentionality and exertion are of course a part of it, but they should not push mindfulness into the background. Without mindfulness the exercise leads to uncontrolled action and exertion. That is a problem with all exercise that requires a lot of activity.

It is important that there is no path in the exercise. Perhaps we can remember climbing a slope without a path. Slowness is very important, as well as simultaneous inner and outer orientation and the adjustment of the body to the slope. The impact of the tranquil gaze from the bottom, from above, and then from the bottom again can be very intense, but also very different. Ascending and descending (when you finally reach the top) can cause different feelings as well. A sharing is therefore very interesting and exciting.

57. Experimenting with Water

Material: none

Location: water

Duration: approximately 20 to 30 minutes

Setting: individual, pair, or group exercise

Age: everyone

Instruction

- experiment with different nature experiences surrounding water

- dissolve substances in water, for example, and a handful of earth or sand

- consciously enter the water with muddy hands or feet

- throw different natural materials into the water and trace their movement in it

- which sounds can you elicit from the water?

- collect objects that have been changed in their form, consistency, or color by the water and order them in a creative way

- change the waterside by building dams, refuges, or branches if possible

Comment

Especially children are attracted to playful interaction with water. Do not let yourself be categorically held back by wetness and mud, and instead review your own attitude at most. Longer contemplations regarding water are suited for adults (see exercise 81).

8. | Shaping Exercises

58. Staging the Unremarkable

Material: different natural objects

Location: anywhere

Duration: approximately 20 to 30 minutes

Age: everyone

Instruction

Look for an "exhibition area" in nature, meaning an empty area of earth, low grass, sand, fine gravel, or snow in winter. It can also be a bench or a table in nature. Now move through the closer environment with open eyes and collect things that can be unremarkable. Collect only a few objects, especially when conducting this exercise with a group. The collected items are "exhibited" together. The individual objects should have a lot of free space around them so that they can be showcased. You can also choose a different specimen of each type in order to clarify their small differences and variability.

Variation "More is Less"

Let yourself be inspired by your current environment by one singe natural material with which you wish to experiment creatively. This can perhaps be a material that is typical of the environment, such as rocks in the mountains, seashells by the ocean, or leaves in the forest. You can also, of course, simply choose an object that you find stimulating. On which uniform surface does the material of your choice sufficiently come to bear? On the forest floor you can, for example, remove the leaves. Now choose a style of arrangement, such as simply laying it down, placing it together, piling it, etc. Try to work without a fully formed idea of how it should look. Make use of the "and-techniques" for this. Allow yourself to be absorbed with your hands and the contact with the material you have chosen on your predetermined surface.

Comment

It is not about finding special objects but about lifting them up from their obviousness and insignificance. It conforms to the attitude of mindfulness to interest one's self for everyday phenomena and to observe them more differentiated than usual.

59. Sketching

Material: simple drawing pads, pencils, sharpeners

Location: anywhere

Duration: approximately 20 to 30 minutes

Age: everyone

Instruction

Choose a specific object in nature, such as a tree, a rock, bark, tracks, or a segment of a meadow or landscape. Take in this view for at least 5 minutes. Pay attention to the lines, forms, patterns, distribution of colors, etc.

As group leader, you can of course specify the suggestion to, for example, a view of a landscape: "I suggest to only sketch the horizontal structures and then to add some vertical ones." Or you recommend to only sketch a flower or a blade of grass. You will not be able to circumvent the possible pressure to perform that some participants might feel. So emphasize the attitude of mindfulness, especially presence of mind and effortlessness. It is not about the result, but about taking a closer look. It is important to not simply push the pressure to perform to the side, but to recognize it without amplifying or holding on to it. Remind everyone of the "and-techniques": noticing pressure to perform and returning to viewing and sketching. In order to generally reduce pressure while sketching, you can make use of natural materials that stain. The rough lines of a landscape can also be brought to paper fairly well this way. Sketch the brown of the earth with, for example, the green juice of leaves or a piece of coal from a cool fire, etc.

The participants can later display their pictures (without names), which is especially interesting when everyone has sketched the same object.

Variation 1

Look at the object, the landscape, etc. Sit down in a way that the object remains in your line of sight. Now sketch what is important to you without looking at the object again. Then you take another look, memorize further details, and, without looking, add them to your sketch. Look as much as you want, but do not copy what you see, and instead sketch from memory.

Variation 2

Another possibility is to sketch objects that have been felt with closed eyes.

Variation 3

Lay out the most important contours with natural materials or strengthen and decorate small structures in the area.

Comment

Sketching fosters our perception. It challenges us time and time again to take another look and observe great lines and structures, as well as details.

Sight is often intensified in variation 1, as the sketchers are motivated to take a closer look. They have to memorize individual aspects of the object first. We took the idea for variation 1 from Kriebel (2007-10, p. 25). Variation 2 can be found in Joller (2008, p. 70). I (V.S.) was introduced to variation 3 during a Land Art workshop by SILVIVA, which was conducted by Monica Jäger and Nicole Schwery.

60. Shaping Lines in the Landscape with Movements

Material: none

Location: dynamic environment with hills, valleys, paths, trees, rocks, etc.

Duration: 5 minutes or longer

Age: everyone, especially adults

Instruction

Stand in a chosen area in which the topography and the lines of the landscape are clearly visible. Look around you and decide on a point on the horizon. From this point you follow the lines of the landscape with your eyes, as slowly and continually as possible. Follow the contours with your eyes first. Then add the movement of your head as well. You move your upper body next and then "sketch" the landscape with you hands, arms, and finally your entire body.

Comment

This idea can be traced back to Juliane Teuscher. This exercise is a challenge, but easier to accomplish than one might think. Many people do not like moving so slowly when others are watching. But everyone is very much occupied with the landscape during this exercise. As always with mindfulness, it is not about avoiding uncomfortable feelings, but about observing them. Embarrassment would not usually be a good reason to reject or break off the exercise. In the sense of mindfulness it would be better to allow for embarrassment and other uncomfortable feelings and then continue with the exercise, and then see if something has changed in the outer and inner perception and the experience of the connection to the environment.

61. Miniature Landscape

Material: countless natural materials, strings

Location: forest, as diverse as possible, perhaps pieces of deadwood

Duration: approximately 45 minutes

Setting: partner exercise (2 to 4 people)

Age: everyone, with variation for children

Instruction

Form small groups and head out into the forest together. Choose a small and manageable area that you creatively wish to draw attention to as a miniature landscape. It can be an overthrown plate of roots, an enchanted moss landscape, or any other conspicuous "elements of miniature land-scapes". Colored strings are well suited for creating boundaries, but natural materials do as well. The area should be at least 3 square feet in size. The small group deliberates in which part of the landscape which "infra-structure" should be built, or rather which type of use will be allowed. Take at least 20 minutes for this. Now each miniature landscape is visited together. In the first phase, one only looks and does not speak or interpret. Then you discuss. After the spoken tour you remain standing for 2 minutes and take another look at the small landscape in front of you.

Variation for Children

Have the children, depending on their age, build a gnome world, a certain animal habitat, or a miniature national park.

Comment

I (V.S.) first experienced this creative exercise during my internship in the Bavarian forest national park in an educational workshop in 1994 (see

Bavarian forest management 2010). I continued it in the Pro Natura Center in Aletsch. I suggested to the participants to build nature reservations and national parks. The individual groups did not, however, create as large a reservation as possible (which I was hoping for as an environmental activist...), and instead created wonderful worlds with space for humans and nature. Certain elements were always there: Meeting places, quiet spaces, observation points, "wellness" areas, good sources of food, water, wild areas, large animals that you can view, gardens, as well as cultural occasions regarding the ties of humans and nature.

62. Color Palettes

Material: cardboard writing pad in form of painter's palette or coaster, glue stick, or piece of paper with double-sided strong adhesive tape (e.g. for carpets), sand or sawdust

Location: diverse color variations, flowers and buds

Duration: at least 20 minutes, setting of timeline beforehand

Age: everyone, with variation for children

Instruction 1

Collect the diverse colors of nature in form of small colorful pieces of plants.

For the color palettes on cardboard, a glue stick is sufficient to glue the colorful pieces of plants. Press them on the material well, so that no part sticks out. This only works in dry weather.

Instruction 2

For the sand art postcard you take carpet glue (extra strong). You can glue the carpet glue on index cards, for example. It sticks in wet weather even. The pieces of plant are rubbed dry with paper towel or a cloth beforehand. The pieces of plant are firmly glued on the entire area and the free spaces are covered with sand or sawdust (for optical and adhesive reasons). By the complete gluing and firm pressing on of pieces of plant their withering is inhibited and the colors remain for up to 1 year.

All the color arrangements can be exhibited in a group, which strengthens the colorful diverse impression.

Variation for Children

For preschool aged children simply distribute differently colored cards as color patterns. Suggest that they collect similar colors in nature from leaves, buds, barks, stones, etc…

Comment

In our experience, the participants dwell for a long time and immerse themselves in the glorious variety of colors. Emphasize the sight of colorfulness. There is very little pressure to perform, as a simple arrangement already works.

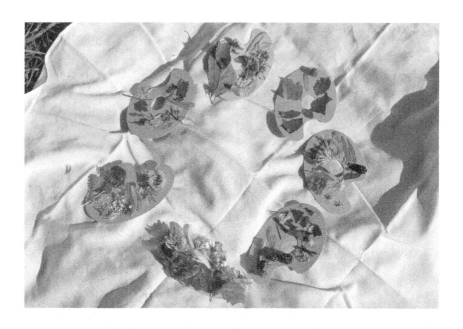

63. Juicing

Material: white cardboard cards, white non-woven fabric for variation for children

Location: diverse colors, flower and buds, berries, not during rain

Duration: at least 20 minutes, give time instructions in the beginning

Age: everyone, variation for children

Instruction

Collect different green leaves from herbs, trees, buds, berries, mushrooms, rotten wood, pine cones, etc. Grind and crush the materials, or rub them on a white piece of paper. For example, observe different variations of the color green in various plant juices, but also the movements and strength of your hand in action. The colors of flowers are well suited in spring, but highly perishable, as they dissolve in sunlight. In late summer berries are well suited, but always remember, especially with children, that they could be poisonous. Bring a moist towel along so the children can wash their hands afterwards.

Variation for Children

You can also have the berries crushed in small white diapers, which is especially fun for children. Elderberries are well suited for this. Since many of us believe that we should not make our hands "dirty", make it clear to yourself that it is not dirt or filth, but just plant juice, no more and no less. (Suitable clothing would be good however, as elderberry stains are difficult to remove from clothing). Your hands will regain their normal color sometime...

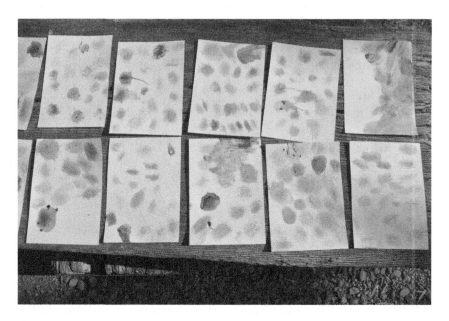

Comment

Crushing beautiful flowers in order to have a colorful dab in the end is not easy for many people. It often feels more appropriate with leaves and berries. Many people like to collect berries very much and coloration is a harmless method to do something with them (the fear of berries is widespread). The pressure to perform is relatively low when coloring with leaves and berries, as it is difficult to really color with them.

64. Arrangement on the Water

Material: natural materials in the area, perhaps the transparent cut off bottoms of plastic bottles or some form of wide water bowl or outdoor pot or soup bowl, water

Location: anywhere, in the best case slightly downward sloping waterside of a calm body of water, puddle

Duration: 10 minutes or more

Age: everyone

Instruction

Collect different light natural objects that do not sink in water such as seeds, leaves, and buds. Experiment beforehand with the weight and current, as well as the formation of waves due to contact with the material. Then display your findings together on the surface of the water, with a creative eye and active hand, so that it is connected to each other. Observe the slight movements of the colors and patterns. Water intensifies patterns, colors, and movements through contrasts.

Comment

Many small objects in nature have beautiful intricate patterns, structures, and forms that we often overlook in their diversity in our environment. This exercise exemplifies them with simple methods. In contrast to the previous exercise, the arrangement can seldom be brought home. The end result has a very fleeting character.

64. Lighting

Material: leaves with special patterns, forms, colors - for variation: old slides that can be opened, sunlight

Location: anywhere

Duration: 10 minutes or more

Age: everyone

Instruction

Collect leaves in the fall and connect them to form a necklace by running the stem through the leaves. This necklace can then be hung on a sunbathed tree. If this is difficult due to the consistency of the leaves or their stems, simply span a thin nylon string between two trees. Now you can hang the leaves with clothespins (everything not too serious) and let them flutter in the wind. A form of leaf gallery is created.

Variation with Slides

If you still have openable slides or can organize some: A richly structured or colored leaf is placed inside and looked at against the sunlight. You can pass the slide around in a group. This is especially coherent, if everyone passes their slide to their neighbor. If the group has more than 12 participants, we recommend splitting up the group, as it is to exhausting otherwise.

Comment

The idea for the slides comes from the Earth Education of Steve van Martre.

66. De-Familiarize

Material: natural materials in the area, perhaps thread, pins

Location: forest

Duration: 10 minutes or longer

Setting: partner or group exercise

Age: everyone

Instruction

Mark a relatively manageable area of 15'x15'. Explore why the discovered natural objects such as leaves, pine cones, stones, etc. are where they are. Leaves usually hang on "their" trees or have fallen off and are lying on the ground close to their original tree. Pine cones hang or stand on the branches of the trees or can be found intact (for example spruce) or splintered (for example fir) on the ground. Defamliarize the natural arrangements now in the chosen area and place something in a spot where it does not naturally exist. Perhaps you can use the thread or the pins to make it easier. There are no limits to the imagination. All participants are supposed to find the defamiliarization afterwards.

Comment

Through the placement of a natural material in an unfamiliar place we focus our attention and perception on salience, but also on the laws of nature that are so self-evident to us that they leave our consciousness.

67. Forest Net or Mandala

Material: natural materials in the area, perhaps string

Location: diverse materials on the forest floor

Duration: 30 minutes or longer

Setting: group exercise

Age: everyone

Forest Net Instruction

Search for one to two bigger sticks in the closer area. As group leader you lay your two sticks on the ground at an angle first. The participants lay their two sticks in connection to them and thereby define differently sized areas on the ground. Afterwards everyone heads out and explores the natural materials that are available. Each person decides on a single material in order to fill a sub-area with.

In a simpler version, you cross your sticks when you lay them on the ground, so that four (open) fields are formed. The group fills out each field with a different material. A mindful observation that includes one's own resonance to the work is recommended afterwards, as well as a sharing.

Mandala Instruction

With a mandala in the form of a circle you can define the forms, circles, and areas with string beforehand. Fill the areas from the inside to the outside, for example, using one natural material for each area.

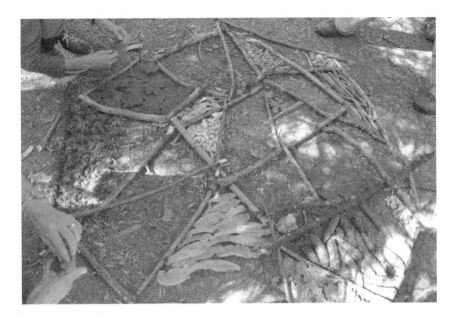

Variation for Children

The contours of a mandala or an animal are layed out with straight sticks, stones, and strings. Define a basic form beforehand. The silhouettes of animals or plants are well suited for children. These could include snails, worms, butterflies, pill bugs, spiders, flowers, trees, etc. Small groups can work on different subjects as well.

Comment

This is a powerful group exercise and especially the mandala is a classic of forest pedagogy. I (V.S.) encountered the forest net during a SILVIVA workshop on land art, which was conducted by Monica Jäger and Nicole Schwery. Creative exercises in groups bind the participants together and relieve the individual.

68. Three Dimensions

Material: sticks and wood and further material in the area

Location: forest or clearing

Duration: 30 minutes or longer

Setting: group exercise

Age: everyone, with variation for children

Instruction

Two or three sticks are rammed straight into the ground as a starting impulse. You can sharpen them beforehand if necessary. Now all participants search for further material in the area. Do not follow an inner picture of how it could look especially artistic. Begin with the place that you are in now. A material will catch your attention. Take it and head back to your collective work. Choose a place there where you wish to place your piece of moss, flower, deadwood, etc. Observe the change and see what the others have brought. This should not put you under pressure though, perhaps because the material of someone else might look much better. Leave your judgment of the actions of other behind you, even if you find that the brown piece of wood does not look good next to your beautiful flower. The new arrangement gives you the chance to be mindful of something that you have not noticed before. We recommend a sharing after creating this together.

Variation for Children

Build a climbing frame or parcours for squirrels.

Comment

This exercise is very binding for a group and works with the diversity of material and principles of construction. I (V.S.) learned about them from Kari Joller.

69. Connecting

Material: none

Location: forest

Duration: 20 minutes or longer

Setting: individual, partner, or group exercise

Age: everyone

Instruction

Begin to "optically connect" and "create contacts" between natural objects you notice in your immediate environment on your own, so for example lay a third tree trunk on top of two others or lay a line of leaves from one tree to the next.

Where is another participant in the group working? Contact them and signalize that you wish to create a connection with natural materials. In the end there will be many visible connections between individual natural objects, but also between the works of the individuals in the area. Follow these connections and trace the "system" that has been created.

Comment

An individual exercise often spontaneously becomes a partner or group exercise in the process of connecting.

70. Cleaning Up

Material: available in the area

Location: forest

Duration: 20 minutes or longer

Setting: individual, partner, or group exercise

Age: everyone, especially adults

Instruction

Choose a forest floor with many different forest materials, an area with as much "chaos" as possible. Mark the area that you will clean up with sticks, so that your work will not be endless. You can change your boundaries at any time, either making it smaller if everything is becoming too much or making it larger. Lay brown leaves with leaves, moss with moss, pine cones with pine cones, and stones with stones. Choose a system of organization for each material.

Comment

This exercise never ends and could be extended indefinitely, especially in the forest. Since it is so senseless and has no aesthetic demands it is easy to access and one quickly becomes involved in the work. An intense contact with the materials and the existing diversity develops. One's own organization system is constantly questioned and adjusted to the situation. The exercise is also fun as a partner or group exercise. Pressure to perform seldom develops, as nothing new is supposed to be developed and instead "old things can be cleaned up".

71. Archaeological Field

Material: perhaps a stick, small stones

Location: especially well-suited for the forest

Duration: 10 minutes or more

Setting: individual or partner exercise

Age: everyone, especially children

Instruction

Head out into the forest with an exploratory look at the forest floor. Where are immersions, uneven ground, interesting structures, or diverse materials? Choose an area of, for example, 3'x3'. Begin with your dig from the center, in order to showcase something like an archaeologist. You clean the area, shove, dig, shovel, scratch, and smooth. Small flat edged stones or twigs can be used as tools. Create your own "tools for a dig".

Consciously observe what you remove, but also what is brought to light. Trace the changes and pay attention to small things and details like an archaeologist. Take a look around from time to time to see where you are at that moment.

Comment

An intense contact with the ground is created by poking around, digging, or scratching the ground. We recommend a sharing when working with adults for this unusual exercise. Especially children love this exercise. Emphasize that the roots of trees should remain unharmed during this exercise.

72. Forest Art

Material: available in the area, white cards and marker

Location: forest

Duration: 20 minutes or more

Setting: individual, partner, or group exercise

Age: everyone

Instruction

Search for a tree trunk, branch, or tree stump that you wish to change. Position it differently, decorate it, "destroy" it, create something with it, leave it the way it is, or do whatever else you may wish with it. Observe associations and scenarios that arise and play with them. Give your work a title and yourself an artistic name. Afterwards you visit the different objects together as a group. Perhaps the artists even present their work.

Comment

I (V.S.) have taken this exercise from the work of my colleagues Silvia Fux, Regula Guyer, and Tatiana Heimer. With the naming of their work and the assuming of an artistic name the artists hint at how they understand their work. They encourage further interpretation.

73. My Barefoot Path

Material: available in the area, perhaps a rope

Location: forest with little undergrowth

Duration: 10 to 30 minutes and longer

Setting: partner or group exercise, individual exercise as well

Age: everyone, with variation for children

Instruction

Explore the forest floor beneath your feet in order to find out how it would
be to walk barefoot on it. Where do you recognize an area with soft moss?
Where are pine cones lying on the ground, where is an accumulation of
rocks or leaves? Observe your expectations. Choose a stretch of path and
mark it with sticks or stones. Now attempt to adjust the stretch of path to
your needs with as little creative intervention as possible. For example,
remove thorns, sharp rocks, or annoying branches. Take things away instead
of building something completely new. Now choose a partner to lead you
on your own path. Then the roles are reversed.

Variation for Children

Animals do not wear shoes! And people also often walk barefoot in the summer. How does this feel? Create a barefoot path with children using materials they wish to try. Is there a suitable stretch where the ground itself already promises diverse sensual experiences? You can span a rope tightly between two trees for this purpose. The ground beneath the rope is then covered with different forest materials, always 1,5' of the same material. The children collect materials such as moss, stones, pine cones, and leaves for this. To conclude the exercise, the children can walk the path barefoot with their eyes covered while holding on to the rope. While building, you should make sure that the barefoot path does not become an obstacle course.

Comment

We recommend to base this exercise on what the ground offers us. The already existing should be emphasized by removing materials. For example, moss is freed from branches or the rocky underground is freed from other materials. The reverse is also possible, namely placing rocks on moss or offering moss islands on top of rocks. This exercise has an exploratory component, as we base it on things that are already there. The exercise also has a strong sensual-receptive component.

74. Coloring Bark Beetle Branches

Material: bark beetle branches, water-soluble paint, paintbrush, water

Location: forest

Duration: 30 minutes

Age: everyone

Instruction

Look for a bark beetle branch with visible eating marks in the forest. Allow for enough time for the search. Compare the depth of the paths, the patterns and structures, the chambers, and escape holes. Now choose the deepest eating trail and color it with paint. Allow the color to dry for approximately an hour. Then dip the branch in water and rub away the paint that is outside of the indentions. Dip the branch in water again to rinse it. Make sure the paint in the eating paths is not washed away.

Comment

No comment necessary.

75. Nature Concerts

Material: natural materials and objects in the area, perhaps elastic bands or wire for instruction 5

Location: anywhere

Duration: 15 minutes or longer

Setting: group exercise in pairs of two or three

Age: everyone

Instruction 1: "Playing Music Together"

Give a concert with natural materials. Choose a place for the concert. Then choose the "musical instruments" that it offers. Head out and explore on your own for this. Try to make sounds with natural materials. Experiment: rub or knock stones together, rustle and crackle with leaves, throw things into the water, or drum with sticks. Now you choose some "instruments". Natural materials that can be transported can be brought to the place of the concert. Sitting or standing in a circle together you begin to play. Take in the sound impulses of the others and pass on some of your own. These can be shorter or longer, depending on our wishes. Take breaks, change your rhythm and volume, and try to somehow participate in the developing sound space. Do not lose contact with the natural materials that create these sounds.

Also pay attention to what you see, feel, and which inner pictures or fantasies develop etc. All this is part of listening and constitutes your resonance.

Instruction 2: "Concert goer"

Form small groups, for example with four participants. One is the concert goer. That person sits down and closes their eyes while the others play a nature concert for them. After, for example, 5 minutes a different participant becomes the concert goer.

Instruction 3: "Stone Concerts"

Search for differently sized and formed stones. Experiment with different sounds that you can create with these stones. You can perform circle movements with a small stone on a slab of rock. How does the sound change over time, as uneven areas are ground away?

The entire group can play an improvised piece using only rocks. Of course, other materials are conceivable as well, but rocks create an astounding sound.

How do the letters of our name sound when we write them on the slab with the small stone? The O is usually recognized, as it is a circular movement of stone. Is it different with U, I, or E?

Instruction 4: "Noise Orchestra"

What is suited for rustling, crackling, creaking, banging, ringing, drumming, howling, clapping, trampling, or clanking?

Instruction 5: "Plucked Concert"

The thin branches of a spruce can be plucked as well. We hold our ear to the trunk during this. We can span wire or an elastic band very tightly between two or three thin branches. One person can then listen with their ear against the trunk.

Instruction 6: "Wooden Xylophone"

Choose straight, branchless, at least arm thick pieces of wood. Hazel wood is very well suited, which can also be sawed and carved beforehand. Experiment with old dry wood and with fresh wood. You can hang the wood in different lengths on a string or just lay it on your upper leg. It is only important that they can swing freely. It is also conceivable to spread them out on the ground, on a rope as a display area, or just on pine cones. Small thin branches of hazel are suited as cleaves.

Comment

Very connecting, creative, and lively exercise. Personal resonance in form of thoughts, associations, memories, feelings, etc. belong to humans making music and listening. To make mindful music and listening as well! We are not physical objects or recording devices. The resonance should only be in reference to the current music or making of music and not to move away from it too far. This happens, for example, when you form a new focus that leads out of the present ("This scraping reminds me of the cat that I used to have, how is Carl doing?", etc.).

A concert with stones can be found in "The Great Learning", a composition by Cornelius Cardew (1971). Instruction 4 is especially suited for children, but adults should have fun as well! Writing on stone can be found in Joller (2008, p. 131).

9. | Contemplative Exercises

76. Contemplations in Nature

Material: none

Location: variable by subject

Duration: 20 to 45 minutes

Age: more suitable for adults

General Instructions on Contemplation

By "contemplation" we mean free non goal-oriented associations, thoughts, and feelings regarding a specifically defined existential subject. The subject can consist of a term, but also a sentence, a story, an image, a natural object, a landscape, an atmosphere, or a process in nature.

A General Instruction on Contemplation Could Look Like the Following:

"We suggest that you contemplate on subject x. Observe all your associations, so thoughts, inner pictures, memories, fantasies, and feelings regarding this subject. Do not attempt to reach a goal, for example, gaining insight. When you feel such an urge recognize it and return to the natural phenomena with an 'and'. Allow yourself to be inspired without exertion."

It can occur that new topics with new focuses evolve from the original topic or that you waste too much energy on an image, a memory, or a thought. Trying to find something out can also be exerting. If you notice this, then return from this specific focus to the subject and the natural objects, processes, or atmospheres that somehow represent this subject for you. Every time you move too far away from the subject you return with an "and". Or decide on a new topic if the original one does not fit to you and the natural environment that you are in at the moment.

End your contemplation with a short phase of wide mindfulness. For more on "wide mindfulness" see exercise 23.

This detailed explanation should also be given by a group leader to the participants and the leader should ask if everyone has understood the principle.

Contemplation is well suited for nature experiences (see exercise 77). But it is also possible to link everyday natural phenomena with terms. We either search for objects that subjectively fit to a certain topic and carry it further (variation 1), or we dwell in a place that hints at a certain topic (variation 2). So follow instruction 1 or 2.

A detailed sharing and discussion of the exercise are strongly recommended. An important opportunity for the participants to discuss existential subjects in a group results from this exercise. A large amount of time should be planned in for these conversations, of course depending on the size of the group.

Instruction 1: "Contemplating with Natural Objects"

The group leader names one subject (or several) for the group and the participants look for natural objects and phenomena which represent, encourage, or enrich this subject for them. The subjects can be relatively closely linked to natural phenomena, as they are specifically being searched for.

Instruction 2: "Contemplating with Natural Objects"

The group leader has thought about which subject of contemplation fits to the place beforehand. They let themselves be inspired by it. The selection of course is a matter of their subjective feelings, but many atmospheres of places are more or less inter-subjective.

Every participant now looks for a place, but also moves as far as they can still hear a signal calling the group together. Also, give clear time instructions. This will mostly vary by weather and should not be too short. The participants should now take in a relaxed stance in which they are not unnecessarily tense, but also not so relaxed that they fall asleep. A medium state of bodily tension and normal alertness are just right. The participants sit on the ground, on a tree, on a rock, etc. in nature. They can also lie down and of course they can move. It can also be good to walk a little in between.

Subjects

Some subjects are emphasized by every natural environment, and objects and environments can easily be found, for example "attachment", "solitude", "trust", or "thankfulness". They are suited for both of the described variants. Subjects such as "destruction" or "weakness" require a search to begin. For the second exercise variation subjects should be chosen that correspond with the atmosphere of the place and are supported by it. Boredom, for example, is induced more by gazing at a rocky cliff than by gazing at a wide open landscape, which itself suggests the subjects of "dependence and freedom", but not safety, for which a well lighted forest with troughs is suited, etc.

Decide for yourself which variation you would associate with a subject. This list can of course be easily extended and some subjects can be combined well.

Recommended Subjects

Lightness, Diversity, Becoming, Transience, Strength, Weakness, Beauty, Weakness, Struggle, Change, Harmony, Ability, Transitions, Slowness, Waiting, Death, Stability, Vitality, Departure, Destruction, Joy of Being, Creativity, Violence, Affection, Connectedness, Work, Cooperation, Symbiosis, Boredom, Happiness, Safety, Trust, The Power of Growth, Silence, Dependence and Freedom, Solitude, Sense of Security, Peace, Gratitude, Nature/Culture.

One Example: "Death and Life"

Begin this contemplation with a walk in the woods, by a lake, along the coast of the sea, or across a meadow. Look for a dead natural object. Do not only think of dead animals, but also of plant material, fallen trees, etc. Quickly examine it with your senses (one or two minutes). What does it look like? Can and do I want to touch it? What are the traces of transience? How long has it probably been dead? How long will it take until all traces of this life form have disappeared? Allow yourself to be inspired to the subject of "death" by the dead life forms and continue it as long as possible.

Observe which thoughts, feelings, images, and bodily feelings it causes. Take at least 15 minutes time for this. Afterwards, please look for a living plant or animal and change your contemplation to the subject of "life". Dwell for 15 minutes during this as well.

Comment

Contemplations are primarily known from religious contexts.[23] We surely practice such contemplations spontaneously in nature. Countless examples can also be found in natural philosophical, spiritual, and belletristic literature. A mindful and explicit practice will generally be longer and more disciplined.

We recommend to go without directives as much as possible and to simply name the subject. The sharing should also be limited to the exchange of experiences as far as possible. There is room for further ideological discussion in the discussion phase. We think they are important and interesting time and time again, but a time-limit is necessary here and they tend to take longer than expected.

---

23. They used to be called "meditations" in the Christian tradition (Baier 2009).

77. Nature Experiences

Material: none

Location: depending on subject, for example waterfall, cave, rocks, mountain tops, quarries

Duration: 30 to 60 minutes

Age: everyone, especially adults

Instruction

Plan in an occasion or phenomenon for your time in nature, in which nature has strong expressive power. Take your time to focus on this phenomenon in detail and observe what it causes in you. Reactions will vary greatly with different participants, as will the amount of self-experience in this exercise. There are endless possibilities for the practice of this exercise. Some are not planned or plannable, but appear spontaneously, as we experience during every longer hike.

This is one form of approaching nature that is familiar to all of us. Therefore, it is almost more important to remind participants of the attitude of mindfulness. It is about not wanting to increase the specialness of the situation, or develop any goals. Do not begin any special or even risky activities during the practice of mindfulness, and instead proceed more playfully with the situation and let go of special expectations as well.

Give yourself time, remain in the present and the natural phenomenon, and remain in contact with yourself. What do you feel and what does this

nature experience mean to you? Perhaps you momentarily only perceive.
Do not exert yourself. Perhaps nature does not matter to you in this
situation. Then leave it like that and observe what happens next.

Extension: Collecting Themes in the Group

Collect the subjects that have developed for the participants through this
natural experience in a sharing after an action-oriented contemplation. The
subjects are then summarized by the group leader and suggested to the
group as a collection of ideas. Then the participants can choose a subject
and then contemplate on that subject. In this case, we recommend to shorten
the time for both exercises.

Comment

"Adventures" are experiences which leave traces and are lasting and change
our life, more or less. This exercise is more about the attitude of mindfulness in contact with nature, everything else develops from there. An
extensive sharing is sensible, because intense individual or emotional
subjects can occur. Furthermore, sharings always mean stimulation as well,
as they make aspects of the situation able to be experienced by others.

The following exercises (78 and 79) are examples of nature experiences.
As they are fairly complex, we have described them in a special manner.

78. Sunset or Sunrise, Twilight and Night

Material: flashlight, seat cushion, warm clothes, map of the stars if necessary

Location: should be relatively safe to traverse in twilight and at night as well

Duration: dusk, twilight, night

Age: everyone

Preparation

Explore the area in which you wish to experience the darkness and perhaps the stars during the day, so that hazards can be excluded beforehand. This, of course, is especially important for group leaders. Places far from light and settlements are ideal, from which you can reach a safe place, for example, from a storm within 15 minutes. Bring along sufficient warm clothing and a seat cushion. Observe not only the weather forecast, but also the times of the moon. From new moon to the first half of the rising moon, the moon remains visible for the first half of the night. It is visible for the entire night during full moon. If you wish to experience true darkness with a cloudless sky then choose days between the setting moon and the new moon.

Twilight

Sit in your own safe place where you feel comfortable and wish to ex-perience the twilight. Places at the edge of the forest, side of the path, or a clearing in which the trees are easy to discern are well suited. If you wish to experience the sunset you need a respective view and suitable weather. Do not make it reliant on the weather, as it will always be lighter or darker.

Now pay attention to how the light complexions change, the colors of the vegetation or the sky, the contrasts, trees, sounds like fading birdcalls, the call of the blackbird, or barking deers and foxes. Do not only observe the change in nature, but also pay attention to your feelings and thoughts. Does "twilight" also have a metaphorical or existential meaning to you? How do you deal with the transitions? If you think of something then trace these meanings, but also let go of them again and focus on the twilight. Does dark nature cause other thoughts and feelings in you than light nature? Observe the sounds around you, the earth on which you sit, and the trees that have stood for decades. If you feel scared, then accept it and observe it, but do not act. Observe how it continues – with your feelings and the twilight. Only react with a termination of the exercise if a real danger exists. With increasing darkness and a cloudless sky you can watch the light of the moon and the stars in the sky above you increase.

Sunrise

It is of course beneficial to have a place with a respective view. But it is not necessary, as it becoming lighter is stimulus enough. Begin on time with sunrises, because it is exciting to hear the birds announce the rising sun and the first signs appear that something is happening. If possible, choose a place with many birds and make use of the spring.

Night

After a sunset it can be nice to make a fire (see exercise 79) and add a hike through the night. Observe safety measures, especially if older participants are with you.

It makes a big difference how you light the path: with a lantern, with one or more flashlights, with torches, etc. How fast you move depends on this, as well as if the darkness becomes more prominent or the feeling of togetherness. A lantern reduces the experience of darkness, but leads to a sense of safety in the group, whereas a flashlight lights selectively outwards and leaves more darkness. Switch between the different forms of lighting! Also, from time to time, stop and turn off all the lights. Emphasize other sensual qualities, especially hearing. This happens on its own, but can be emphasized nonetheless. A walk at night causes many emotions and memories. As a group leader, stay in contact with your group. If necessary, stop and conduct flashlights or sharings. But do not get lost in individual reports. Always return to outer mindfulness and indicate the interactive aspects (How do I move in the dark, how do I feel as part of the night or the group?).

Comment

Experiences of twilight and night can lead to unusual experiences. Especially at night, many people react to nature with associations, thoughts, and feelings that seldom arise during the day. If this experience is unusual for you, we recommend going with a group the first time. Depending on where you are, it is also recommended for safety reasons. It is sometimes a motivation for participants (especially women) to take part in nature groups in order to be able to visit nature at unusual times (and in unusual places).

As group leader, allow enough time for a sharing.

79. Fire

Material: dry wood, material in the area, matchbox

Location: campfire

Duration: 60 minutes or longer

Setting: individual, partner, or group exercise

Age: everyone

Instruction

Go to an officially designated campfire site. Ask your local officials where such a site might be in your area. Make sure that there are no tree roots underneath it. Look for suitable dry non-rotting wood in the area and for fire starters like dried grass, dried buds, birch bark, or dry fir brushwood. Collect sufficient material so that you have everything available and do not have to head out again. Is there water nearby in order to extinguish the fire? If not, you can prepare a supply of earth or sand in order to extinguish the final embers.

Experiment with different materials: Throw different materials in the fire to cure them: sage, mugwort, rosemary, resin, or grains of corn. Place different types of wood on the fire one after the other, for example beech, birch, oak, spruce, or willow. Which wood burns fastest, burns longest, smokes, gives light, and how does this atmosphere change with the respective wood? How does the color, light, smell, or sound change? Poke around in the fire, make smoke signals, trace the path of the smoke into the sky, etc.

Follow the play of the flames, its movements, colors and sounds, smells, and its waves of warmth with all your senses.

Remember to extinguish the fire well. Do not simply leave glowing embers behind. Use earth, sand, or water and observe how the fire goes out.

Extension: "Going into the Dark"

The group stays at the fire. One participant enters the darkness for several minutes – as far as they wish. When they return, they tap a different participant who now heads out on their own. The participants observe how this makes them feel. Various reactions are possible, from fear to the question: Do I even wish to return?

Comment

The transformation process of burning wood to light and warmth, rising smoke, and the constant transformation of flames to gray ash is one of the most fascinating natural phenomena that few people can stay away from. Fire creates atmosphere and causes a number of moods in us: comfort, liveliness, sense of community, confidence, arriving, but also menacing and uncontrollable energy. Plan in sufficient time for a campfire.

80. Small World

Material: none

Location: anywhere

Duration: 20 minutes or more

Age: primarily for adults

Instruction

Take a seat in nature, if possible in an area that offers some (!) diversion. Mark an area of about 1'x1' with a twig or by different means. Now spend the planned amount of time with viewing the area. You can gladly examine it more closely. But remain focused on the area. If your gaze or thoughts drift away it is fine. Observe it, allow yourself some time for this diversion, and return with an "and" to your area. Which associations, thoughts, and feelings do you have during this observation? Accept boredom and annoyance as you would exploration and surprise. Take the recommendations in the instructions in exercise 76 to heart.

Conclude the exercise by walking around for some minutes in wide mindfulness, observing everything that is happening at the moment (see exercise 23).

Comment

A possibility to explore how diverse nature is and observe different emotions and mixtures of feelings (happiness, gratitude, but also impatience, curiosity, boredom, etc., let us leave this open). What does the experience of boundaries and vastness tell me?

81. Water

Material: none

Location: by the water or during rain

Duration: 20 minutes or more

Age: everyone, especially adults

Instruction

Sit or stand by a body of water (creek, pond, ocean, etc.) or observe the rain. Take in the water in all its facets: color, transparency, smell, mobility, liveliness of the water, etc. (see also exercise 19), possibly also waves, vortexes, or the sound of rain. Keep the general explanation to contemplation in exercise 76 in mind.

Comment

The water can – if you take time for silent observation – initiate existential themes. The general prevalence of water inside and outside of organisms as a "life elixir", its power through consistency, its flow and mobility, its adaptability, and the transparency of the water – all this can cause associations and thoughts on life topics. Water especially offers us experiences related to time such as rhythm, pace, flow, consistency, and transience. Water intuitively lures people to it and plays an important role in nature experiences.

We use *everyday* phenomena with the exercises including trees or water (see exercise 83) that are especially suited for a contemplative exercise without a predefined topic. Of course, you can also conduct this exercise with other widespread natural phenomena, for example:

• roots

- blossoms
- earth
- rocks, stones, cliffs
- clouds
- colors (green tones, autumn colors)
- snow
- wind
- frozen things (different levels of icing)
- rain
- etc.

82. Bridge Exercise

Material: none

Location: on a bridge

Duration: approximately 10 minutes

Age: everyone, more for adults

Instruction

Stand in the middle of a bridge above a creek or a river. First, look at the side where the water is flowing towards you and gaze at the water for approximately 5 minutes. Afterwards, you gaze at the water flowing away from you on the other side for the same amount of time. Pay attention to the resonance that these different perspectives cause in you.

Comment

A sharing is very helpful for this exercise. The order in which you gaze at the water can also be reversed. It is important to be in contact with the water flowing towards and away from you and your resonance (associations, feelings, etc.) at the same time. A simple exercise with surprisingly different and sometimes intense reactions by participants. We wish to thank Juliane Teuscher for this exercise.

83. Underneath Trees

Material: none

Location: underneath trees

Duration: 20 minutes or longer

Age: everyone, especially adults

Instruction

Choose a tree and regard it from a distance first, in order to consciously observe its phenotype. Does it stand alone or blend with other trees in its vicinity? Take in the tree from different perspectives. Then stand directly by its trunk and look upwards along it. Which structure does the bark have, how does it feel? Which side of the trunk is perhaps covered in moss? Where do branches grow, how do they intertwine with the finer branches and twigs? Take a closer look at the leaves. What is their size, form, and color? How do they feel – soft and smooth, or rough and leathery? Which notion of the roots do you have? Walk around the ground in the area of crown of the tree, as this is approximately where the roots should be. Which animals visit this tree? Do birds sing in it, do insects nibble on its leaves, or do they crawl along the bark? Perceive this tree in its wide range of shapes and colors. Then play with your own associations with this tree. This way the oak often seems stable, wayward, gnarled, persistent, and strongly defensive, the birch tree light, lovely, dancing, soft, etc. Does the tree have metaphorical meaning or a "message" for you?

Lie or sit under the tree and observe the light and shade that the tree offers for approximately 5 minutes. Pay attention to the gaps and to conclude, observe the movements of the tree, its twigs, and leaves.

Comment

Trees play a special role in nature experiences (Kaplan&Kaplan 1989, p. 48&77; Eggmann&Steiner 1995, Schreier 2005). They often have strong radiance (physiognomy), are the source of many metaphors, fantasies, anthropomorphisms, and possibilities of identification. All these processes should find a place in the practice of mindfulness (see chapter 13).

84. Seasons

Material: none

Location: anywhere

Duration: 30 to 60 minutes

Age: everyone

Instruction

Explore the diverse phenomena of the season in which you currently are (see exercise 31). What is special about this season? Is it the temperature, the colors, the light, the phase of the plants, the birdcalls, the smell, or the entire atmosphere? Is the season just beginning, is it midway through, or in transition to the next? How do you feel at the beginning and end of the season? Anticipation, regret, or indifference?

How are you dressed, how do you act, how is your stance, your movements, your breathing, you level of energy, and your mood?

(Not only, but especially for children): How do animals behave? Think about which animal you would like to switch with and with which you would not.

Which associations, fantasies, memories, expectations, and feeling do you have? Innumerable poems and songs deal with the seasons. Can you understand that yourself? Do these seasons mean anything to you? How do you interpret them? Which metaphor? Which personal resonance?

How do you fare with the constant change of seasons, the slowness of these changes? How does the cyclical process, transience, and the return of the seasons make you feel?

Do you have impulses to flee, do you wish to avoid the seasons? Do you want to go on vacation or stay in the house more? What are your preferences and dislikes? Discover your own valuations!

Always return to your observations and your contemporary resonances and allow yourself (as with every contemplation in nature) to be inspired by nature experiences over and over again. See what happens: In nature and for yourself, stay open to new experiences and allow yourself to be surprised.

Comment

Seasons are often very poignant and atmospheric. They are experienced by the body first-hand and are important to our mood. They are rich with metaphors from a cultural and individual perspective. The seasons make it clear that nature experiences are also culturally transmitted. At the same time, each nature experience is more than a cultural mode of interpretation. It is never confined to it.

Part 3 | Background

10. | Mindfulness in Nature Education

Verena Schatanek

My work in nature education began 25 years ago in the Pro Natura nature reserve "Aletschwald" (Aletsch forest, own translation, GZ)[24] in the Swiss alps. For all these years two central ideas have guided me: "We are only ready to protect that which we know and love" and "learning with your head, hands, and heart".[25] A hint of mindfulness intuitively became a part of my daily work. We tried to create "atmospheres" in which nature could speak for itself. Words and explanations almost became unnecessary, the soul and the body could be replenished. These were the intense moments that we wanted. An intuitive knowledge of which methods, exercises, and settings were received well developed through working with different groups and in different locations in nature, from the wilderness to nature in cities. Part of this knowledge lead to the insight that activity in nature affects the participants most profoundly, if contemplative moments of silence and awe are conducted along with interactive moments.

My career transition from the Aletsch area with its spectacular mountain landscape to a Nature School in Zurich[26], with its forest strongly influenced by humans, confronted me with an unexpected conclusion: The creation of the previously described intense moments, which used to be almost auto-matic (with school classes as well), became a challenge. The question arose:

24. A 1200 acre nature reserve of the Swiss environmental organization Pro Natura, arolla pine-larch forest above the great Aletsch glacier, removed from operation since 1933. Educational work since 1976 by the Pro Natura center Aletsch in the villa Cassel/ Riederalp.
25. This central idea of many nature educators dates back to the Swiss educators Johann Friedrich Pestalozzi (1746-1827).
26. The Nature Schools of the Office of Parks and Open Spaces were established in 1986 in the Sihl forest (known today as the Sihl forest wilderness park Zurich) thanks to the dedication of the former forest conservationist of the city of Zurich, Andreas Speich. They are a city service and are addressed to school classes and teachers of the city of Zurich, from kindergarten to 9th grade, who can book nature education courses or continuing professional development courses.

Are moments of existential pause mainly possible in wild untouched locations in nature, or is it possible to create them in an "average" everyday environment as well? For years I had a clear position on this: It was pure nature with its diversity in small and large things and its majesty that touched me and could irreversibly bring me into the present. The larger, wilder, more silent, or more secluded, the better! I could relate to nature adjacent to civilization and its noises much less on an emotional level: The noise of traffic, for example, regularly absorbed so much of my attention that it was difficult for me to take in nature and its moods in an unbiased manner.

Meeting my fellow author, Michael, opened a new perspective to me in this respect: During simple mindfulness exercises ("and-techniques"; 3-2-1 exercise) near a frequented street whose noise bothered me I realized what the attitude of mindfulness could mean for working with people in nature in a practical and conceptional sense: If one succeeds in not denying emotional filters in one's own perception, and instead to consciously recognize and therefore relativize them, an intense moving nature experience is also possible where personal judgments previously stood in the way. I felt that the attitude of mindfulness was a key to a more deep effect: Nature experiences become more intense, durable, connected, grounded, and momentous, as well as serving as an opposite pol to superficial fleeting nature experiences.

I was surprised in the coming months how easy it was for me to consciously take in the attitude of mindfulness in nature. I noticed that I was accustomed to many mindfulness exercises, because the approach was already part of the nature education work with all senses – old wine in new wineskin so to speak. With nature education I mean a practice that deals with nature in order to strengthen the relationship between humans and nature, invigorate education, and understand nature. In practice, almost noone in the field of nature education will strictly only apply one of the many educational concepts[27] related to nature. Usually different elements of

27. For example Earth Education (Van Matre 1998), earth protector project (Müller-Schöll 2010), nature-oriented education (Goepfert 1998), nature education

these different streams of thought are combined with another depending on the group, moods, situations, landscapes, weather, and educational goals.

Despite the abundance of nature education concepts worldwide, too many occasions in nature for adults are merely natural history tours with "educational elements" in my experience. The focus is on the outer world with its diverse manifestations. Natural objects and individual species with their interrelations are in the foreground more than aesthetic and emotional aspects. Natural history wishes to remain objective and present facts. The more expert knowledge a person has, the more suited they seem to lead a natural history tour. If someone can speak in a fascinating and enthusiastic manner it is wonderful as well. It is about recognizing the spectacular and rare in nature and to inform the participants. "What have you seen that is special?" is a question often asked after excursions. If it is simply general things, then that it is already often considered as a flaw: natural objects and observed species are judged as "average" or "special" specimen. Knowledge of the species is central and it is about naming the observed species. This attitude is partially understandable. Nature education tours often have the aim to promote environmental protection. On the basis of Red Lists and so called flag ship species, which functions as a "lead animal" in the sense of a common thread throughout the event, these measures can be demanded in a political sense. Nature education, species conservation, and landscape conservation are closely linked in the German-speaking world, evidenced by environmental protection organizations such as "Friends of the Earth", WWF, Greenpeace, and Bird Life. Nature experiences are legitimized, as they are supposed to lead to more environmentally friendly and conservationist behavior.[28]

Many offers are based on the conviction that we only protect that which

---

(Trommer&Janssen 1998), nature-oriented environmental education (SILVIVA), nature experience education (Cornell 1991, Kalff 1994), nature interpretations (Tilden 1977), holistic environmental education (Jung 2005), environmental education PLUS (Gugerli&Frischknecht 2011), forest education (Bolay 2012), wilderness education (BUND Friends of the Earth Germany 2002) wilderness awareness school (Young et al. 2014), and several more.

28. For example the Bavarian Forest Administration 2010, Kyburz et al. 2001, Wüst et al. 2012.

we know and cherish. Especially cherishing contains several aspects of a mindful attitude. Many environmental protection organizations, organizers, and excursion leaders are not conceptionally aware enough of this. Natural history occasions are therefore often in danger of being everything but the practice of a mindful attitude that would strengthen its deep effect. I would like to exemplify this based on the example of a fictitious bird excursion.

A group is underway in a nature reserve in which very rare species of bird are often spotted. The occasion is public and the audience is very heterogeneous in their prior knowledge. The leader is an acclaimed bird specialist who is especially interested in rare species. He therefore passes by the blackcaps, blackbirds, and calling sparrows without comment, since they are only common species. As a result, most participants are soon engaged in private conversations. Those in the front are able to enjoy the casual comments of the group leader, who happens to actually find the exclusively searched species. It can only be observed for a moment and then flies away. This is no reason for disappointment for the group leader, on the contrary: All participants can now make a mark on their observation lists, which is a satisfactory end to the excursion in their opinion. Additionally, the group leader now holds a longer talk on this species and successful environmental protection, emptying a sack of words and knowledge on the audience. With so much expert knowledge it is clear that countless other birds that are calling at that moment cannot be mentioned and that even eagles pass over the group in that time.

I am surprised time and time again how cognitive and frontal many excursions are, how much one's own knowledge is presented, and how little attention is payed if the presented material even reaches and touches the audience. That the focus is only on the outer world can be of advantage: On natural history excursions, the intense perception of individual natural elements can lead to a shift in perspective and regeneration for many par-ticipants. They enjoy leaving everyday life behind them. It is very often experienced as liberating that inner feelings are not a topic and that we can simply immerse ourself in nature.

An especially pleasant example of natural history that is seen as a precursor to mindfulness was described by Jean-Jacques Rousseau in *Reveries of a Solitary Walker* (Rousseau 2003 [1782], 86/90). In his fifth "walk" on Peter island in the Bieler lake he dedicates his morning to botany[29] and his afternoon to the cultivation of extended moments of broad mindfulness:

"No longer wanting to work, I needed an entertaining pastime that I liked and what would not require any more effort than an idler could happily devote to it. I decided to compose a flora petrinsularis and to describe all the plants on the island, not leaving a single one out, in sufficient detail to keep me busy for the rest of my days... The forking of the self-heal's two long stamens, the springiness of those of the nettle and the wall pellitory, the way the fruit of the balsam and the fruit capsule of the box burst open, and the thousand little tricks of fertilization which I was observing for the first time filled me with joy, and I went about asking people if they had seen the horns of the self-heal, just La Fontaine asked if they had read the Habakkuk...As evening approached, I would come down from the heights of the island, and I liked to go and sit at the lakeside in some secluded spot on the single; there the sound of the waves and the movement of the water, gripping my senses and ridding my soul of all other agitation, plunged it into a delicious reverie,...The ebb and flow of the water and its continuous yet constantly varying sound, ever breaking against my ears and my eyes, took the place of the movements inside me that reverie did away with and were enough to make me pleasantly aware of my existence, without my having to take the trouble of think. From time to time there came to mind some slight and brief reflection on the instability of this world, the image of which I saw in the surface of the water: but soon these fragile impressions faded away before the steadiness of the continuous move-ment which lulled me and which, without my soul actively doing any-thing, kept me transfixed, so much that, when time and the agreed signal called me home, I struggled to tear myself away. " (Rousseau 2011, p. 51-54)

---

29. Also see Amthor 2012.

The cultivation of the knowledge of species is not simply a superficial accumulation of knowledge, but the expression of a conscious ability to perceive and cherish – in the sense of "you as my non-human opposite are worth looking at and getting to know". Moments of presentness, which are filled with intense feelings and vibrations in nature, are formed during the search for mushrooms, birds, orchids, etc., and through constant pauses and attention. It is pleasant to combine this being underway in nature with other elements of the practice of mindfulness. Many streams of thought within nature education in the last 100 years have done the same, as I will exemplify in the following based on selected approaches and experiences and observations of it from experience.

10.1. Mindfulness in Different Teaching Traditions of Nature Education

10.1.1. Nature Interpretations

Nature interpretation is an almost 100 year old nature education concept that originated in the U.S., but was only able to establish itself much later in the German-speaking world. The beginnings of conservationism in the U.S. and the founding of national parks[30] went hand in hand with the development of nature interpretation. This educational concept goes back to the ideas of John Muirs (1838-1914), the founding father of North American nature conservation, who was strongly influenced by the natural philosophers Emerson and Thoreau.[31] Muir felt strongly moved by the remaining areas of wilderness and supposedly used the term "interpretation" in 1871 for the first time in his diary during a visit to the later Yosemite National Park. John Muir "interpreted the language of natural phenomena" for himself, as he spent enough time in these landscapes. Freeman Tilden (1883-1980) formulated for the first time in the 1950s that a certain

---

30. The U.S. National Park Service was founded in 1916. Education in nature is the task of interpretive Rangers, a sort of Park Ranger, who are responsible for the care of visitors and receive special training for this.
31. Ralph Waldo Emerson (1803-1882) and Henry David Thoreau (1817-1862) were the founders of the philosophic, religious, and literary movement of transcendentalism (from the Latin term "transcendere" – to transcend).

translation is needed for visitors thoroughly alienated from nature, in order to offer room for the subjective nature experiences of each individual. He published a small practical basic work of nature interpretations in 1957 to increase the quality of nature education work of Rangers in National Parks.[32] Nature interpretation emphasizes that nature must be brought into relation with the personality and experiences of humans and founds this on European romanticists (for example Novalis) or European natural philosophy (for example Goethe).

The development of nature education was different in Europe. This is perhaps because wilderness had mostly vanished from Central Europe. Nature was strongly influenced by cultural landscapes. The growing idea of conservationism in Europe for this reason manifested itself in the sense of active landscape conservation and a mostly cognitive teaching of natural history, with a certain scientific distance and an emphasis on the outer world.[33] However, nature interpretation integrated the subjective nature experience into the education offered by National Parks in the U.S., in which visitors are only visiting nature for a relatively short amount of time. In this context, the guide of an excursion has the role of an interpreter or translator between humans and natural phenomena. The guide does not simply present the information, but always includes the available natural phenomena. When the participants notice that the excursion is not only about outer nature but themselves as well, they are much more open to environmental concerns. In the sense of deep effects it is about searching for messages that are transmitted by natural phenomena and are meaningful for the everyday life of the participants. These messages are developed into central thematic and conceptional ideas. Central ideas are often existential themes overriding natural historical facts and represent a deeper truth according to nature interpreters. Central ideas are general aspects of human life that are meaningful for most people such as growth and decay, vitality, development, etc. Aesthetic and symbolic existential dimensions of nature experiences are thereby opened to be experienced. Nature interpretation already contains many aspects of a mindful attitude, which however in practice is too often shifted towards knowledge transfer in my opinion.

---

32. Tilden 1977.
33. Kyburz-Graber et al. 2001, Ludwig 2003, 2011.

Nature interpretation could only establish itself in the German-speaking world at the end of the 20th century. Today its central principles are as relevant as ever and have been included in the educational policies of nature reserves and the training of Rangers.

10.1.2. Nature Awareness Education

Nature awareness education swept over from the U.S. to Europe much earlier than the older understanding of nature interpretation, namely in the 1970s. The merit of nature awareness education is that not only cognitive aspects are included in education, but also that it contributed to the renaissance of subjective feelings in the German-speaking world.

Joseph Cornell is one of the most well-known nature awareness educators. His playful exercises to increase perception ability with all senses are almost a standard repertoire of every nature educator, even if many where developed further in practice by many nature educators. The central aspect of his educational concept are direct nature experiences that are supposed to lead humans of all ages to develop a more personal under-standing of nature and in the end take personal responsibility for nature.

Cornell relies on differentiated perception and arriving in the present. He moves the self-evident and often overlooked into focus and does not only work with the majestic, rare, large, or wild. He asserts a more playful handling of nature. His educational concept of "Flow Learning" consists of four different steps of learning: Arousing enthusiasm, concentrated per-ception, immediate experiences in nature, and the collecting and sharing of inspiration.

It is suited for nature education work with groups and all four steps are introduced in the following in the words Cornell.

Flow Learning

Stage One: Awaken Enthusiasm *Stage Two: Focus Attention Stage Three: Offer Direct Experience Stage Four: Share Inspiration*

1. Awaken Enthusiasm – Without enthusiasm, people learn very little, and can never have a meaningful experience of nature. By enthusiasm, I don't mean jumping-up-and-down excitement, but an intense flow of personal interest and alertness.

    Awaken Enthusiasm games make learning fun, instructive, and experiential-and establish a rapport between teacher, student, and subject.

2. Focus Attention – Learning depends on focused attention. Enthusiasm alone isn't enough. If our thoughts are scattered, we can't be intensely aware of nature, nor of anything else. As leaders, we want to bring students' enthusiasm toward a calm focus.

    Focus Attention activities help students become attentive and receptive to nature.

3. Offer Direct Experience – During immersive nature experiences, students make a deep connection with an aspect of nature. Offer Direct Experience activities are built on the students' enthusiasm and receptivity, and are generally quiet and profoundly meaningful.

    By bringing us face to face with a bird, a wooded hill, or any natural subject, Offer Direct Experience activities give us intuitive experiences of nature.

Intuitive experiences are non-rational and provide us with inner, direct knowledge of nature. Henry David Thoreau called intuitive learning

"Beautiful Knowledge."

4. *Share Inspiration – Reflecting and sharing with others strengthen and clarify one's experience. Sharing brings to the surface unspoken but often universal feelings that—once communicated—allow people to feel a closer bond with the topic and with one another* (Cornell 2015, p. 28-29)

Many elements of "Flow Learning" can be transferred and adjusted to a nature-oriented practice of mindfulness. Cornell recognized that humans are not automatically ready to open themselves to immediate nature experiences. They are often still caught in everyday life in their thoughts and must first be brought into the present. In order to raise awareness and avert the digression of thoughts, he suggests focused attention and perception exercises. His games for the senses are easy, fun, experimental, and unusual in the beginning. Often senses are used in an isolated manner in stage 2 or the dominant sense of sight is turned off. Participants, for example, have their eyes covered, in order to bring the other senses to bear on the exploration of the outer environment, for example hearing birds, feeling bark, tasting fruits, and smelling herbs. It also animates the obser-vation of the body and feelings in nature – the temperature or wind on the skin, as well as moods and associations in nature. For Cornell, it is often about the perception of beauty and power in nature and the experience of silence. In stage 3 Cornell wishes to make a deeper experience possible with which we immerse ourselves with all our senses at the same time in nature. In the language of mindfulness, he goes from focused to broad mindfulness. The introduction to Cornell's suggested inspiring exchange of experience in stage 4 is partially almost dramatically staged and clearly serves the purpose of deepening the connection to nature and motivating others to follow this path as well. People are supposed to share their positive experiences in order to further strengthen the effect within the group. His descriptions of stage 2, 3, and 4 allow for the reverse assumption that he primarily hoped for pleasant, happy, and euphoric emotions. Unpleasant negative emotions or conflicts with nature are not envisioned by him. Cornell also works a lot with fantasy journeys and imaginations, which however bring the participants away from the scene, differentiating his approach to that of mindfulness.

In his third book *Listening to Nature: How to Deepen Your Awareness of Nature* (Cornell 1991c) he shifts the focus from "play and drama" to the attitude of mindfulness. His suggestions are directed towards individuals wishing to connect their everyday life with nature, who open their perception to processes, animals, moods, and overlooked details and are prepared for existential questions in nature. Thoughts, meditative texts, poems, and photographs prepare these adults for the spiritual dimension. Mindfulness in nature however, only reaches the necessary tuning through the conscious taking in of the attitude of mindfulness. But a cognitive understanding of the concept of mindfulness is recommended.

In Germany, Michael Kalff, one of the founders of the Nature School in Freiburg, published a handbook that is broadly used in nature and environmental education. In contrast to Cornell, he includes that nature can be frightening (Kalff 1994, 45) and includes existential questions more in his work. Fear is a sign of alienation from nature and resulting personal insecurity for him, but also a healthy reaction in nature that protects us and helps us to not overestimate ourselves. He demands a conscious and reflective handling of these emotions and characterizes twelve important aspects of nature education (1994, 41 et seq.): "recognizing the diversity of life, learning to listen and look more closely, having sensual experiences, recognizing living processes, nature as a mirror of one's soul, experiences of existence, life and death, perceiving time as life, security in existence, beauty and vulnerability, reverence of life, love". In my experience, this approach was implemented especially in the wilderness and National Parks with a large amount of deadwood, a dynamic of processes, natural origins, and diversity in educational practices, as these themes are determined by natural phenomena and humans have spontaneously and unconsciously taken in an attitude of existential observation.

However, Kalff's viewpoint is also mainly focused on the positive, harmonic, and happy aspects of nature. Like Cornell, he suggest a four step methodology that, however, differs from "Flow Learning". The introduction, in contrast to Cornell, does not begin with strongly activating playful exercises, as adults are often too reserved and children become too "hyperactive". Kalff uses introductory rituals (often in the sense of "Mother Earth") and sensually-oriented perception exercises. The second step of nature encounters allows room for nature explorations and an increase in knowledge, as many people feel familiar and safe in such settings due to their school experience. The third step is a more deep sensual experience "through isolated senses, inclusion of imagination, formative creativity, listening, and seeing – the silent, small, unremarkable." (Kalff 1994, p. 53, own translation, GZ) The fourth step should round up the exercise and is a meditative encounter with nature: "Playful dissolution of the border between humans and nature, identification with nature, and conscious ex-perience´of being a part of nature" (Kalff 1994, p. 54; for a critical examination of this view see chapters 12 and 13 of this book, own trans-lation, GZ). He also understands nature meditations as imagined fantasy journeys, for example the growth of a tree from a seed, the cycle of the seasons, etc. with narrated images and moods, and requests for body move-ments and observations of the body.

This approach to silent exercises (Kalff 1998) is widespread in the German-speaking world. Children can be reached on these spiritual jour-neys depending on the group and how keyed they are, because they are a sort of inner story. However, they are very demanding on the group leader and often do not fit based on the dynamic of the group. The hesitation and resistance to closing their eyes in front of other children and just be still should not be underestimated. There are always participants who will not or cannot accept this silent mood. Today, these meditation journeys are often called mindfulness exercises, which they are not in the actual sense. They are basically "suggested" fantasy journeys and not the perceiving of one's own observations, resonances, moods, or thoughts on nature. They certainly have their place, but should not be confused with mindfulness. They lead away from the location of natural phenomena and away from the present. Mindfulness exercises, as we suggest in chapters 4 to 9, are much more relevant to present times, realistic, and practical, especially with adults.

The trend in the practice of nature education has barely developed into this more "spiritual" direction. It can be found in some publications, but it cannot be found in the online database "Datenbank Waldmeister", which has collected the most relevant nature and forest education activities in the entire German-speaking world. Despite the multitude of conceptual impulses, there seems to be a "spiritual vacuum" (Gugerli&Frischknecht 2011, p. 165) in the practice of nature education. The concept of mindfulness in nature could fill this vacuum.

10.1.3. Creative and Formative Nature Education

The formative and creative aspect has gained importance in the past few years. Animated by the high motivation of many people to not only be in nature and explore it, but to form and change it as well, many creative offers in nature now exist. Inspired by Land Art artists such as Goldworthy[34], who passionately address the aesthetic senses of many with their fleeting artistic works with natural materials in nature, nature education tries to make a new creative nature experience possible and thereby address a different audience.[35] Nature should not just be understood as a nice backdrop for arrangements.

> "Nature is observed, experienced, and through creative intervention tested and changed. Land Art allows the creator to recognize their own relationship to nature not only to attain a picture of nature for themselves, but also to practice an appreciative non-egocentric handling of nature. By perceiving nature aesthetically, we experience the possibilities and impossibilities of our life and that of life in nature. Art thereby shows, how nature and culture are inseparably linked. (Jäger 2011, p. 4, own translation, GZ)

Focused, but also broad suggestions for observation are consciously used beforehand in order to be able to even deduce the available natural materials and the location in nature, as well as to be open to nature.

---

34. Goldworthy 1991, 1994, 1996.
35. For example Bestle-Körfer et al. 2010, Güthler&Lacher 2005, Güthler 2011, Häfele 2011, Poyet 2008.

Associations, metaphors, and inner pictures are expressed and shared with others.[36] A "vernissage" of the works with concise titles is a humorous way to make playful sharings possible. Having enough time for oneself, free space, playful elements, and one's own activities is more important than the result. It is recommended to keep the pressure to perform as low as possible.

This formative aspect uses many aspects of mindfulness for its creative process, which is seen time and time again as an expression of inner impressions, feelings and relational experiences. It is its strength that people really open themselves to nature and dwell in it for a while: while observing, examining materials, exploring the area, and during their own activities.

10.1.4. Wilderness Awareness School in the Tradition of Coyote Mentoring

This form of contemporary form of wilderness education was created in the U.S. and has increasingly been used in Europe for the past few years. It is strongly influenced by the teaching method of Coyote Mentoring (Young et al. 2014) and basic ecological and natural historical knowledge that allows people to cultivate their knowledge of the local area and nature. This form of learning is based on the vast nature experiences of American Indians. It has its origin in American Indian traditions, but many elements can be found around the world. I myself have experienced this "school of aware-ness", for example, with desert tribes in North Africa. Instead of a coyote they use a jackal (Schatanek, Elkharassi 2006) to teach their children with similar methods to feel at home in a certain area. Coyote Mentoring is a central part of practicing so called attentiveness. The coyote as a symbolic animal of this exercise practice can be equated to the European "Reinecke Fuchs" (an epos with a fox as its main character, GZ). He is considered smart, spontaneous, humorous, and versatile while going beyond fixed roles and behavioral patterns.[37] With Coyote Mentoring the participants learn to

---

36. Also see the approaches of Jäger 2011 and Joller 2008.
37. Young et al. 2014, p. 10-13.

regain a close relationship to a social world assumed to be inhabited by spirits.

Awareness in nature was pure necessity for thousands of years. In the U.S., Tom Brown Jr. and his student Jon Young are considered to be masters of this. Tom Brown is the founder of the "Tracker School" and his student Jon Young followed his suit with the "Wilderness Awareness School" in 1983. Natural things, natural phenomena, natural processes, and the entire environment with the individual at its center are to be directly experienced and understood. It is about sharpening and perfecting sensory perception in nature and its resonances in us. The constant reading and interpreting of tracks in the landscape trains the attentiveness wished for in students, makes the attitude of mindfulness possible, and is therefore seen as personality development (Young et al. 2014, passim).

A longer or more regular visit to nature and the practicing of so called core routines are prerequisites in order to be able to connect with nature.

These core routines are universal and do not belong to a specific culture.[38] For example, it is a routine to have one's own place to sit, to constantly widen one's senses, to ask questions about nature and to read tracks, to roam without intent or destination, to see with one's inner eye, or to listen to birdcalls. There is quite a list of such core routines in wilderness awareness school which require practice. Sensual attentiveness focuses or broadens automatically, depending on the requirements of the situation. It is about the outer world, but also one's own feelings, stimuli, and the stimuli of other creatures, all at the same time. The group is the place for exchanging individual experiences in nature, it is not a group that listens to a teacher ("mentor"). The mentor does not give answers, and instead asks questions that lead further and inquires about the details of things perceived. Was the flight pattern of the bird wavy or straight? Where the waves at the lake soft or broken? Small details, moods, forms and patterns, aspects and dimensions of mindfulness, and the faintest stirring of life should be recognized and observed. The students are supposed to, as far as possible in the situation, fill themselves with the perception of reality and nature and thereby make the borders between humans and nature weaker on the inside and outside. After an excursion there is "homework", for example finding one's own sitting place weekly.

Barely any other current of nature education practices and emphasizes presentness, the opening of the senses, and the practicing of attentiveness so strongly. However, it is a demanding program that takes time. But "attentiveness" does not explicitly find worth in letting go of judgments or aimlessness itself, as is the case with mindfulness. There are more and more clues from practical experience that perception and actions in everyday life and the relationship with nature change lastingly through mindful and attentive nature experiences and wilderness awareness exercises.[39]

38. Young et al. 2014.
39. Chawla 2002, Kaplan&Kaplan 1989, Erxleben 2008, Müller 2011, Fischer-Rizzi 2007, Kriebel 2007-2010, Young et al. 2014.

10.2. Education for Sustainable Development

Around the turn of the century, the insight grew in educational policy circles that a strong sensory- and experience-oriented nature education could be unsatisfactory and depoliticizing.[40] In the face of growing ecological problems this was seen as a great deficiency. The concept of "Education for Sustainable Development" (abbreviated "ESD" in the following) was seen as a solution, which first established itself in political circles after the United Nations Conference on Sustainable Development in Rio de Janeiro in 1992.

> "Environmental education in the sense of ESD deals with the relationship between humans and nature. Humans shall be competent to handle natural resources respectfully. Thereby, humans stand between the priorities of economical and ecological interests." (Swiss Symposium on the Environment 2014 [2011], p. 5, own translation, GZ)

The following practical requirements were derived from this in the German-speaking world: Contemporary environmental education should no longer be geared to experiences and adventures, but to capabilities (competences). The offers that are still to be developed should lead into the future, give the participants the capabilities to be active and creative in their everyday life[41], make space and time for discussions on values and reflecting, as well as allow the participants to participate and cooperate. Problems and their solutions are approached through multi-perspective and interdisciplinary exploratory learning.

---

40. Unterbrunner 2005, p. 11.
41. In Germany, "creative competence" is the central term of ESD. Creative competence means that which leads forward, a future of communities in which we live and actively participate for the purpose of sustainable development. There are ten competencies formulated, which are mainly used for educational purposes at schools (DE HAAN 2002): open-minded and attaining knowledge while integrating other perspectives, anticipatory thinking and acting, gaining insight interdisciplinarily and acting, planning and acting with others, participating in decision making processes, motivating others to become active, reflecting on one's own ideals and those of others, planning and acting independently, showing empathy and solidarity for the underprivileged, motivating oneself to be active.

The concerns of Education for Sustainable Development are more than legitimate. In my opinion, the direct experience of nature in the sense of an explicit nature orientation falls too short. The resonance of nature experiences in the form of emotions with personal, existential, or spiritual themes are lost, even though UNESCO in its preamble to higher education formulated a vision of "deeper dimensions of morality and spirituality" (UNESCO 1998, Preamble). Direct immediate nature experiences, a term that was brought into the environmental education debate by Kellert, play a lesser role conceptually and practically and are often replaced by guided indirect (media, books, etc.) and even symbolic nature experiences (Kellert 2002, passim). It is often unknown to the political actors of an Education for Sustainable Development that the extensive thematization of environmental problems can be counterproductive, depending on the person. More and more people and children block themselves to this out of emotional overextension. However, suppression processes only lead people further away from nature. Some projects for an Education for Sustainable Development therefore sadly lead to alienation from nature and barely help to build a sustainable relationship with nature, which however is an important basis for a relevant commitment to nature.[42] In practice it has been shown that the offers become more distant from nature, more cognitive, less rich in experience, less emotional, and less sensual when global aspects and the problems to be solved are placed in the foreground. These critical remarks do not mean that ESD leads in the wrong direction. A synthesis of the practice of ESD until now and the demands of a contemporary nature-oriented environmental education is possible. There are several examples in Germany and Switzerland that lead in this direction and that primarily integrate aspects of a mindful attitude or even of mindfulness in the conceptual sense.[43]

"The Education for Sustainable Development, which is on everyone's lips as commanded from above, conceptually neglects the side that makes a sustainable attitude possible in the first place, as well as competence and familiarity with nature.

---

42. Also compare Ludwig 2010 and Louv 2011, 2012, and others.
43. For nature-oriented approaches of ESD see Corleis et al. 2006, Kohler&Lude 2012, Stoltenberg 2009, Trommer 1998, Ludwig 2010, for nature-and Mindfulness-oriented approaches see Jung 2005, 2011, 2012, Gugerli&Frischknecht 2011, Symposium on Environmental Education 2014, p. 21.

Nature as a teacher of intuition and thought, as creator and therapist of our psyche – this has proven itself countless times (…) All activities and suggestions that lead to the creation and development of a differentiated and rich relationship and communication between humans and nature and fellow humans are a part of holistic environmental education. It creates emotional relationships with nature, awareness, consciousness, ideals, and alertness, its goal is living in harmony with the interests of humans and the social world surrounding them." (Jung 2008, p. 8, own translation, GZ)

Theoretical and practical stimuli from nature phenomenology, nature interpretation, forest-oriented environmental education[44], environmental psychology, deep ecology, and forest education which take subjective experience into account flow into projects and works of "holistic"[45] or "integral environmental education".[46]

A research project by the university of St. Gallen is researching the affect of this integral environmental education with 4th and 5th grade school children.[47] A special focus is layed by Gugerli and Frischknecht on the sequential combination of the following aspects: "Conscious and constructive handling of pleasant and unpleasant emotions, systematic thinking and feeling, active implementation in everyday life, a culture of mindfulness and connectedness [to nature]." (Gugerli&Frischknecht 2011, p. 21, own translation, GZ). The Nature Schools of the Office of Parks and Open Spaces in Zurich differentiate their offers for city schools depending on the age of the children. When working with younger children (kindergarten to 3rd grade) building a relationship with nature is in the foreground, which are supported by age appropriate mindfulness exercises. Only beginning in the 4th grade do the requirements of ESD grow more and more in importance and complement nature-oriented activities.[48]

---

44. Bolay 2007.
45. Also see Jung 2005, Erxleben 2008, Wolter 2004.
46. Gugerli&Frischknecht 2011.
47. The approaches from "environmental education plus" by Gugerli&Frischknecht 2011 are developed further and evaluated for their practical application.
48. Compare to Schatanek et al. 2010, Hofstetter&Schatanek 2014.

10.3. Environmental Psychology Perspectives

Direct immediate nature experiences disappear from our daily life and they are also not conceptually grounded enough within an Education for Sustainable Development. These direct nature experiences however play a large role in motorical, cognitive, social, and spiritual development.[49] Guided structured nature experiences (also called indirect nature exper-iences) increase dramatically, as do symbolic nature experiences in which nature often is not even present anymore and only appears as an image in the form of pictures or movies.[50] But not only the degree of immediacy of nature influences our experience, but also the natural environment itself. Which places do we humans prefer and therefore contribute towards?[51] What do we do when and at which age in nature and what influences us? Which things do we turn towards and which do we turn from, consciously but also unconsciously? Which natural phenomena create fear and which fascinate us? What are human likes and dislikes?[52] All these evolutionary biology and environmental psychology facets of natural relationships and nature exper-iences give nature educators valuable and important stimuli for nature education stemming from experience in the context of Education for Sustainable Development.

Beginning in the 1970s, the environmental psychologists Rachel and Stephan Kaplan from the university of Michigan began to research how nature encounters should be structured, so that lasting nature experiences and relationships with nature influence our environmental behavior. They were also very interested in the influences of various landscapes on our psyche and our ability to recuperate. In many regions of the world they re-searched which natural spaces were preferred and which positive and negative emotions are connected to specific natural structures, in a sense they research the biological and cultural conditions of subjective feelings towards nature. They showed that there are widespread typically human and

---

49. Gebhard 2013.
50. For thorough developmental psychological aspects of direct, indirect, and symbolic nature experiences see Kellert 2002.
51. Kaplan&Kaplan 1989.
52. Also see Kellert 2002 and Gebhard 2013.

cultural patterns: water, forests, savannas, and parks principally seem attractive to humans. But not all forests are the same. Monotonous and predictable structures are mundane and boring for most people. Markedly wild landscape elements may be inviting for exploration, but their dangers are so impenetrable that they are only attractive to those that find their way in them. However, a landscape that is too open does not offer points of orientation and can therefore seem dangerous or simply boring. A landscape that is too dense blocks our view and our way out. We must be able to orient ourselves when we are searching for hidden things and feel relatively safe. Diversely structured landscapes with their various colors, forms, niches, and hidden things promise us future exploration. Natural spaces with the following "flaws" are intuitively not valued and are even disliked:

- Lack of coherence: makes it harder to understand what is in front of us.

- Lack of complexity: lowers the probability that we are fascinated.

- Lack of legibility: lowers the trust to understand the environment.

- Lack of mystery: lowers the probability that we are tempted to explore.

The Kaplans were able to discern the structures need for people to be able to relax and regenerate in this complex interrelation of general patterns and individual preferences and dislikes. They differentiate between arbitrary and involuntary forms of attention and consider them to hold a central role in recuperativeness ("attention restoration theory", see chapter 11).

During my work in National Parks and wilderness areas, I have experienced time and time again that humans can spontaneously take in the relaxed attitude of mindfulness in untouched landscapes, as long as the involuntary attention is not constantly aroused by exciting, strange, dangerous, or unassessable things. Then we can form our attention consciously and on the one hand direct it pointedly towards phenomena, and on the other hand open them for a state of broad mindfulness. In these open moments we are especially receptive for existential questions (becoming and withering, phases of life, meaning of life, what is really important in life, etc.). The practice of nature education has shown that the wilderness makes mindful existential experiences possible, as long as the context is adequate. The Kaplans verify this experience of many of my colleagues. Through years of research they showed how important longer wilderness experiences are for long term effectiveness in everyday life, and how great their influence on our life's journey and our attitudes towards life can be.

The available time in nature is a factor: In the beginning, they experimented with 15 days in the wilderness and reduced this duration in the sense of a minimum to 9 days after several years. Since, in their opinion, the duration of nature contact is so important for our attitude towards nature and our environmental behavior, they see a large additional field of action for nature experiences in the cultivated and closely located nature of our life environment: Silence and routine nature experiences that are emotionally meaningful are also possible here. These nature experiences may not necessarily be existential and lofty, but therefore close to daily life. In my experience, mindfulness exercises in their simplicity offer more ideas for this. One's own relationship with nature is thereby further strengthened, which does not remain without consequences for individual environmental behavior.

It is crucial that both pillars, meaning wilderness experiences on the one hand, and the experience of cultivated nature in everyday life on the other hand, complement each other: Those who can have existential nature experiences are more likely to rethink their environmental behavior, due to the experience of natural spaces and phenomena close to everyday life. This con-nection is often underestimated in practice.

The question arises, which structure a stay outside must have in order to make a deeper nature experience possible. Kaplan and Kaplan therefore speak of compatibility in the sense of a resonance between the outer and inner world.

A practical example: When it is about making the emotional approach to nature easier and allowing children to become open and attentive, then certain activities prove themselves very effective. In the context of offers by the Nature Schools of the Office of Parks and Open Spaces in Zurich, we make the following observation regularly: People (especially children) show greater devotion during "simple fundamentally human activities", for example when collecting, sorting, building with and forming natural materials, manipulating and changing, playing with fire, hunting and caching animals, exploring freely, active by the water, handling poisonous plants and mushrooms, or collecting and utilizing wild plants and herbs. During such activities, you show a noticeable amount of presence, attentiveness, alertness, concentration, and emotions, which are precursors for the attitude of mindfulness. If this observation is taken seriously, then it becomes clear that certain restrictions can be counterproductive for the establishment of relationships with nature: Children should hold a frog into their hands or be allowed to pick flowers. They should also be allowed to hit trees with sticks and pluck leaves. Instead of forbidding it, they should be taught which tree is strong enough for this "treatment" and can spare a few leaves. The U.S. author Richard Louv[53], whose books are popular beyond a nature education audience at the moment, recommends cultivating different facets of a bond to nature with the children. It is about direct immediate contact with the wilderness and the diversity of nature for him, in order to establish a connection to the animals, plants, and the sources of food. Children should be able to be as free as possible to become active and influential in nature. He challenges society to create more spaces and possibilities for the autonomous playing of children in nature.[54] Louv pleas for the possibility of open experimentation and individual approaches to nature, detached from well meaning educational aspirations. The different facets of the relationship between humans and nature influence cognitive, motorical, and spiritual aspects of our lives. In this context Louv speaks of "mind/body/ nature connection" or "Vitamin N" (n for nature) (Louv 2012, p. 61).

In the end, the following can be summarized: The environmental psychology perspective has strengthened nature educators in a way that

53. Louv 2011, 2012.
54. Also see Hoppe 1998, Berthold&Ziegenspeck 2003, Gebhard 2013.

they realized how, depending on the group and the natural space, one could come into contact with natural spaces and creatures through various activities, and how the emotional relationship with nature is strengthened by different approaches, which is supposed to be an essential influence on our environmental behavior. The term mindfulness is seldom listed as a conscious attitude or competence within environmental psychology, but it seems to me that this attitude is implicit. Environmental psychology also justifiably points out that nature education offers and nature experiences are not only legitimized by dealing with environmental behavior and the preservation of the outer world in the sense of environmental protection. According to our concept, nature experiences and mindfulness promote the relationship with oneself, nature, and others.

10.4. Mindfulness in Nature Education – Practical Experiences

10.4.1. The Practice of Mindfulness with Children

Love of movement, curiosity, thirst for knowledge, liveliness, and spontaneity are basic needs of children that need to be integrated into an age-appropriate practice of mindfulness.[55] It is relatively easy to consciously observe nature with children, especially when it concerns objects and phenomena that fascinate children. The impulse and urge to name, sort, and judge is already existent. I elaborate on this in my work, so that children can let go of their uncertainty and tensions, but I always return to differentiated perception. In my opinion, mindfulness should be practiced in lively and real situations with children. In connection with nature experiences and natural phenomena children are open to it. A comparison with the own body seems obvious, when beginning with a natural history introduction on the hibernation and dormancy of animals: children love to observe their own heartbeat and to compare it with acoustic exemplifications of those of hedgehogs, bats, and dormice in hibernation, or those of bears, squirrels, and badgers in dormancy. It is the same with the sensation of heat. The children recognize the sense of the exercise and are open to it.

---

55. Compare Berthold&Ziegenspeck 2002, Jackel 2011.

A second grade class spends one of four "season days" on the same "hidden path of the fox" in the forest. A stuffed animal fox at the edge of the forest welcomes the class, and the class greats it with a fitting song that they brought with them and gives it a name. The class then immediately immerses itself in the life of the fox with me…

> "The fox leads a completely different life, perceives the world completely differently…Can see so well that it sees a mouse scurry away at the edge of the forest, can hear so well that it hears the patter of the mice in their holes, can smell so well that it could pick up the scent of the sick rabbit at the edge of the forest with its nose…Come along everyone, explore its world. Foxes do not get annoyed with homework, do not have a warm home with books, TVs, or video games, nor do they have sport practice or music class, they always live in this forest, observe everything that is happening at the moment, where something is moving, where they hear something, what they smell with their noses…Foxes cannot speak or whisper, do not complain when they are shoved, they are simply present in the forest with their eyes, ears, nose, paws, breath…We sneak behind the fox and do as it does: We see three thins in the forest, hear three sounds, feel our breathing and our silent steps…Then try out two things, two things to see, to hear, to feel, then try one and when everything is done at the same time the world seems more fox-like to you…"

The class of 24 children silently walks one after another through the forest, only occasional shoves can be heard and quiet protests, while the other children shush them. An atmosphere of alertness and of arriving unfolds and the children consciously observe the world around them.

Afterwards, they talk about their experiences in a sharing. Those that had a similar experience of that of the speaking child can silently raise their hands…

We later sneak to the fox's favorite spot:

> "Heal, outer side, inner side, feel your foot, it is different than the fox's paw, but you can still sneak silently. How far apart must your

legs be so that your rain pants do not rustle?...The fox likes to lie in front of its den with its siblings, it perceives everything that happens near the den and pays attention to even the slightest movement...It could be a mouse moving on the ground, a squirrel or a bird in the trees, or is it just a leaf swaying with the wind? Arrive, everyone for themselves, silently, like the fox, lie on the ground and observe every-thing that moves around you...Is a bird calling a warning somewhere? Do you hear a typical alarm sound? Birds do not only react to humans, but to our fox as well…"

The class waits quietly and patiently in front of the den, the children sit or lie on the ground and look up into the trees...listen...At the end of the day the children are clearly moved when saying goodbye...they hug me...they kiss the stuffed animal…

What happened? Why was not only this day so successful, but almost every day that my colleague Regula Guyer developed and which we refined together with more and more mindfulness exercises in the last years? It is surprising that alertness and amplified emotions do not only begin to show after four days, but beginning on the first day. The song that they already knew and practiced offered an emotional introduction and picked the children up in their everyday life. From the beginning, before the class could become loud and restless, we placed the focus on how important it is for the survival of the fox to perceive the present with all its senses. The stuffed animal fox always pokes out of my backpack while we are under-way and serves as an optical sign of the "alertness mode". Switching roles has an almost magical effect and can be very relaxing for the children, as the social rules of the class are thereby relativized. This makes it easier to combine sensory activity that the children recognize in its existential importance to their counterpart with sneaking exercises, breathing exer-cises, and awareness for the body. There is an interest in the fox and the challenges of its life in this forest during this season. Aspects of movement are incorporated with a challenging route and not with movement games, which often lead to a loud and destructive mood. We sneak through small and confusing paths that meander through the forest, instead of broad paths, and we cross creeks, climb cliffs with ropes, and rappel while feeling our own body. In the course of the year the same same places are visited again and again, so that changes are observed over time: "What has changed here since the last visit? What will it look like next time?"

The Nature Schools in Zurich offer a three-day program for third grade classes on the "cycles of birds" with natural historical, musical, and mindful aspects. My colleagues Regula Guyer, Silvia Fux, and myself discuss which abilities nature lovers, nature filmmakers, nature photographers, behavioral scientists, hunters, etc. need, in order to observe, research, film, or hunt birds, with the children. This way, the following exercises in nature make sense to the children and convey a wisp of reality. The consequences of their actions is immediately clear to the children. It is about mindful body movement when tracking birds, which allows the students to really observe the birds without them immediately flying away. The children feel deeply connected to nature when they successfully observe animals.

10.4.2. The Practice of Mindfulness with Adults

Mindfulness in nature education unfolds its full impact as an explicit concept especially well in adults. They often only come into contact with nature education for training purposes or as visitors of nature reserves. Many visitors only spend a few hours or, at best, a few days in nature before returning to their everyday life.

My colleague Rita Schneider and I began offering an all-day mindfulness workshop and a two-hour mindful evening hike at the changing of the seasons in the wilderness park Sihlwald in Zurich in 2013[56]: People from the closer area were interested, but also people from the city who came to the "Sihlwald" for a different kind of "after work" event. Some even came at every occasion. They enjoy being underway with like-minded people without an excursion leader they have to "follow".

---

56. The approximately 3000 acre large wilderness park in Zurich with its branches "Sihlwald" and "Tierpark Langenberg" is the first natural experience park in Switzerland with a unique combination of forests, wilderness, and animals within the metropolitan area of Zurich, Zug, and Lucerne.

These mindfulness exercises offered by the wilderness park Sihlwald in Zurich are addressed to people who already know a great deal about nature on the one hand, or those who for whatever reason do not wish to learn more *about* nature on the other hand. They enjoy being in nature, wish to calm down, and savor its relaxing effect, but they do not wish to head out on their own. Extraordinary times like dusk and darkness are avoided by many people in my experience, especially women. A challenge for me and my colleague Rita Schneider in the practice of explicit mindfulness was the cultivation of a different language. We wanted to cast off our role of animating people and instead build bridges. Being used to bringing along a lot of didactic and educational material, we were pleased at how little effort the occasions needed. The participants have everything along that they need: their senses for perceiving nature, their bodies to move around, their hands to form, and their minds to reflect. We do not need large accessible spaces for games or athletic approaches, nor do we need permission to collect or utilize, etc. We only need people and nature, as well as courage and time to give this relationship a chance.

Especially at the center of nature reserves with path restrictions, the possibilities for nature education approaches such as movement, collection, utilization, creation, etc. are limited. However, these central areas have such a strong radiance that we can allow them to speak for themselves with the help of mindfulness exercises. The widely known wilderness slogan "Natur Natur sein lassen" ("letting nature be nature", own translation, GZ), coined by the former director of the Bavarian Forest National Park Hans Bibelriether, can be deepened with contemplative mindfulness exercises and the participants can discuss what they experienced afterwards. We see a potential for nature reserves, nature parks, biosphere reserve, national parks, etc. to enlarge the number of their visitors with mindfulness-oriented nature education and to lead more people to nature. We were thinking of workshops lasting several hours, mindfulness hikes of two to three hours, or also a combination of mindfulness with decidedly nature education projects such as land art, collecting herbs, tracking, etc.

During several professional development courses of the Nature Schools of the Office of Parks and Open Spaces in Zurich regarding the themes above we, the team of the Nature Schools of the Office of Parks and Open Spaces in Zurich, observed time and time again that suggestions for mindful perception, exploration, but also creation in and with nature where gladly accepted by teachers, not only in light of its applicability to students.

10.5. The Contribution of Mindfulness in Nature to Education for Sustainable Development

Mindfulness exercises in nature allow for a deep effect in a relatively short amount of time, which is usually reached by long continuing education, workshops, etc. This can lead to a rise in quality of short-time offers. We also expect better self-care of nature education, an improvement of communication with the participants, and a more relaxed approach to sophisticated groups. It is not about only practicing mindfulness during the entire educational process and losing sight of other educational goals. The case for more mindfulness does not mean that we see the attainment of knowledge and strategies of action, as well as the ability and willingness to actively form one's own environment, as unimportant. In this field of environmental education, mindfulness is not nearly sufficient. In our experience, mindfulness deepens one's own natural competence before educational efforts, but also self- and social competences, and it enriches and deepens nature education in the sense of ESD. Passing through forms of Mindfulness in phases can strengthen the ability to perform: I found it helpful that through inner and outer pauses and alertness we can observe sensory, motorical, emotional, social-communicative, and cognitive processes differentially. This allows a change in perspective, empathy, and to think of further options. This way, more mindful and altruistic, meaning more selfless, authentic, cannier, and flexible activity is possible.[57]

Mindfulness in nature education makes it easier to deduce the outer and inner world and deepens the relationship that we have towards it. Nature prompts us to cultivate all dimensions of Mindfulness.

10.5.1. Deducing and Observing Nature as the Foundation of Human Existence with all Senses

Many nature education hope that the experience that the participants have in the context of their work will have an effect on their everyday lives after the occasion. This aspiration is a tremendous challenge in nature education on a daily basis and can unfold its effect over a long period of time, which the following feedback from our survey (see Introduction) illustrates:

> "...I always enjoyed being in nature, but could not perceive it in its diversity. Especially the acoustical dimension remained closed to me – I did not hear many things, unless someone explicitly asked me about it. When I began immersing myself into the world of animal voices with my ears, something incredible happened. My entire perception changed and the world became bigger and more differentiated. Today, nature is very familiar to me: The practice of Mindfulness over several years contributed to recognizing and reflecting on my search patterns in nature, to not lose myself in nature, and to observe my bodily feelings, moods, and needs better. Mindfulness showed me time and time again how quickly we primarily see what we want to see at that moment in nature and how relative much of my perception is. This

---

57. A similar categorization can be found in Jackel 2011.

relativization helps me to recognize the needs of others and to respect
them. I do not mean only humans, but also the other living beings.
This influences my daily life: how I travel, how I shop, how many
resources I want to claim for myself."

Demanding and especially adequately implemented sensual perception
exercises and activities are getting fewer and fewer when working with
adults and on thematic excursions, as neither providers nor participants
wish to find themselves in the "feel me, touch me" corner. When the skeptic
has accepted the term Mindfulness they feel comfortable with the more un-
emotional descriptions and notice that Mindfulness in nature is not a "doctrine of harmony". Events markedly oriented towards natural history can
benefit from mindful perception as well. Let us remember the fictitious
example of a natural history bird excursion at the beginning of the chapter.
In consideration of the practice of Mindfulness, the sequence would appear
in the following way:

The focus during the hike through the nature reserve is not only one
especially rare type of bird, but the diversity of the birds in general. Before
the name of the bird is given by the leader of the excursion, the group
observes the appearance and behavior of the bird. Which colors and
patterns do its feather, eyes, and legs have? If we closed our eyes, could we
sketch it? How does the bird behave? Is its flight pattern straight or is it
very wavy? Does it beat its wings fast and hastily or slow and carefully?
How does its call effect us? How does it effect others? Is it even a call?
Why do we think so? Can it be a warning call, a begging call, or a contact
call? Do the birds feel bothered by us? Do they move back and forth hastily
and are about to fly away? How can we change our movements and our
stance, in order to get closer to the animals? Where is the necessary
distance? Can we influence it through our own actions? What feeling do I
have when I discover a rare bird? Am I happy about the observation or am I
sad that they have become so rare? The participants are invited to observe
birdcalls at home, to practice getting closer to birds with modified movements, and to observe which birds call a certain place in nature home.
Suggestions are given, how interesting structures can be created for birds in
your environment.

With such a setting, participants with various amounts of previous knowledge are addressed. That beginners get their money's worth is obvious. But interestingly, many very experienced ornithologists are impressed by the many details that had eluded them previously.

The approach chosen above can be generalized detached from the subject of an excursion. The "object" is not simply observed on its own, but experienced in its situative context. A further line can be drawn nicely here: The participants of our fictitious excursion described above have perceived the environment more broadly, deeper, and more differentiated. The foundation for systems thinking[58] is thereby trained, as required by ESD. Thanks to the specific use of elements of mindfulness, the preconditions are created for the occasion to have a long-term effect on the participants that enables them to perceive and recognize analogous time, space, and relational patterns in their everyday life: The perceived objects are interdependent and clearly part of the ecological system. A mental map can develop and real systems thinking has become possible. The ability to analyze risk is thereby schooled, which has become rare ability. Situations can once again be adequately judged. It is recognized when caution is needed in nature and adequate conclusions are drawn.[59]

Mindfulness exercises in nature allow enough free space to process, reflect, and emotionally trace the experience on one's own. A mutual exchange or one in a group adds a new dimension. It brings different patterns of perception together with playful ease. Such an exchange deepens the experience. Do the perceptions of others amount to a comprehensive impression for me? The following example shows this descriptively and makes it clear that cognitive elements have their place in a sharing as well.

Michael and I prepared nature- and mindfulness-oriented workshop in the Odenwald forest in Germany. Michael admired a large amount of plants with striking violet flowers at the edge of the forest. I was underway with a

---

58. Frischknecht-Tobler et al. 2008.
59. Also see Einwanger 2012.

natural history perspective and he with a mindful one. I was silent for a time and felt helpless. As a biologist I knew that we were dealing with invasive neophytes (bobby tops). I had seen this plant as negative until now and seldom took the time to regard it more closely. I tried to take in Michaels beginner's perspective. The flower was beautiful. After a while of almost amazed admiration I consciously left this attitude again and told Michael about the problem of the neophytes overgrowing everything. With the attitude of mindfulness we can find the individual plant beautiful in its appearance and observe the resonance of the flower in ourselves. At the same time, this should not obscure one's perception of processes and developments. We can perceive the loss of diversity with this knowledge and recognize what is important to us, as well as what we wish to apply ourselves to, through the resonance to this.

10.5.2. Consciously Observing Bodily Feelings and Emotions in Nature and Recognizing Valuations

Most nature educators do not only work towards a cognitive and perception enhancing effects. They wish to turn "simple nature experiences" into "nature adventures", and to touch the participants emotionally by being in nature. The events are not supposed to be cool in a tentative way and be fun, but is supposed to touch the participants emotionally in a positive way. Sometimes it is simply about perceiving your own body, for example when working with children or with athletically influenced offers in nature education. A passionate mountain hiker describes his mindfulness experiences with the following words:

> "I enjoy the silence in and surrounding me, allow myself to be fascinated by a variety of completely unremarkable insects and plants, am amazed by the clouds on the rugged mountain cliffs, feel myself intensely at precarious passages where every step must be made cautiously. I experience exhilarating moments when the landscape unexpectedly opens up or an ibex crosses my path. Hunger, thirst, sweat, and breathlessness are part of being underway without dampening the mood. Sometimes small stones crunch under my feet, or I walk over humus-rich ground – I always feel like I am part of the land-

scape."

Observations of the inner and outer world meet at eye level in this description. Nature in its three-dimensional structure, with its heights and depths and unevenness, effects the body and sequence of movements directly, and thereby also influences the psyche.[60] Own movement attuned to nature and just being underway is meaningful and sensible.

There are good reasons why a more conscious feeling of the body is to be striven for in nature education with the help of elements of the practice of mindfulness. If children and adults find themselves in an unknown area, they often move awkwardly. This includes the placing of individual steps on the one hand, as well as the division of one's own strength during a longer distance on the other hand. Here, the specific use of mindfulness can be helpful: Those that consciously observe their breath and heartbeat adjust their pace instinctively to ascent and slope of the terrain. Those that perceive themselves as part of the three-dimensional space adjust their stance and sequence of movements to the requirements of the area.

It is often easy in the practice of nature education to lead the participants to a conscious observation of their own body. However, a greater challenge is to include feeling. In my experience, mainly positive impressions are expressed in feedback rounds. But positive impressions are mostly not there from the beginning. Fascination, awe, and respect namely are often first reached through acquired basic knowledge in natural history, own observations, and experiences in nature. Especially with children and adults alienated from nature, emotions such as disgust, fear, aggression, and timidity can also be encountered at the beginning. The emotional experience of nature is dependent on the challenges of the situation: The group can be content and relaxed or tense and fearful. This is where I see a great opportunity for nature education. It allows one to become aware of one's own moods, sensitivities, and feelings caused by nature in all its facets. Mindfulness exercises explicitly challenge us to accurately observe the full

---

60. Compare Storch et al. 2010.

range of emotions from fear, rejection, disgust, and anger to exuberant joy. That certain natural elements partially encounter spontaneous dislike is completely normal and is of evolutionary importance. Emotions are often divided into positive and negative or comfortable and uncomfortable categories in discussions in the field of nature education.[61] These divisions do not do justice to the complexity of these emotions, as often more than one emotion is prevalent. The following example of an excursion in the mountains will clarify this:

> "We are freezing! It is colder than we imagined in the summer at 6500 feet above sea level. The glacier in this grand landscape is truly amazing, but it is also freezing. Too bad that I am wearing shorts. My bottle of water is empty, my hiking boots are too tight, and my only sandwich has already been eaten. Does the fox tapeworm exist in this area? I just ate blueberries. And do ticks still exist at this altitude? The leader of the excursion shows us moraines where one can see the last peak of the glaciers, thereby clarifying the consequences of climate change – it is interesting, but somehow I cannot appreciate this at the moment: Thunderclouds are forming above the summits of the Matterhorn, Weißhorn, and others on the horizon. I want to return to our shelter. Luckily, the path to the idyllically located mountain lake we planned on visiting tomorrow has been closed due to the danger of an avalanche, although I was looking forward to it. These majestic mountains are also uncanny..."

Mixed feelings of every kind can be observed and accepted especially well with the attitude of mindfulness. The tension between such feelings can cause deep existential and spiritual experiences. The feeling of majesty in nature as a mixture of happiness and fear is often described as a "great" experience. If we feel secure enough, we can endure these tensions and open ourselves to them (see chapter 13). Such emotional experiences are not only pleasant memories, as they shape the foundation of many environmental activists interactions with themselves and nature.[62]

---

61. On emotions in environmental education see also Gugerli&Frischknecht 2011, Kals et al. 2000.
62. Chawla 2002.

Although we naturally prefer pleasant feelings, it is helpful and relieving to accept unpleasant feelings in nature. They do not always have to be grand emotions: Subtle and unremarkable feelings are just as important in order to relate to nature. We can trace them especially well with the attitude of mindfulness. There is often a lack of words fur such subtle things. When it is about learning thoughtful interaction with one's emotions, terms for possible feelings are often playfully introduced beforehand. This approach is also chosen in educational programs in which participants are supposed to learn a different way to deal with their emotions in order to prevent violence. It is easier for many people to consciously observe emotions if they are introduced to the terms beforehand. Description can help with differentiated feelings, as it is thereby consciously observed.[63] Naming can certainly be helpful, but it also holds the danger that people are categorized and that moments of observation are neglected.

Another rewarding goal of mindfulness-oriented nature education is to make the valuations connected to existing moods and feelings clear. Many valuations are thereby recognized as relative, possibly even as fleeting personal perspectives, and frustration tolerance improves. This change in perspective works well with and enriches children and youths. As part of the "Wiese: Lebensraum oder Futtertraum?" ("Meadow: Habitat or Feeding Dream?", own translation, GZ) curriculum of the Nature Schools in Zurich, fifth grade students are asked to emotionally evaluate different types of meadows from various perspectives. A uniform green meadow is initially most attractive to the students, according to my colleague Rita Schneider – probably because soccer can be played on it. After a change in perspective to the world of butterflies, the emotional importance of green areas changes severely. We experienced something similar in the program "Wald und Mensch" ("Forest and Humans", own translation, GZ). My colleague Urs Hofstetter from the wilderness park Zurich reports that the uniform spruce forest is significantly more liked by children than the impenetrable mixed forest Sihlwald. Does familiarity play a role here? Or is a uniform and easily accessible spruce forest more inviting for free and undirected play?[64]

---

63. Rosenberg 2005.
64. Concerning the topic of free unstructured play in nature see Gebhard 2013.

I remember a workshop on values, valuation, and decisions during the exhibition "Entscheidungen" ("Decisions", own translation, GZ) in the museum of Lenzburg in Switzerland. Based on the presentation of various scenes we, a group of nature educators, were encouraged to emotionally evaluate these scenes intuitively with the help of red and green cards. Green stood for positive, red for negative. We "conservationists" showed the red card the entire time when a uniform lawn was shown, which confused the leader of our workshop. This picture was actually supposed to symbolize "nature", which is why she expected us to show the green card. Even if the meadow was covered with dandelions none of us would have shown the green card. Our natural historical value system clearly influenced our emotional valuation. We missed the diversity of species, the colors, the flowers, flying butterflies, etc. The perception of what is, as well the observation of what is missing, but still inside of us in form of knowledge, expectations, memories, and inner pictures, in reality can be made clear through the attitude of mindfulness. This is an indispensable part of an education for sustainable development.

10.5.3. Building, Advancing, and Deepening Bonds and Ties with Nature

The great opportunity of mindfulness in the context of nature education is that it causes a strengthening of relationships and ties with nature independent from ethical concepts and ideologies. The following citation of a nature educators with decades of experience underlines this:

> "...I sit motionless at my favorite place in the forest. A mouse walks around my shoes and does not notice that I am there. At that moment I feel that I am a part of nature..."' (Own translation, GZ)

This description shows that the experience of ties with nature has room in everyday life. Perhaps it was a crucial spiritual experience for my colleague. This simplicity and presence corresponds to what is achieved with the attitude of mindfulness.

Ties with nature are often based on the fact that we feel connected to other living beings and can interact with them. But this assumes that we perceive other creatures as living beings with needs and sensitivities of their own. Most people, especially children, must first learn the necessary ability needed to change perspectives. With many animals it quickly becomes clear that our counterpart has different needs than we do.[65]

Empathetic abilities increase through contact with animals (Gebhard 2013, p. 129 et seq.). Contact with animals is especially intense when we are perceived as a self-evident part of the environment by them. Such moments arouse a deep feeling of attachment to nature in many people. This is already shown in the citation above.

Many people feel a strong connection to plants such as trees or flowers. Here, interaction shifts towards the aspect nurturing and maintaining. The importance of gardens is a good example for this. One's own influence becomes visible in the garden: We recognize consequences, inter-relationships, and contexts. Garden work is often uncontrollable, as the results are often different than we intended: Hail, beetles, caterpillars, snails, and frost are a part of it. Garden work thereby becomes participation in nature. By connecting it with the concept of mindfulness student gardens, urban gardening projects, environmental protection measures, etc. receive a new meaning within ESD. The mindful observation of before and after leads us away from blind actions. The actors, for example, take the time to return to places that were modified and recognize the consequences of their actions.

When we ask people which aspects of nature they feel connected to, they often do not mention living beings, but entire landscapes that can be explored on one's own or together. They are often familiar landscapes from our childhood in which we feel safe, but also landscapes that are so im-pressive that they have meaning for our life. Symbols and metaphors in

65. Concerning the importance in the development of children see Gebhard 2013, Weber 2012, Myers&Saunders 2002, and Katcher 2002.

nature allow us to reflect, think of new possibilities, and strengthen ties. Rather untouched landscapes through their multidimensionality, diversity, liveliness, unpredictability, and inconsistency make it clear for many people what it means to be alive and connected with others. The foundation for this deep emotional connection with nature and the feeling of belonging is already layed in childhood[66] and is considered to be one of the most effective factors for sustainable environmental behavior today.[67] Emotional connections with nature develop through visits to nature, mindful observation with all senses, and especially by sharing these experiences with people that are important to you. The practice of mindfulness in nature includes nature as well as people and intensifies the relationship, familiarity, and connectedness with nature.

---

66. Kellert 2002, Chawla 2002, Gebhard 2013, Weber 2011.
67. Kaplan&Kaplan 1989, Kals et al. 1998.

11. The Importance of Mindfulness in Nature to Well-Being and Mental Health

Michael Huppertz

This chapter will not deal with the healing powers of nature, but instead with the healing powers of nature experiences. Of course I am most interested in which connections exist, or can be created, between the healing power of nature experiences and the healing power of mindfulness, and possible synergies between the two. It is only possible to follow certain strains of this topic at this point and to find scattered starting points in history and the present in order to answer this question. This suggests an essay structure, rather than a systematic consideration. Not only is there not enough room at this point, it also seems too early. The positive influences of "mindfulness in nature" on well-being and health are not a relevant scientific topic yet, but nature's influence in general is more so.

Richard Louv spoke of a "nature deficit disorder" (Louv 2008, p. 99 et seq.) with all the magic of naturalism, a sort of basic fault in relation to nature which supposedly affects many people in industrialized societies that do not spend much time in nature. In his opinion, many children in the United States suffer from a lack of "N vitamins". It is not only about protecting nature from humans for him, but also protecting people in nature: "If we are going to save environmentalism and the environment, we must also save an endangered indicator species: the child in nature" (Louv 2011, p. 159).

In fact, there are countless studies that verify *positive influences on well-being and efficiency from contact with nature*:

- an improvement of cognitive abilities, especially a regeneration of attentiveness;

- less development of and quicker recovery from stress, measured in vegetative parameters;

- a quicker convalescence;

- an improvement of well-being and mood;

- a lessening of aggression and possibly criminal behavior;

- an improvement of self-confidence, especially through active contact with nature.[68]

It is difficult to find the factors that cause these soothing and healing aspects of being in nature. Being in nature is often connected with specific social contacts, more movement, or simply diversions, but also with smells, noise levels, lighting conditions, temperature, and much more which all has an influence on our mood and our social behavior (Guéguen&Meineri 2013).

Attention restoration theory (Kaplan&Kaplan 1989) is an interesting attempt to explain the soothing effect of being in nature in regard to the concept of mindfulness. An exhaustion of attentiveness is made responsible for numerous disorders and health hazards. Rachel and Stephen Kaplan differentiate between two basic forms of human attentiveness: directed and undirected modes of attentiveness. Our daily life usually requires directed mindfulness. It focuses, evaluates, considers, and analyses. It offers us orientation, but makes us very tired as well. It is hard to maintain this level of attentiveness for several hours without becoming tired. On one hand, we now recuperate by sleeping, but on the other hand, we also recuperate through phases of the second form of attentiveness, namely, effortless un-directed attentiveness. Under *fascination*, nature is understood as a realm of experience which can be experienced in the mode of effortless undirected attentiveness and supports this mode. Natural phenomena that cause a slight fascination are, for example, glittering, moving, lively, and recurring

---

68. Overviews in Brämer 2008, 2011, 2012, Flade 2010, Louv 2011, Guéguen&Meineri 2013, Gebhard 2013.

undramatic spectacles of nature like sunsets, waves, etc. According to this theory, people recuperate especially well if natural areas are harmonious (*coherent*). This is also the case when the requirements of the situation are in harmony with the purposes of the person (*compatibility*). The practice of mindfulness and natural experiences equally support the change to an effortless directed and undirected attentiveness. Therefore, this hypothesis is an interesting attempt to explain the synergyzing effects of both ways of life.

Nature as a realm of experience and relational object has had a shadowy existence in *psychiatry and psychotherapy*. Since antiquity, there have repeatedly been ideas in the history of medicine that the experience of nature has a healing effect on the psyche of patients[69]. In the 19th century, "romantic psychiatry" was accompanied by the suspicion that early industrialization was the cause of many mental illnesses, due to its overstimulation and hecticness. From a romantic perspective, nature was the alternative model to a degenerated society. This is one of the reasons – though certainly not the most important – why large psychiatric clinics where built in the countryside. There was much expected from fresh air, agrarian or horticultural activity, the spectacle of vegetation, healthy nutrition, and abstinence. Sometimes a rigid course of isolation was accordingly pursued from former living environments was accordingly pursued[70]. Today, the experience of nature plays a minor role in psychiatry. Horticultural therapy and animal-assisted therapies are the exception.

Horticultural therapy has secured itself a solid position in the fields of psychiatry and rehabilitation. Here, the diagnosis is not paramount, and the therapy usually concerns the preservation and development of general human abilities and those of the individual patient. Provided that patient and client groups are examined, it can be said that especially patients suffering from dementia benefit from this form of therapy. They show an improvement of mood, less behavior disorders, and can come into contact

---

69. Regarding the history of horticultural therapy, see Neuberger&Putz 2010, Niepel&Pfister 2010.
70. Halemeyer 1996, Beck 1983.

better[71]. This form of therapy also seems to prove itself in the field of youth psychiatry, drug therapy, and with physical and mental disabilities.

Horticultural therapy has a history in the United States, England, Spain, and Germany that reaches back to the beginning of the 19th century, and whose predecessors can be traced to Galen in the 2nd century A.D. The aspect of work, the distraction, the general positive effect of fresh air, plants and the sun, and later also the receptive (contemplative, sensory) aspects of working in the garden stood in the foreground. organizations and specific education on horticultural therapy first emerged in the United States in 1972, in England in 1993, and since then has emerged in many other countries. In accordance with this professionalization, horticultural therapy is understood as a "planned and goal-oriented process" (own translation, GZ), in which "garden oriented activities and experiences" (Niepel&Pfister 2010, p. 17, own translation, GZ) are utilized to improve quality of life and for therapeutic purposes. It is about the preservation of motor skills, sensuality and reality orientation, but also the increase of self-worth, responsibility and communication that makes collective work in the garden possible. Horticultural therapy groups meet regularly over an extended period of time. Its practice is very diverse and includes almost all of the not too difficult work that can be done with plants and their products. Especially the gardens of clinics are utilized and shaped accordingly.

Today, receptive processes and activity itself are usually more prominent in horticultural therapy than the result. Therefore, mindfulness implicitly has a strong presence in horticultural therapy, but it does not play a role so far as an explicit concept or practice of exercises. I would like to demonstrate how great its implicit meaning for specific therapeutic work can be in the context of horticultural therapy with an example that impressed me very much.

There is an organization in England that has been advocating the therapy of torture victims worldwide since 1985. It was founded under the name *The Medical Foundation for the Care of Victims of Torture*, and is known as

---

71. Beck&Karn 2012.

Freedom from Torture today. Beginning in London, it now has five centers in England that have treated more than 50.000 victims over the years. More than 200 employees and volunteers offer psychotherapy, physical therapy, other medical treatment, consultation, as well as assistance regarding integration into English society. In 2002, a report was published by Sonja Linden and Jenny Grut[72] on a horticultural therapy project within the framework of this aid group. It began in 1992 under the name *Natural Growth Project*. During this reference period, 40 victims were treated by three employees at any given moment. Most patients were given a parcel of land (approximately 10'x3') to take care of a larger allotment within a garden community. They were allowed to use their products for themselves, their friends, and family. There were individual and group conversations during, as well as accompanying, this garden work, in which experiences or memories were discussed that developed or surfaced while working in the garden.

The *Natural Growth Project* assumes that torture victims

- often have difficulty to communicate with other people in a confident and open manner;

- suffer under their memories and cannot adequately control them;

- have difficulty to verbalize, share, and process these memories;

- cannot dwell easily in the present;

- do not automatically believe in and shape their future;

- therefore have enormous difficulty to establish themselves in an alien and new culture.

---

72. Linden&Grut 2002, regarding its current status see:
http://www.freedomfromtorture.org/what-we-do/10/11/5109

As with all traumatized people, it is first important to stabilize them in the present. Being in nature can contribute to this, as can working in nature. The self-dependency and stability of nature with its rhythms, sensual fascinations, and relationships offer the necessary foothold. Thereby, spaces and security are created for an examination of the past:

> "From my observations, people who have difficulty in relating to other people seem to find it easier to caress a leaf, smell a flower, talk to a bird, and once this is established and feels safe they can move on to people. Concentration, physical exercise, peaceful sounds and open spaces seem to help break down psychological defenses and allow the more vulnerable, hurt or angry aspects to emerge." (Grut&Linden 2002, p. 9)

It is easy to understand that contact, open spaces, peaceful sounds, and freedom of movement have a special meaning to people, who were confined under constant threat and mistreated. According to this report, memories were initiated by the metaphoric potential of nature, comparisons to earlier nature experiences, physical processes, etc. Working in the garden made one's own abilities and possibilities palpable.

All of this was addressed in individual and group conversations, but also through cooperation and communication, both gestural and non-verbal, while working. The therapists consciously refrained from the use of translators. For people whose plans in life had been partially destroyed, the future became livable again: "Planning in the garden and on the allotments is therefore a highly symbolic and charged activity, representing as it does the present beckoning the future" (Grut&Linden 2002, p. 41). Nature contributes to this through its reliable rhythms (seasons) and growth. Nature is simultaneously predictable and unpredictable, but never static or backward-looking. Many activities and difficulties that arise while working in the garden have a symbolic and generalizable content. They require controlled aggression, patience, care, optimism, cooperation, etc.

Working in the garden has created many possibilities to arrive in the new environment that refugees have to live in at first, whether they want to or not: engaging with the weather and vegetation, visiting garden centers, communicating with neighbors who are defensive and critical, but also offering guidance and assistance, and many other aspects. Here, working in the garden opened up a very concrete entry into English society and it was important for those affected to be able to bid farewell from their former home in a positive sense with this new path.

At this point, it is not possible to address the multitude of experiences and interpretations that the authors describe in their book. They have created a "remembrance garden" for physically impaired patients and founded a gardening group for the children of traumatized parents. Furthermore, one patient created a medicinal garden and processed its harvest, and there are many more examples. I hope that it has become clear how horticultural therapy can be interpreted in regard to the problems of clients or patients. In this case, caring for one's own parcel of land was certainly a decisive point.

The elements of mindfulness which serve as a precondition for working on these trauma are obvious: presentness, sensuality, feeling oneself, handling emotions, patience, recognizing one's own possibilities and boundaries, improving one's self-worth, connectedness and relational mindfulness, acceptance, gratitude, and opening oneself for the future. In the case histories and scenes documented in the book, such elements of mindfulness are described repeatedly, even though they are not connected in an overall concept or term. It is not only the parties concerned or the therapists, but especially nature which initiates healing experiences, keeps alive, shapes, and encourages through its qualities. The therapy consists of engaging in reflected relationships with nature.

Studies show that even encounters with nature via media (pictures, movies, etc.) can have a positive effect on the well-being of individuals (see Flade 2010)[73]. In 2014, Susanne Moser-Patuzzi und Marion Jettenberger created a very nice practical book with picture cards and a multimedia CD

---

73. This is used in psychological research, so far as it pertains only to individual sensory channels (especially if they are optical or olfactory) which are relatively easy to stimulate.

that is suited to bring people back into contact with nature, who due to immobility and supply problems can only visit a park or garden in a limited manner or not at all. Besides using large picture cards with typical nature motifs, they also work with natural materials and essential oils. But it is not only the material itself and its meticulous arrangement according to themes such as seasons or slowness that makes their work so interesting. It is how they show how the material can be transferred into a conversation through precise observation, remembering, recounting, and open questions. It is a practical book of mindfulness, even if this concept is only passingly referenced.

Another form of green care which has been elaborated, well organized, and by now saturated with experience is *animal-assisted or animal-transferred therapy*. Even though there were already institutions that used animals therapeutically, for example in Belgium in the 8th century, at the end of the 17th century (and 1942) in the U.S., and at the end of the 18th century in Germany (Bethel), the beginnings of animal-assisted therapy in the narrower sense are seen in the consultations of Dr. Boris M. Levinson. In 1960, he wished to treat a young boy with psychotherapy, who was seen as very withdrawn and unapproachable and already had several failed attempts of treatment behind him. The following scene influenced animal-assisted therapy for a long time. The parents arrived too early for the appointment, so that Levinson's retriever was still lying in the back of the office. The dog ran to the child and caressed its face. The boy surprisingly did not show any sign of fear and remained in close contact with the dog. Finally, he breathed the wish to come back and to play again with the dog. (Greiffenhagen&Buck-Werner 2007, p. 16). Levinson published the case several years later and experiences were confirmed time and time again, in which dogs served as door openers with patients who had difficulty with interpersonal contact.

It was also increasingly recognized that contact with animals could not only be helpful for therapeutic relationships, but also benefit life quality and therapeutic processes in general. In this way, therapeutic forms developed that are today known under the term "animal-assisted therapy", in which animals either function as a catalyst to allow the patient to merge in a therapeutic relationship or have a central therapeutic function as therapeutic partners. Especially dogs, horses, alpacas, and dolphins are used in "animal-transferred therapy". Working with horses is most prevalent and well-known.

Overall, a broad array has developed for the involvement of animals in educational, rehabilitative, and therapeutic processes. This ranges from the simple presence of animals in institutions (pen, aquarium, house pet) to pointed therapeutic interventions, for example with neurological illnesses and patients who are disabled, fearful, or suffer from a borderline-personality disorder.[74] One focus remains therapeutic work with children, and people whose behavior in relationships and communication is significantly impaired.

Even though sophisticated methodological considerations show that the state of research regarding the efficiency of such methods of therapy is

74. Lederbogen 2012, Greiffenhagen&Buck-Werner 2007, Fachgruppe 2005.

tenuous[75], there are countless reports and case reports which show positive effect in the following areas:

- motor function and physical feeling

- attentiveness and concentration

- sensory perception

- empathy (more precise perception of the behavior of other beings, recognition of non-verbal signals)

- ability to communicate (with the animal, with people about the animal, and finally with people)

- expression of personal wishes and emotions

- emotionality (experience of acceptance by the animal, coping with anxiety, improvement of feeling of self-esteem)

- improvement of social skills (trust, overcoming contact anxiety, taking over responsibility, care)

This array in turn makes it clear, how strongly mindfulness – inner, outer, and relational – is implicitly benefited by this work. However, it does not play any role in the countless explanatory models of educational and therapeutic work with animals.[76] It immediately suggests itself to strengthen and also formulate the aspect of mindfulness in the cases of animal-assisted therapy. This could contribute to making the aspects of presentness, aim-

---

75. Pottmann-Knapp 2013.
76. The explanatory models are very diverse. Deliberations on attachment theory, which mostly stem from psychoanalytical development research, and other concepts of depth analysis (identity and personality development) are dominant, but there are also phenomenological and naturalistic-genetic approaches in anthropology ("biophilia"), as well as neuroscientific, behavior therapeutic, act-theoretical, and further explanatory models (Olbrich&Otterstett 2007, Vernooj&Schneider 2013).

lessness, openness, eagerness to experiment, acceptance, connectedness, empathy, thankfulness, and joy of being – which already play such a large role in this work – clearer, and contribute to raising consciousness in this regard, thereby purposefully promoting them within and outside of the therapeutic setting.

We did not present any horticultural or animal-assisted therapeutic exercises in this book, because they contradict our principle of simple implementability for all participants. They require many prerequisites. The corresponding therapists are specialized and professionalized in the meantime, and the authors do not posses the necessary competencies. It becomes clear through horticultural and animal-assisted therapy that mindfulness in consultation and therapy should not primarily be about developing new mindfulness procedures. Instead, it is more about making the aspect of mindfulness clear and strengthening it in existing procedures conceptually, as well as through suitable exercises. Mindfulness is a contribution to the practical philosophy of educational, consultation, and therapeutic work, and to the practical philosophy of patients and clients. Everyone who works in these fields can develop it with their clients and patients. Only as an exception is it a new procedure that can be distinguished and isolated from traditional approaches.

Today, nature remains less important in ambulant *psychotherapy* than in institutionalized psychiatry, psycho-somatics, or rehabilitation. The pre-history of psychotherapy took place outdoors and included nature. For example, Count Puységur gathered a group under an old lime tree in the tradition mesmerism under which a spring originated. He connected the participants to the tree with ropes, and he put them in a trance. In this state of somnambulism, people spoke about their problems with unusual openness.[77] "Psychotherapy" only established itself as a term and method of healing with psychological remedies when Freud attempted to quasi isolate a "psyche" in the laboratory of his doctor's office and to examine it under experimental conditions – as he was familiar with from his

---

77. Ellenberger 1985, Sloterdijk 1987, Huppertz 2003. Freud certainly did not only hold himself to this setting, and instead often held his therapeutic conversations outdoors.

neurophysiological research.[78] He was the first to speak of a "scientific psychotherapy". There was no room for outer nature in this form of scientific setting, and inner nature as well should only come to light in form of symbolic representations (language, dreams), according to this theory. It took a long time before psychotherapy was able to break away from these specifications and appreciate the importance of bodies, movement, expression, behavior, and scenic events – in- and outside of psychoanalysis.

Behavioral therapy reoriented perception back to the behavior of people in their environment. Though this led to treatment outside of doctor's offices ("in-vivo expositions"), the perspective of diagnostic-therapeutic was directed towards symptoms and not nature's resources. With the triumph of cognitive behavioral therapy, a mentalization also began. Its practice was reinforced in doctor's offices. When people now speak of a "third wave" of behavioral therapy and explicitly reference the inclusion of experience through mindfulness, then the hope can theoretically be attached to this that therapeutic settings will be extended and be open towards nature. Sadly, this has barely been practiced in mindfulness-based therapies. Due to its connection to cognitive behavioral therapy, the main interests until now have been mental processes, physical feelings, or sensory exercises that do not rely on nature. This restriction to familiar settings is reinforced by the fact that many of the concepts of mindfulness which are used have a preference towards inner mindfulness, because they mainly adhere to or interpret a Hindu or Buddhist tradition. Here, a widespread concept within the world of mindfulness is also a hindrance, namely that it is first necessary to work on one's self before it is possible to correctly interact with the outer world.[79] Therapeutic work in nature is more obvious, if one has a more interactive concept of man and accords reality therapeutic (and spiritual) relevance. For this reason, there is only occasionally room for actual (and not just imaginary!) nature experiences and direct interaction with nature in mindfulness-based therapy so far.[80]

---

78. Huppertz 2003. For the construction of "psyche" in the history of ideas see Schmitz 1992, p. 93 et seq.
79. For a critique of this concept see Huppertz 2014a.
80. Coleman (2006) portrays countless meditations in nature, but limits himself to using nature only as an occasion for complex instructed mental exercises.

In humanist psychotherapy, the experience of nature had and continues to have a special significance. Here, the influences of the life reform movement – especially the work of Elsa Gindler and Heinrich Jacoby – and Charlotte Selver's "sensory awareness training" had a deep effect. In this tradition, nature appears as an enrichment of sensuality through outer nature and the wisdom of the body.[81] Mindfulness should catalyze both these processes. From a therapeutic perspective (which was not the original perspective of the movement), the limitations of humanist interests in nature lie in the very general orientation towards personal growth and the idealized orientation towards the wisdom of nature.

In the past decades, *ecopsychology* has developed in the United States. It criticizes the fact that psychology and psychotherapy show enormous interest in interpersonal relationships, but not in the relationship between humans and nature. Aldo Leopold made the case in the field of nature ethics to broaden the ethics of human communities: "The land ethic simply enlarges the boundaries of the community to include soils, waters, plants, and animals, or collectively: the land." (Leopold 1969 [1949], p. 204) Similarly, ecopsychologists argue that psychotherapy first addressed inner psychological processes, then interpersonal problems and family systems , and that it is now time to include the natural environment in psychotherapy.[82] This logic has a fascinating quality. Inner and interpersonal themes are indeed dominant in psychotherapy to a degree which – considering real cross-linkages – seems very limited. The evasion and denial of more complex and less private coherencies, as well as the distress which exists in the world, can impede the patient's sense of reality. Many people feel that retreating to entirely private issues such as relationships, biographies, experience deficits, personal material worries, physical illnesses, etc. is unsatisfactory.

But the problem arises in practice that openness towards nature and ecological problems are insights of the therapist, which the person concerned must first be familiarized with. Here, the danger exists that

---

81. Brooks&Selver 1979, Stevens 1996 [1971].
82. Roszak et al. 1995, Roszak 1997. In this sense, also see Gebhard 2013 [1994], 2005.

ecological themes are prioritized before intra-psychic and micro-sociological themes, which the patients subjectively suffer from. This problem is reinforced by the fact that ecopsychologists usually feel obliged towards holistic conceptions, in which systems can be joined in ever larger totalities and finally to a whole.[83] The subjectivity and individuality of those concerned becomes less important from a holistic-systematic perspective. Accordingly, medical models are questioned for individuals as well: "At the heart of the coming environmental revolution is a change in values, one that derives from a growing appreciation of our dependence on nature. Without it there is no hope. In simple terms, we cannot restore our own health, our sense of well-being, unless we restore the health of the planet." (Brown 1995, xvi). But not only individual features, dramas, and intra-psychic processes become unnecessarily reliant on planetary developments, but also the possibilities of patients to help themselves and take responsibility for portions of their suffering that mainly have to do with them. The respective therapy options expire as well. That is why it will be difficult to join ecopsychology in its contemporary form with existing psychotherapeutic and psychiatric knowledge. Nonetheless, therapeutic work with mindfulness in nature should conform to its purpose to broaden the intellectual, sensual, moral, and practical horizon of therapy and prevention.

In Darmstadt, we try to include Mindfulness in nature in our therapeutic work. Our ambulant network in Darmstadt, the *Arbeitsgemeinschaft Achtsamkeit* ("The Mindfulness Working Group", own translation G.Z.), was founded in 2009.[84] Most members were previously involved in the ambulant DBT-Network (Dialectic-behavioral therapy for patients with Borderline personality disorders), founded in 1996, and some have continued this involvement.[85] It was our desire to deepen our work with mindfulness and to make it available to additional patients as well. For this reason, we work with groups of patients with specific symptoms and suffer from depression, anxiety, psychoses, or addictions. But we also offer preventive and open meditation groups. Many of us offer professional

---

83. For a criticism of this concept, see chapters 12 and 13.
84. For a detailed description of the project, see Huppertz et al. 2013; also see http://www.ag-achtsamkeit.de
85. Gunia&Huppertz 2007.

development courses. We wish to expound the practice of mindfulness in a diverse, lively, and simple manner that is close to everyday life, so that it can help patients with different disorders of varying severity. Our working group meets in order to discuss organizational questions, share experiences, and also to practice and share new exercises. We have different psychotherapeutic educations, there are no hierarchical structures, and no formal organization. The development of individual therapy programs takes place in small groups with two to four therapists, which address a specific topic. However, no therapy manuals are created here. Instead, drafts are created, corrected in the course of the group, and adjusted to the development of the working group. We accept a maximum of 14 registrations per group and the participants to a large degree are able to decide how much they wish to pay for joining the group.

We have already often worked in a (flower) garden with DBT-groups and individual patients. Now we go to individual meetings in nature with all of our groups, for which we use a small park that is very close to our exercise room and quickly transitions into a landscape with meadows, forests, and creeks.

We regularly offer a group under the title "mindfulness in nature". This group has no explicit therapeutic or preventive aspirations. However, the context of the group in our working group brings with it that several participants find themselves in psychotherapeutic treatment or participate in one of our other groups at the same time. At the moment, the group meets during the late morning on a Saturday every month and is a half-open group. The participants then register for six sessions each, and open spaces are continuously filled with new participants. It is also financed within a certain framework through self-assessment. This group activity takes place exclusively outdoors, even in the winter and when it rains. A meeting lasted six hours in the beginning, but we have shortened it to four hours in the meantime. At first, we did this because we ascertained that the energy of participants decreases after approximately four hours, and secondly because it becomes too uncomfortable for almost all of the participants when the weather is bad. At the same time it must be taken into consideration that we go into nature with people, who partially do not have any experience with mindfulness or psychological problems and do not posses a particularly intense relationship with nature. The group meets at different times of day, meaning sometimes from 5 to 9 a.m. in order to experience a sunrise, and sometimes from 7 to 11 p.m. to include a sunset and darkness. We move around within a few miles of the area surrounding Darmstadt-Eberstadt, a suburb of Darmstadt that borders on the Odenwald. Here we find forests, and also a city forest, smaller lakes, vineyards, creeks, etc. and generally not typical natural scenery. Our equipment includes appropriate clothing, rain shelters, aluminum covered seating material, drawing materials, food, and drinks. Many participants enjoy the possibility to be in nature for a long time in the safety of a group – even at unusual times of day and in places that they may not be accustomed to - and to be able to follow a structured path and order. We do not cross any great distances, and instead dwell in many places, making the physical burden small. In principle, these nature exercises should be able to be continued in a similar form in everyday life. Therefore, the group is not comparable with retreats, wilderness groups, or anything similar, though we do sometimes use opportunities for special nature experiences (night walk, sunrise).

We present the attitude of mindfulness in detail and repeatedly in these groups as well and work with the mindfulness exercises presented in this book. On principle, we ask the participants to remain in the attitude of mindfulness the entire time and to only speak with each other about what is happening at the moment. We include natural materials, geological formations, seasons, courses of the day, the atmosphere of places, and landscapes in our work. The group leaders always scout out the areas for the next meeting beforehand and develop the program at the same time. Every meeting includes a revision of one's own practice of exercises in the time between meetings and a contemplation of 20 to 45 minutes. We have exchanges with one another after every exercise, both in the sense of a sharing, as well as in the sense of discussions on the sense and usefulness of exercises.

The participants are very engaged. Everyone realizes that we accept the inhospitable and adverse aspects of nature as well. We already reported on individual feedback in the introduction. The impact of the groups seems to be lasting and many experiences are also repeated alone. We unfortunately do not have any external evaluations, which we are wishful for, as only they could give us reliable statements on the effect of our work. Our experiences, the portrayals of experiences from different fields, and the reflections on the synergy of nature experiences and mindfulness lead to the following questions, in my opinion:

- Do exercises in nature promote mindfulness and thereby contribute to the recovery or cure of psychological illnesses?

- Does mindfulness in nature strengthen the healing effect of nature experiences? If yes, then how and which ones?

Working in the nature group has lead to us also increasingly performing exercises outdoors in other groups as well. If we examined the personal experiences of patients in nature, we could find out how it varies in different disorders and how its positive effects can be supported during the practice of exercises. For convincing concepts it would be necessary to create a plausible theoretical connection between the syndromes which need to be treated and helpful interventions, as it is done in classical therapy processes and partially in mindfulness-based processes.[86] We would require convincing theories, which are able to explain which factors of mindfulness in nature help with certain syndromes and why they do so. At the same time it would be necessary to consider which forms of mindfulness and which exercises in nature are especially helpful or also contraindicated with specific disorders.[87]

Effective factors could be general recovery effects (relaxation, recovery of mindfulness), relief from expectations, distance from interpersonal con-

---

86. Huppertz 2012.
87. For several basic rules and experiences, see Huppertz 2009 and Huppertz et al. 2013.

flicts and self-examination, the mood-enhancing and aggression-curbing effects of nature, the improvement of one's feeling of self-worth in nature, the experience of dependencies, one's own limitations, existential realities, humility and thankfulness, the experience of majesty and the extension of self connected to it, proving oneself in new and sometimes challenging situations, the experience of one's own resilience, effectivity, or care, the experience of tranquility, safety, and connectedness, the rediscovery of one's own creativity and playfulness, or spiritual experiences in nature. Undesirable side effects pertaining to this work are – with general thera-peutic experience and consideration of several basic rules (see annotation 96)- barely to be expected. So there are many hypotheses. This speaks for the fruitfulness of the idea to include nature experiences in psychothera-peutic and consultative work.

12. | Mindfulness and Nature Ethics

Michael Huppertz

12.1. The Ethical Aspect of Mindfulness

In Chapter one, we showed that the attitude of mindfulness should not be understood as an attitude of non-judgment, and instead should be seen as an attitude of skepticism towards spontaneous judgments. Reality can be understood, but also misrepresented, by judgments. Without judgments. all feelings in the narrower sense are lost – such as love, fear, anger, hope, etc. - and no involvement for or against something is possible. Mindfulness can lead to appropriate judgments. and is thereby able to influence our moral orientation. Therefore, the attitude of mindfulness is ethically relevant.

When we attribute value to something this can simply be due to the fact that we hold on to a preference, over which an argument could be held. "[P]eople cherish and value things that they do not really think good, things that they would not be prepared to commend as good to others. Often they love a person, or a house, or a country, just because it is theirs, the one the have grown up with." (Nussbaum 2001, p. 51).

It could also be that we strive for interpersonal understandings – so, universal validity - with our judgments., for example when we advocate for something and believe that others should do so as well. In this case, we speak of moral judgments. In this sense, people hold justice, the protection of life, or the humane treatment of animals for morally important. The question of how moral values develop, what characterizes them, how they are transported, and how they can be justified is an ethical question, and if it pertains to the value of nature, we enter the field of "nature ethics" or "environmental ethics".

In this chapter, I would like to address the following question: Does the idea and practice of mindfulness in nature have ramifications for nature ethics?

12.2. Mindfulness and the Intrinsic Value of Nature

If we are directly in front of an animal that is suffering or hungry, we will probably feel affected by this and try to help the animal if possible. When we see the ocean we do not wish it to be polluted, and when we see the forest we do not want it to be cut down. The valences and impulses that are connected to this are not experienced by us because we quickly calculate whether the animal, ocean, or forest can still be utilized, but instead due to the fact that we wish to leave them the way they are.[88] We encounter such moral impressions in the form of scenes, as well as designs, stories, etc. When we wish to protect, preserve, or promote something we do not even require the conception or term of a value, because we simply wish to get involved in the issues that are important to us and not for their "value". The term value itself already assumes a duality of value and fact, of being and ought, which is not created through our experiences, but through a certain form of reflection which separates between objective and subjective facts. In our experiences, descriptions and judgments. are not separated (Fischer 2015). We directly experience a scene as cruel or caring, as violent or exhilarating, and we experience a direct stimulus for action.

If we however wish for others to share our perceptions, we must communicate them, reference them, etc. If we wish to go beyond this and for other people to follow our procedures, or finally if this does not happen spontaneously and we must weigh preferences, we are forced to create comparability, I.e. they must be related to one another as values. We then cannot avoid turning "felt preferences" into "considered preferences"[89] and representing them as values.

In ethics the term "intrinsic value" is used, if we cherish something for

---

88. Regarding the topic of moral impressions and intrinsic values, as well as the diverse possibilities of experiencing and conveying them, see Taylor 1997 [1981], Nussbaum 2000, Hauskeller 2001, Fischer 2012.
89. Bryan F. Norton, according to Niebrügge 2007, p. 39.

its own sake and not because it fulfills a certain purpose. Intrinsic values are not functional values. Something does not have intrinsic value because it is beneficial for something or someone, and instead has value because it is the way it is.

Every time we experience something as intrinsically valuable, mindfulness is involved to a certain extent. This does not mean that someone consciously practices mindfulness in this moment. But values that we experience as "inherent" to a thing, person, etc. can only be experienced, if we respond to them with an aimless, open, and recipient attitude. If we do not turn to a person or a thing in an attentive and interested manner, and do not give them our time, energy, and attention for their own sake, we cannot recognize them as intrinsically valuable. It is also part of aimless attentiveness towards others that we give people and things time. Communication over whether intrinsic values exist or not, which status they have and why certain natural elements should be recognized as intrinsically valuable, is a central issue in nature ethics.

It is a human – probably even specifically human and moreover very adult – position to cherish something without connecting it to a function, even if it is only experiential or entertainment value. Aimless appreciation can arise spontaneously and does not require any training per se. We are all familiar with spontaneous excitement without purpose for natural phenomena such as a sunrise, waterfall, starlit sky, or the feeling of spontaneous affection towards animals or landscapes. The practice of mindfulness can cultivate and strengthen this attitude. It allows us to recognize intrinsic value in nature where this has not been possible so far. Not only mindfulness towards the things themselves is helpful in this regard, but also the sensing of one's personal resonance. A "mental state" can literally arise through mindfulness, which can be described as "the physical-sensual experience that a person has, who is, lives, works, or moves around in a certain part of nature" (Böhme 1989, p. 12, own translation, GZ). Through this mental state a cultivation of sensuality and being open to non-functional relationships with nature, and thereby a "cultivation of appreciation...as a search process within one's way of living" (K. Ott 2010, p. 81, own translation, GZ), develops in connection with the practice of mindfulness. In this way, mindfulness becomes an element of ethical intelligence.[90]

A problem arises for mindfulness as an ethical competence: Those who wish to be mindful towards something for the sake of being mindful run the danger of paying attention to their attitude instead of the matter itself.[91] It is very sensible to emphasize the attitude in the practical application of exercises and to place them in the foreground, but lastly mindfulness is realized as a new habit, as a way of being, with a dedication which is not directed towards itself, but towards the present moment and the object of mindfulness.[92] The seriousness of the moment counts in morals and ethics, not the spirit of the practice of exercises.

12.3. The Necessity of Moral Reflection

In many cases, more than sensual cultivation is part of the experience – and especially the communication – of intrinsic values. Often knowledge, as well as the "recourse to appreciation" and the "reflection of value standards" (K. Ott 2010, p. 81, own translation, GZ), is necessary. Concrete moral problems originate beyond the experience of intrinsic values, because no moral obligations result from them alone, at least not if we only speak of "obligations" and "moral values" if they are intended to be more or less generally binding. In order for them to be generally applicable and thereby be able to become effective, it is necessary for them to be substantiated as much as possible.[93] The "reasoning" begins with the premise that experiences underlying appreciation can be communicated and possibly even shared. "That which was a formative experience for one person should be

---

90. Huppertz 2014.
91. Louden 1998 [1984]: "The orientation towards virtues cannot in itself provide consistent ethical orientation. Through the term virtue we push a certain aspect into the foreground which undermines that which makes a virtue virtuous, namely the meaning of a value which the attitude or action is aimed towards. Those that carry out a virtuous action because they wish to be virtuous are not virtuous. We are helpful, because the fate of the one in need is near to our heart, and not because we follow the voice of virtue and wish to be virtuous." (Own translation, GZ)
92. That is how the dislike of some authors towards the word "exercise" can be explained, for example in Jacoby 2004 [1945] or Baier 2001.
93. For a detailed account, see Nussbaum 2000.

able to become a comprehensible insight for everyone else. The meaning of such formative experiences is therefore directed towards all moral persons, who of course have the right to take in a critical position towards these descriptions" (K. Ott 2010, p. 66).

Furthermore, the experiences should be able to be placed in a moral context (different values, duties, rules), which is, or could be, shared by a community. A statement like the following would otherwise remain the heroic decision of an individual: "If I could only rescue my life in exchange for the price that an intact biocenosis, such as a real forest (not a plantation), would die, then I would consider the cost of my life not too high" (Meyer-Abich 2006, p. 33, own translation, GZ). Though an ethical theory or a moral mindset which does not imply any inherent value would be up in the air, we would not be able to go far with this intuitive foundation alone. The perception of inherent values is anything but dependable. It includes – as do our feelings – cognitive portions which could be false. A beggar can be part of a profitable enterprise, a victim, a perpetrator, an attractive plant can be an existential threat for entire biotopes. There are also cognitively complex and simultaneously firm moral impressions which are unwittingly inherited in the framework of traditions, and can only be recognized as valueless or immoral in a further context or through a historical perspective. The worship of a leader, enthusiasm for a fatherland and a war, as well as the love of another person may be subjectively evident, but can be blind from a different perspective. Even within an individual moral or a relative community of shared values moral conflicts can arise, especially when intuitions come into conflict with one another, for example when we generally reject the killing of animals but wish to preserve forests at the same time, or when we think about the conservation or utilization of resources. We clearly require a considerable amount of rational effort to weigh values against one another and develop something like binding moral rules, obligations, convincing moral conceptions.[94] A diversity of nature ethical positions have arisen from this necessity.

---

94. Nussbaum 2000, K. Ott 2010.

12.4. Nature Ethical Positions

In its largest dimension, positions in environmental ethics can be divided in the following way[95]:

1.   Anthropocentric Positions

2.   Pathocentristic Positions

3.   Biocentric Positions

4.   Holistic Positions

This division may be fundamentally unsatisfactory as will be shown in the following, but captures the essential traditions and makes the relevant problems clear. Positions 2,3, and 4 can also be summarized as "physio-centric" positions, as they accord intrinsic value to non-human natural beings and objects, which are not derived from their important contribution to human life.

The anthropocentric *position* is very familiar to us: we are obligated to protect nature, because

•   it is indispensable for the preservation of the human species;

•   it is beneficial to human well-being and health;

•   it brings us joy, for example through its beauty;

•   it contributes to moral and personal development, or leads to spiritual experiences;

•   we are attracted to it (biophilia hypothesis).

All these arguments are based on the assumption that the value of nature

---

95. In reference to Krebs 1997, p. 337 et seq.

can be functionally measured in regard to the idea of a happy, or from the extended anthropocentric perspective, a successful human life. I will come back to this extension. All other positions reject this functionalization.

The *pathocentristic position* states that the interests of all sensible life forms should be protected and that we are obligated to promote their well-being, regardless whether it is beneficial to us or not. There is no substantial reason to lift humans out of nature in regard to well-being and suffering. If we consider our well-being to be of value, why not that of other beings, as far as they can want (or not want) something and are able to feel and suffer? The following epistemological problem arises from this demand: intrinsic values in nature have to do with the properties of natural beings. In order to capture and consider them, it is also necessary to consider what is good for the animals and which needs they may have. In turn, this is dependent on our communication with them.[96] In the simplest case, we are able to understand the sensibility of an animal in direct communication, as we do in the case of cats, dogs, horses, and great apes. In other cases, we infer it from their behavior, through defensive or responsive reactions, sounds, etc. This way, it can be unproblematic for some animals to live in a zoo, while it is torture for others. In order to be able to assess this, knowledge on the biological (especially neurobiological) properties is certainly one approach. It is clear that we consider higher developed animals to be capable of suffering, but not organisms which do not have a central nervous system, such as bacteria or plants.

The position is unsatisfactory, due to this necessity to find a plausible hierarchy (or forgo them). But is also unsatisfactory, because we thereby make a characteristic derived from our own constitution to the foundation of environmental preservation, namely our own sensibility. Furthermore, inanimate nature disappears from ethical considerations in this perspective. As practice of mindfulness shows, this is a substantial deficit, as especially landscapes, atmospheres, biotopes, stones, rivers, etc. play a large role in mindfulness in nature.

---

96. See Habermas 1997.

The *biocentric position* does not limit itself to the ability to suffer as the criteria for worthiness of protection, and instead takes "liveliness" as its essential criteria. Everything that is alive is valuable in principle and entitled to protection. Which reasons speak for this position? Why are we inclined to attribute an intrinsic value to beings? What clearly morally impresses us, is the goal orientation and purposeful behavior that animals show. If we wish to critically review this, we must first understand wherein this goal-orientation exists. Living organisms are systems, in which individual behavior fulfills a function. Although these functions can be described in causal sequence, there is a consensus that functional observation does not thereby become superfluous.[97] The organization and growth of processes first becomes understandable through this. Sadly however, the description of functional processes is not a sufficient source from which to derive moral obligations. Descriptions must be able to be formulated with an ascription of value, in order to make the leap from is to ought to be. Obligatory rules cannot be derived from descriptions without a value component.[98] But purposes can only then become values when they are important to someone and they commit themselves to it. Only beings that can have interests can also create values, and only humans can articulate them in a way that allows them to be handed down and discussed. "If plants or ecosystems only follow purposes in the functional sense, then their purposes consequently have no moral value" (Krebs 1997, p. 354, own translation, GZ). In purely functional perspectives, life cannot be treated differently than any other system. It is not understandable, why terms such as "metabolism" or "reproduction" should obligate us to something.

Even the attempt to substantiate biocentric positions through such elementary ethical impressions as Albert Schweitzer's "Reverence for Life" is not self-evident, as it is not intuitive for many people. There are many forms of life whose continued existence we do not welcome – from the

---

97. Mutschler 2002.

98. Rules cannot be derived from descriptions, normative statements cannot be concluded from descriptive statements (Hepfer 2008, p. 24 et seq., K. Ott 2010, p. 121 et seq.). But normative statements can already be integrated into descriptive statements for example by using functional terms (MacIntyre 1987). One should however be aware of these normative implications when using terms such as "human" or "nature" in this sense.

bramble bush that overgrows our garden, to cancer cells, or the Anopheles mosquito that carries malaria and costs millions of people their lives every year. Here, Reverence for Life is too abstract because it does not consider the various relationships that we have to the living. Even for Albert Schweitzer, *nature* is sometimes gruesome and it is incumbent to *humans* for him as well to first develop Reverence for Life and assert it versus nature. But also as humans, if we see ourselves as creatures as well, we currently still require plants in order to nourish ourselves, and it is questionable whether it can be considered progress if we free ourselves from this dependency and proceed to purely chemical nourishment. The inescapable guilty conscious that arises from the unavoidable destruction of plants, insects, worms, and bacteria seems to be a form of perfectionism or exaggerated and harmful negative self-referentiality (guilt). But what remains of the biocentric position is the maxim of protecting life wherever it is possible and wherever – to be legitimized – human interests allow it. The biocentric position can also be criticized for not considering inanimate nature in its conception. It could be argued that inanimate nature is always part of considerations, as no life is imaginable without it. However, this argument would functionally bind the value of inanimate nature to its benefit for living beings, constituting an unacceptable dependency and limitation. Therefore, I will now address the holistic position in environmental ethics which has no problem with such limitations.

The most well-known and influential formulation of the holistic position came from Arno Naess and his colleagues. Naess referred to it as "deep ecology" and saw it as part of a "deep ecology movement" (Naess 1995, p. 64). He characterized it in the following way: "The well-being and flourishing of human and non-human life on Earth have value on themselves (synonyms: intrinsic value, inherent worth). These values are independent of the usefulness of the non-human world for human purposes" (p. 68). In the clarification of this point, it is stated that: "This formulation refers to the biosphere, or more professionally, to the ecosphere as a whole (this is also referred to as "ecocentrism"). This includes individuals, species, populations, habitat, as well as humans and non humans cultures. Given our current knowledge of all-pervasive intimate relationships, this implies a fundamental concern and respect. The term 'life' is used here in a more non-technical comprehensive way also to refer to what biologists classify as "non-living": rivers (watersheds), landscapes, ecosystems. For supporters of deep ecology, slogans such as 'let the river live' illustrate this broader usage so common in many cultures" (p. 68). The appreciation of the diversity of nature and an accordingly critical limitation of human activity results from this basic assumption, which also includes a "substantially smaller human population" (p. 68). Human needs are respected, so long as they are necessary for survival (p. 68). Naess' argument does not proceed from "is" to "ought to be" (see annotation 102). Naess underlines: "Thus, there are 'ought to be's in our promises as well as in our conclusions. We never move from an 'is' to an 'ought to be', or vice versa. From a logical standpoint, this is decisive" (p. 76-77). "The main difference, however, is that some sentences at the top (I.e. deepest) level are normative, and preferably are expressed as imperatives" (p. 76).

In this chapter, I would like to limit myself to critical considerations that are relevant to nature ethics, and defer other critical objections to this influential position – for example epistemological ones – to the following chapter on spiritual searches in nature. If we assume that it is even possible to understand and sensibly describe the "entire biosphere" that we would belong to, the question arises why the entirety of nature should have a moral value. This question does not pose itself to Arno Naess and other holistic thinkers, because for them the intrinsic value of nature exists independently from humans and human knowledge and therefore cannot be reasoned (Naess 1997, p. 189, in connection with T. Regan)[!]. Nature would also have value if humans did not exist and were able to recognize it, so for example before the appearance of humans on planet earth. However, this position finds little approval, as only few philosophers can imagine a value that is not at least reliant on human knowledge and the ability to formulate. Usually at least a so-called epistemic anthropocentrism is acknowledged: there are no values, if they are not embraced by humans. "Values" are a human category.[99]

99. For example, see Krebs 1997, p. 343 or Hauskeller 2009, p. 116 et seq. Nonetheless we experience them as properties of *things and humans* like all other properties that we ascribe to nature. It is impossible to discard our common "realistic" intuitions (that things and humans exist independently from us as subjects) without becoming contradictory. Our intuitions are indispensable for our everyday observations and

To proclaim nature "as a whole" to an ethical value will further remain problematic, even if we take the concept back in a critical epistemological manner. Systems cannot exist if they are not supported by their elements. The function of these elements is not dependent on its specific content. Systems survive through "functional equivalence" (Luhmann 1970, p. 14, own translation, GZ). If 90 out of 100 turtle hatchlings are eaten on land and in water then that makes systemic sense, as they are a great source of protein for seabirds. From a holistic perspective, it is never about an individual or an individual species in nature. There can also be conflicts between species conservation and ecosystems. 90% of all the species that ever existed are extinct, for the most part due to natural developments and disasters. The recognition of the value of an individual is the achievement of cognitively differentiated living beings (not only humans), and as a moral principle is a cultural achievement. A systemic contradiction exists between a whole and the *singularity* of its parts which cannot be resolved. If one proclaims a value for the "whole", one must accept the functionalization of these elements and must live with the possibility that their potential self-interest cannot be equally appreciated if it is not functional. Furthermore, singularity is endless, whereas functions are limited. Mindfulness stands on the side of singularity. It opens up possibilities for encounters that are principally still ongoing. Because the one thing or the other continuously evolves with me and the circumstances, perspectives, and the encounter itself.[100] For radical holism, the otherness of the other and the characteristicness of characteristics are inevitably only second class truths.

There is so much suffering of animals and humans in nature, because living beings wish to resist the logic of the system but are not able to do so.

---

actions, and are irrefutable in this sense. Furthermore, every statement and line of argument is inter-subjective and assumes at least the existence of other humans, one's own existence, and the existence of a third party that we collectively refer to. After all, it is also plausible to assume that our picture of reality and how we experience it develops out of the synergy of (inter-)subjects and nature. We thereby always subtract out our constructive efforts, as we do in sight (our eye movements), the lifting of objects (our muscular pretension), etc.

100 . This correlates with the structure of encounters according to Buber, in reference to the participants and their "qualitative endlessness" (Huppertz 2009, own translation, GZ).

What would the rabbit in the fangs of the python, the young lion in the jaws of a full-grown lion, or the people caught in the floods of the tsunami in Thailand say? "Ecologically meaningful"? "Nice that life always wins in this universe" (Weber 2011, p. 142, own translation, GZ)? That a child dying from cancer is part of a vast network, a great symbiosis? "Through that vast network all forms arose, intelligence arose...There is nowhere you can go where you're not held in the web that sustains us all...What are you? What am I? Intersection cycles of water, earth, air and fire, that´s what I am, that's what you are" (Macy&Brown 1998, p. 184-185). .... "The great symbiosis that is you" (Macy&Brown 1998, p. 187). The holistic perspective helps to harmonize and idealize Nature and to eliminate the inextricably conflict between humans – being more than cycles of elements – and nature. However, nature is beautiful, admirable, important, nourishing, comforting, etc., but it is also gruesome and naturally blind for the interests of persons.

For individual people as part of an ecosystem, nature means embedding, supply, and harmony, but also a series of conflicts and the certainty of defeat as a being. Every individual dies and makes room for the following generation, and everyone begins the fight against the dangers that nature – including the nature inherent to humans – holds anew. Of course holistic positions recognize "eat or be eaten", the dangers that nature poses to humans, etc., for example very clearly in so-called wilderness encounters.

Holistic theories must however defer the accepted gruesomeness of nature to a non-existent realm. Harmony and beauty are considered to be central to the determination of nature, which derives a certain credibility from the image of recreational nature in industrialized cultures. Furthermore, nature is not only regarded as harmonic in these cultures, but is stylized (and anthropomorphized) as a victim. Storms and floods, droughts and parasites, or even larger dangers such as meteor impacts, which nearly wiped out all life forms in earlier times, are excluded in contrast. Many natural phenomena (volcano eruptions, meteor impacts, the dominance of certain animals) do not have a recognizable function for the whole in the sense of species conservation or biodiversity. There is also no mention of

AIDS viruses, Alzheimer's disease, Chorea Huntington, or cancer cells in holistic conceptions of nature, only naming such sicknesses which cannot be blamed on a misdirected society. The vulnerability and disfunctionality of inner nature are left out in holistic positions, because they would make the topics of transience, decay, and danger through nature clear for every individual. People protecting the environment are in their prime and underway in a powerful and good-hearted manner to protect endangered nature.

One can try to advocate a softer holistic theory by underlining that the whole and its individual components are equally ethically important. Martin Gorke calls this (his) position "pluralistic holism" (2006, p. 261, own translation, GZ). Such a position creates an area of tension. It inevitably leads to conflicts of interest, for example, when individuals have to yield or suffer harm for the benefit of the whole, or because an entire species, such as neophytes (migratory species that often displace indigenous species), disturbs an ecosystem, or currently where gray squirrels are decimating red squirrels (they die of a smallpox virus that gray squirrels import). The whole now has no absolute value anymore and the question of criteria for intrinsic values within nature arises, for example regarding the developmental stage of an animal, its social organization, or its cognitive abilities, or its complexity or rarity in general. Gorke discusses such possibilities, but ultimately discards them all.[101] Indeed, such criteria would destroy the essence of intrinsic values that cannot be measured on a scale. However, if one discards the positioning of a harmonic whole in nature and also does not gain any immanent criteria for values from nature, then the only path remaining is to acknowledge all which exists in its intrinsic value, as Gorke suggests as well.[102] Now it is easily recognizable that this will not help us in practice.[103] But this consequence also raises the question, why one should even think in a physiocentric frame.

The danger of physiocentric theories lies in the fact that they devalue culture towards nature. Culture is measured in deep ecology in regard to how far it is integrated in nature. Nature is nature, and culture serves the purpose of nature. Culture is seen as a servient maid or as a continuation of nature with other means, and it should not stand in the way of the diversity of nature. The threat that holistic theories pose to individual freedom and culture can be seen in the propagation of the reduction of global population by at least 90% and the general subordination of culture in regard to nature. The drastic reduction of humanity would surely only be possible, if the rights of individual people or couples to procreate and the complexity of cultural achievements, which are also dependent on the vast number of humans, are greatly limited for the benefit of the biosphere as a whole. According to Gorke, "marginal interests ('luxury interests') must take a second place with respect to existential interests" (Gorke 2006, p. 271, own translation, GZ). This initially sounds harmless, as there must surely be some form of weighing interests if one wishes to protect nature. But the author further states that:

> "From this perspective it can surely not remain hidden that a large
> portion of human culture is not justifiable, if one takes the principle of

---

101. Gorke 2006, p. 266 et seq.
102. Gorke 2006, p. 265.
103. Gorke recognizes this as well, which is why he attempts to supplement absolute ethics with relative ethics (2006, p. 269 et seq.).

proportionality seriously. Hiking paths, museums, swimming pools,
and musical instruments do not constitute an indispensable foundation
of human life." (p. 271, own translation, GZ)

Those who believe to know the interests of the whole can often take
very little consideration of particular and procedural values such as free
elections, freedom of the press and of expression, or communication free of
domination, meaning the open-ended negotiation of different and con-
flicting interests required in a democracy. Because one does not wish to
think this through to the end with all its consequences, the question of how
such a reduction of the global population and cultural treasures could ever
by achieved is only marginally addressed.[104] Like every other fundamen-
talism, holistic nature ethics is idealistic in tone, but potentially dangerous
in its actions. And yet there is presently little to fear, because the conception
is mainly relevant in a scene in which people are otherwise democrats and
humanists. It may be that the "rhetoric" of deep ecology nonetheless fulfills
"the essential function in keeping members fighting together under the
same banner" (Naess 1995, p. 76) in the world, but I doubt that it is also
able to "provoke interests among outsiders" (Naess 1995, p. 76).

But how can we use this critical depiction to solve the problems presented?

12.5. Nature Ethics from the Perspective of Being in Nature and Mindfulness

Our being in nature brings many different kinds of experiences with it,
including moral impressions as well. The attitude of mindfulness draws on
a certain form of being in nature, intensifies it, and strengthens the aspect of
aimless presence. Various intrinsic values of nature thereby become clear,
which however are not ordered in a hierarchy stemming from nature and
cannot be referred back to the big picture. Mindfulness also holds in individual cases, be it the single individual, species, or ecosystem. A consistent
moral orientation that transforms such impressions into binding values,
norms, and actions can profit from biocentric, pathocentric, holistic, and

---

104. Regarding the political implications, see K. Ott 2010, especially p. 193 et seq.

anthropocentric positions.

The biocentric position opens our eyes for the special quality of life. However, appreciating the creatureliness saves us from drawing the boundaries of our values too narrowly, overemphasizing the special position of humans in the known world, and sublimating our way of existence.

The pathocentric position makes it clear that it is part of a comprehensive mindfulness based on contact with nature to empathize with or try to understand sentient nature as much as possible, and derive intrinsic values and rights from this empathy.

The holistic way of thinking is an important contribution, if it refers to definable ecological systems, landscapes, and natural atmospheres. Then it broadens our understanding of what nature is. Moreover, it invites us to recognize ourselves as part of ecosystems and to act accordingly. In this form it is not reliant on the conception of an overriding whole in nature, and should therefore rather be called "ecocentric".

We can gain a consciousness for the special status of humans in nature from an anthropocentric position. In order to have a humane understanding of ethics, and we cannot imagine a different kind of "ethics", humans cannot be one being out of many. Instead, humans can and must be especially sensitive to the intrinsic values which result from the natural coexistent world, but also from the specific needs, feelings, consternations, abilities, and responsibilities that are connected with humans being in nature. A humane nature ethics must convey the intrinsic values of nature with the intrinsic values of human life.

Therefore, the attitude of mindfulness does not support the alternative "anthropocentrism or physiocentrism". Physiocentrism does not have any better arguments than anthropocentrism, because ethics can only be substantiated as relational ethics. "The recognition of an observed other as independently valuable takes place through its perception by a bodily affected subject. It is not based on a definition and the presence of capabilities or characteristics in a candidate" (Rehman-Sutter 1998, p. 208-209, own translation, GZ). Relational thinking is the key to understanding mindfulness, as well as ethics. A moral appreciation of nature can only be gained through the relationships we develop with it. And this relationship can include more or less aspects of mindfulness. The more mindfulness it contains, the more intrinsic value we ascribe to nature. However, mindfulness is by far not the only meaningful relationship we can maintain with it.

Let us take an example: we observe the descent of an avalanche from a safe distance in the alps. We also know that no one is endangered by this avalanche. We can now, if we so wish, remain in or take in a mindful attitude. Presumably, we will experience beauty, majesty, and much more. But there is no reason to leave the attitude of mindfulness in this situation. But let us assume that we see a skier in danger or we witness the destruction of an entire village (like Galtür in 1999), then mindfulness will surely step into the background. We will become active and at least welcome that avalanches will be prevented by fencing and other measures in the future. Other examples: a dog threatens us or a child nearby, Ebola pathogens spread, etc. It may be that we can maintain a certain mindfulness towards a snapping dog by trying to empathize with it, but this becomes difficult with Ebola viruses. But mindfulness would be insufficient here in any case, and it would be in complete contradiction to our moral intuitions.[105]

But what should come instead? The relationship to a dangerous life form will always be characterized by aggression and hostility, and it is good that is! This does not mean that we should live out our aggression without thinking (as little as we should with our love), but that we observe and accept it. Only this makes it possible to handle a hostile relationship that we, for example, have with a snapping dog (from both sides!) - or formulated more carefully and less anthropomorphically, a relationship with contrary interests – in a sensible manner for ourselves or others. However, the

---

105. Mindfulness is only a sufficient moral base for someone, if everything is already connected to each other in a harmonic way and Mindfulness morally functions quasi on its own (see chapter 13).

primary perception is that of danger and fear, as well as an according valuation of natural phenomena. It does not emphasize the intrinsic value of the natural object, but its danger instead, and under circumstances prompts us to corresponding actions. Therefore, it depends on the relationship and even the concrete situation if we ascribe something an intrinsic value, or if the moral impression of the scene or object is entirely different, namely one that prompts us to functional and effective actions. The properties of objects thereby play a role, namely in regard to their potential. We may concede to a snapping dog that we can train it, but it becomes difficult to ascribe the same potential to an avalanche in an inhabited area or an Ebola virus. Unless we are radical holists. Intrinsic values do not simply exist and instead we ascribe them, which requires a certain attitude which is always prepared to abstain from self-interest. It is a choice to do so, it is an attitude which we can consciously take in or not. We can correspondingly position ourselves towards ecosystems, so that we are prepared to protect the underwater world accordingly, even though we do not know the species that live there and do not ascribe them any potential functionality. We cannot continue to do so however (or not primarily), if we recognize that biological entities such as cancer cells or parasites are in the process to spread and unfold their own systemic structures (vascular systems, etc.), thereby killing a patient (unless however we argue in a holistic manner and see a path in every sickness, which in the end brings the patient further).

All intrinsic values are a part of interactions which humans participate in. They can contradict one another, for example cultural and natural intrinsic values do not have to be compatible.[106] But, in principle, there is no contradiction between human interests and the intrinsic values of nature.

> "How should a human being live? The answer to that question is the person's conception of eudaimonia, or human flourishing, a complete human life. A conception of eudaimonia is taken to be inclusive of all to which the agent ascribes intrinsic value (...) Now the important point is this: in a eudaimonistic theory, the actions, relations, and persons that are included in the conception are not all valued simply

---

106. Informative examples fur such conflicts and approaches to the problem can be found in Niebrügge 2007, p. 57 et seq.

on account of some instrumental relation they bear to the agent's
satisfaction. This is a mistake commonly made about such theories,
under the influence of Utilitarianism and the misleading use of
'happiness' as a translation for eudaimonia." (Nussbaum 2001, p. 32)

"Eudaimonia" refers to the orientation of ethics – developed by Aristotle
– along the idea of human flourishing The conception of a good human life
does not have to be limited to interest in survival, the satisfaction of needs,
or personal luck, and instead can include the perception of the intrinsic
values of nature and the dedication for its preservation and development.
According to M. Nussbaum, the conception of a good life should not orient
itself according to the satisfaction of basic needs, which would mean an
impossible and authoritarian simplification, and instead should be oriented
according to possibilities that should be available to every person, whether
they seize them or not.[107]

The perspective of mindfulness is a worm's-eye view, not a glance "sub
specie aeternitatis" (Spinoza, loosely translated as "from the perspective of
eternity"), and cannot offer ultimate groundings. This presumably cannot be
done by ethics. However, mindfulness is connected to sensuality and openness, possibilities, and limitations in a special way. It is not specified to
certain contents, and is instead skeptical towards the validity of experiences
and statements. Even with strong subjective evidence, it is principally regarded as incomplete and preliminary. Mindfulness can illuminate different
intrinsic values in their importance to different situations and approaches to
nature, which form the reference points of every moral stance. It is not contradictory to ascribe an intrinsic value to a landscape and to simultaneously
feel and know that it has an exceptional meaning as part of our lives and
those of others, if we enter into an according relationship with it. As relationships cannot be uniformly harmonious, the necessary alignment of
interests is not free of conflict and requires a tolerance of ambivalence[108],
for which the practice of mindfulness is good training. Moral tensions and
possibly unsolvable contradictions must be endured and accepted, when
they regard topics such as animal testing or the installation of wind farms.

---

107. Nussbaum 1998, 1999.
108. Kruse 1983, Gebhard 1993.

Mindfulness is a contribution to ethical intelligence. It has the decisive advantage that it is learnable. With the practice of mindfulness we take responsibility for our perception, as we can cultivate it and thereby create the basis for moral attitudes: "(…) the subject of observation is, by being active in its perception, potentially a responsible subject" (Rehman-Sutter 1998, 204; own translation, GZ). With the practice of mindfulness we actively sensitize ourselves for the values through which problems in environmental ethics first arise. It makes us aware of and emphatic towards them. Furthermore, it promotes solution-oriented forms of communication and examinations with its pluralistic, accepting, and open basic attitude.

13. | The Spiritual Search in Nature

Michael Huppertz

13.1. Spirituality

Sometimes we conduct "spiritual anamnesis" in our workshops, meaning we ask the participants if, when, and how they have had spiritual experiences in their life. Besides the loss of a relative, life-threatening situations, and the experience of births, experiences in nature are named especially often. In this chapter, I will examine why impressions of nature can cause spiritual experiences in certain cultural and individual circumstances and what the attitude of mindfulness can contribute in a practical and conceptual manner.

But first I must explain how I understand "spirituality". "Spiritual" is an experience which transcends the existential framework (everyday forms of time, space, and identity, the existing structure of worry and the fear of death) and finds new experiences: acceptance, connectedness, trust, safety, thankfulness, composure, cheerfulness, and joy of being. Such experiences used to be instructed in the context of religious belief systems. "Spirituality" has and is understood as the subjective and experienced side of religion, which sometimes stands in conflict with the dogmatic and institutional aspects of religion. Today, the search often breaks away from religious traditions, or it includes different traditions in the sense of an individualized "new spirituality".

In our culture, the path to nature shares in common with the spiritual path that they both mean taking a conscious step out of our everyday life. Both draw their power from the experience of difference in everyday life and the arrival in a world of experience which is obviously suited to offer new answers. They both broaden our horizon in that a feeling of existence in a much broader context ensues , the end of which we are not able to, and do not have to, predict. It requires a special cultural constellation and individual motivation *to search and find the spiritual potential of nature.* This search requires that *personal subjective experiences* discover something *in nature* which allows for a spiritual transformation. However, this also means that personal experiences are taken seriously and attention is really directed towards nature and does not solely see its importance in the context of religious or metaphysical specifications, for example in the magical attempt to appease it or win it over, to subjugate or preserve it, to view it as the robe or creation of God, or the embodiment of a metaphysical principle (Brahman, source, connectedness of everything with everything). A spiritual encounter with nature clearly requires that an individual or a community

- really engages with nature;

- takes its own resonance in nature seriously and

- interprets the resulting experiences in a spiritual manner.

   In the following, I would like to show in which way it is possible to unfold one's own spiritual capabilities through the interdependency of nature experiences and mindfulness. So I will especially be searching for such nature experiences, which promote the attitude of mindfulness and are supported by it.

13.2. Mindfulness and Spirituality in Nature

"'Now we are finally outside of the gates of the town', said Sebastian, while standing still and looking around freely". Ludwig Tieck's novel *Franz Sternbalds Wanderungen* ("Franz Sternbald's Wanderings", own translation, GZ), published in 1798, began with these words (Tieck 1966 [1798], p. 11; own translation, GZ). The step into nature is firstly a step out of civilization and all of its constraints, including those stemming from personal perception. New experiences lift themselves from these constraints, be they commitments or routines. Every parting from routines and familiar orientations is difficult. Nature makes this parting easier through the pull that it exercises. It promises a difference, and the longing for a new way of life, as well as new experiences and encounters, leads the searcher to it.

Nature relieves us from familiar worries and ultimately from the structures of worry themselves. We can experience deep relief in nature. With this step into nature we can leave all of the structures behind us, which either make demands of us or help us to fulfill them: people, institutions, instruments, rules, and norms. Nature itself does not make any demands of us. It does not communicate with us, does not offer any opinions, give any feedbacks, or wish for any changes. All changes in nature occur on their own. It does not exert itself. We do not have to think about it, and instead can just let it happen, assuming that we feel safe. The more we get involved with nature, the more we are in it, the more our familiar programs pale and are relativized.

We open ourselves in nature. We leave our usual focuses behind us, as they are not supported by nature. We are not wedged into narrow rooms, social identities with their problems with roles and recognition, or our own or other people's expectations. Instead, we become broad in nature, feel relieved, and open for new experiences. For us, nature is a space with few social regulations. The more natural it is, the less regulations there are. This is part of what makes the wilderness fascinating.

Nature is vast, mysterious, and unfamiliar. We usually move in familiar, manageable, and functionally organized spaces. We know where things are and where we wish to go. In nature, we accept the limits of our wishes, actions, knowledge, and our human way of living. We cannot understand nature, as perhaps we do the motives, intentions, and feelings of people. In the attitude of mindfulness we do not wish to and cannot trace their regularities either. Instead, we experience that it is partially full of structure and harmony, as well as full of coincidences, chaos, and surprises. The more wild and untouched it is, the more it is so. As long as we do not feel threatened, we allow this unpredictability and enjoy it. The acceptance of one's own limitations and the strangeness and mysteriousness of the other is an important experience for the spiritual path in nature. Experiencing mysteries that do not require solving and that we can accept light heartedly has a relieving and liberating impact on our mind and feelings. We come to peace through the acceptance of these mysteries.

We do not experience ourselves as the center of the situation anymore in nature. In an action-oriented and individualized world, we experience ourselves as the center around which the circumstances are cognitively and instrumentally organized. Everything is within reach at our desk or in our workshop. Our homes are organized according to our needs (the light switches are not too high, the bed is not too low, etc.). As a rule, we perceive the environment from the perspective of an agent. However, nature is not organized according to our needs; it maintains its own relationships. It forces us to relational thinking: nature maintains relationships which include us, not the other way around. It is a wonderful feeling for many people to be able to be part of something, without having to be the center of attention and having to take responsibility. The more untouched the environment, the more we have the feeling that we are a part of the natural situation, into which we integrate ourselves and which is not organized around us. We can focus away from ourselves and encounter other life forms, perhaps even see the world and ourselves through the eyes of other living beings.

Nature does not share our norms. It can be very small, incredibly vast, extremely fast, endlessly slow, endlessly vast, or unfathomably deep. Provided that nature is overwhelming, scary, and fascinating due to its size we speak of *majesty.* Wide landscapes, mountains, cliffs, the ocean, high trees, etc. are majestic. In order to be able to feel majesty, we must be in a safe position ourselves. The horrible must not be a real threat to us. We only experience that as majestic which we can withstand. But then the experience of majesty increases our feeling of self-worth; it lifts us up.[109] Gustave Courbet's painting[110], which we have chosen for the cover of this book, shows the vastness and majesty of the ocean, as well as the resonance of the

---

109. Pries 1989, Hoeps 1989.
110. Gustave Courbet (1819-1877), Le bord de mer à Palavas.

viewer of this natural spectacle who encounters the vastness and dynamic of the ocean in an upright posture and with striding movement.

Majesty brings us into a receptive posture, to stand in awe, and into another world. Our powerlessness to control nature and our experience of dependence on and impotence towards nature mean that we do not have any influence. We are placed in a receptive posture.

In nature we experience endlessness. New focuses develop in nature (landscapes, water, plants, animals, nature sounds), as well as a broadening of one's horizons. Our way of existing changes rapidly through wide views of landscapes or the ocean. Horizons can become broader and more diverse. We feel filled with new meaning and unimportant at the same time.

Nature allows us to experience the incompleteness of space. "Vastness" is often called a specific feature of nature experiences. The popularity of overlooks and vast views is well known in environmental psychology. Even enclosed landscapes maintain the characteristic feature of referring us to another part of nature.[111] Somehow it continues on behind the mountains and the horizon.

A horizon itself cannot be grasped. It wanders with us and could follow us around the globe if it had to. The observable endlessness of space makes us aware of our limitations, relativists our endeavors, and at the same time makes it possible for us to experience ourselves as a part of larger and incomprehensible spatial worlds.

The second form of endlessness is the diversity of animate and inanimate nature in all of its forms of appearance and existence. We cannot exhaust the diversity of a meadow. Every change in perspective is a beginning, as is every change of weather, seasons, or times of day. This may be

---

111. Simmel 2014 [1913].

true in rooms or the city as well, but the experience is more immediate and overwhelming in nature. The composition of nature plays a role in this experience, as do the cognitive abilities of those perceiving. The endless diversity of nature refers us time and time again to unknown objects, new landscapes, and new forms of life. Not only is nature endless in its diversity, our being is able to diversify in it casually and playfully: at one point I am someone who is listening to birds, at another someone who is lying on the ground heavily, at a further point someone who is placing stones on top of each other, and at yet another, someone who is being warmed by the sun.

It is easier to remain in the present in nature. Nature is a wonderful field for the experience of qualitative time. It confronts us with new, surprising rhythms and tempi: the movement of leaves, snails, or clouds, the flowing of water, sunsets, but also the fluttering of butterflies, the speed of swallows, flies, and fish. We change our own rhythm if we attune ourselves to these rhythms. The temporalities which define our everyday life – objective (measured) and social time (day of the week, etc.), but also the past, present, and future (modal time) – thereby lose their meaning. The present only knows time as a process.

In and with nature we are immediate, sensual, and present. Nature has an impressive sensuality. It commands all of our senses – intense, varied, surprising. Its sensual effects are not always pleasant. A cricket can be very annoying and some plants, feces, and ponds can have a deterring smell. Only in its colorfulness does nature seem to be above criticism. As a rule however, the enthusiasm is greater for the sensual qualities of nature and being in nature, especially for its abundance.

"Sensuality" has a double meaning and thereby directly refers to the interactivity of being in nature. Intense sensuality changes being in the world fundamentally because it makes the immediacy plastic, which is the foundation of human life, but is often displaced by everyday symbolic activities. There is no such thing as "pure experience", as is often claimed by spiritual concepts, because our experiences are always influenced by our individual and cultural habits, interests, and modes of behavior, perception, and interpretation. Those that command the according experience see the mushroom and hear the song of a robin immediately, and not only some plant and some chirping. But it is also possible to get thoroughly involved in nature without *active* interpretation. The waiver of interpreting, contextualizing, and analyzing strengthens the sensuality of nature, one's own resonance, and the feeling of an immediate connection with the environment. Unabated by present symbolic activities, an unusually strong sense of reality ensues in the present which captures outer reality, as well as the reality of one's own existence: *presence*[112]. I exist, here and now, in connection with my environment. I feel questionless, grounded, stable, alive, sensual, present.

We can experience a strong connection to nature. This experience is the foundation of many spiritual interpretations and speculations on the unity of humans and nature, the connection of everything with everything, or an essence or reason that underlies all existence.

Intentional actions lead to subject-object distinctions. But processes such as breathing, eating, drinking, and excreting already show us that we interact with nature in form of our *metabolism*, as we are also a part of

---

112. For a more detailed account of this point, see Huppertz 2015.

nature. We also experience connectedness to nature by *interacting with nature* in a preattentive and self-evident manner. When I climb a mountain, I adjust my steps to the incline and uneven ground, and when I plant a tree, I use sufficient strength in order to create space for it in the ground. Usually these interactions do not capture our attention. Sometimes everything overlaps so well that we cannot discern between what nature contributes and what we contribute (for example when breathing or swimming).

But we can also feel connected to nature by *perceiving* it in a certain way. If our perception is connected to movement, it is easy for us to differentiate between our contribution and that of the environment to it, for example when we feel or observe something. It is something entirely different if we lean against a tree, lie on the ground, or lay our hand on a patch of moss without moving. In such cases, the ability to differentiate evaporates quickly, and only a uniform perception remains. Differentiations between the feelings of the body and the perception of the environment only reappear when we move, pain arises, or something new occurs in the environment. It is similar if we look without looking around, or when we listen. Hearing is a very passive form of perception that we cannot escape and can barely change. Atmospheric perceptions are of this holistic nature as well. *Atmospheres* are based on synesthesia, meaning sensory experiences that are aligned with one another, to which also personal bodily resonances belong. They are only possible if we are open to them and allow for feelings and impulses accordingly.

In nature, we easily experience such indistinguishable totalities of experience, because it quickly puts us into a receptive, passive, and sensual mood, in which we behave calmly and dedicate ourselves to its radiance, due to its strong sensual and comprehensively atmospheric radiance. In a similar way, this is also possible when listening to music, dancing, making love, or through collective experiences. It is not sensible to take apart these totalities of experience. But it is also not sensible to draw the conclusion from this totality, in which the distinction between subject and object does not play an important role, that such indistinguishableness is truer than the distinction between the movements of my feet and the texture of the ground, or between Me and You. Indistinguishableness is not a higher or deeper experience, and is instead simply a specific experience. An extensive and permanent dedifferentiation of experience, in which nature is no longer perceived as nature or the other as the other, is no gain, but the situative indistinguishableness of self and nature promotes the experience of connectedness.

We can also experience nature by experiencing nature as *similar and related* in many concerns. A simple excursion to a lake shows us living things, such as fish and water bugs, and dead things, like trees – the seasons, emerging, flourishing, withering, and standing still. We experience creativity, communication, attack and retreat, hiding and showing oneself. These analogies speak to us and change our individual experience. We recognize "that we are integrated into the same regularities which we find as the foundation of life in the elements" (Joller 2008, p. 9, own translation, GZ).

Dead branches in a pond can easily transport to us the certainty, but also the contextuality, of death, and the liveliness of the fish next to the branch can transport the continuity of life or the easiness of the moment. We can discover existential themes when dealing with animals which connect us to them, as we are both subject to the same natural processes.[113] We can even find suggestions and solutions in nature:

> "If we learn how to create a connection with nature, we will be able to recognize ourselves in nature and find suggestions and solutions for our own life and individual path. We enter a connection, which promises our life a sensible and healing effect. In a world which is characterized by rapid changes, we experience the stability of a clear rhythm in nature, based on which we can orient ourselves." (Joller 2008, p. 9, own translation, GZ)

A connection to nature is often created through anthropo-morphisms:

> "Pine-trees marched up the sun-warmed-moraines in long, hopeful files, taking the ground and establishing themselves as soon as it was ready for them; (...) while with quick fertility mellow beds of soil,

---

113. Olbrich 2003.

settling and warming, offered food to multitudes of Nature's waiting
children, great and small, animals as well as plants." (Muir 1997
[1897], p. 324)

It is not always quite clear how literal such anthropomorphisms are meant.
John Muir saw the Creator at work in all natural phenomena, so he
presumably did not understand his formulations as anthropomorphisms. For
him, humans and other living beings were subject to the same processes of
life and forms of expression[114]. Nowadays, most people are aware that
anthropo-morphism is a device, which can certainly be exaggerated.
Anthropomorphisms are a description of properties of expression
("impressions", "physiognomies") in correspondence to human properties.
However, the importance of anthropomorphic experiences and
interpretations is not lessened through this. They create analogies that we
would otherwise not be able to recognize[115].

Projections, idealizations, and fantasies also create a connection. Unlike
analogies and anthropomorphisms, they use natural phenomena as an
opportunity to transfer wishes, needs, and fantasies onto natural
phenomena. They appear, for example, in the form of the idealization of
nature. Nature becomes a visionary image, in which the beauty and
harmony can be found for which the human subject yearns. Projections,
idealizations, and fantasies are experienced as connections based solely on
their structure and independently from their substance. They command
relatively freely over their object, as long as the object does not reveal its
independence with all its might.

In nature, we can more easily be seized by spiritual feelings. Feelings
are usually complex composite entities. They consist of experiences,
interpretations of events, needs, expectations, memories, thoughts,

---

114. Emerson on the other hand saw nature as a miracle of beauty and perfection on the
one hand, and as spiritualized on the other. The spirit of God resides in it, as it does in
the human spirit, but nature is subservient to humans in this regard. Muir was an admirer
of Emerson.
115. A detailed discussion of the dangers and the importance of anthropomorphizing for
nature and the experience of nature can be found in Gebhard 2013, p. 66 et seq.

fantasies, stimuli for acting, facial expressions, gestures, vegetative reactions, and communication with oneself or others. Feelings are part of situations, accompany and define a relationship to the world, and are additionally subject to inner psychological processes. The interpretations with which we may possibly enter into a situation decide if, for example, the feeling of connectedness or the impression of majesty is predominant, if our experience is more calm or more wildly enthusiastic, more filled with fear of the unknown or peaceful recognition.

Spiritual feelings are feelings of liberation and arrival. They relate to the present, and not as most of our feelings (fear, grief, hope) to the past or the future. That is why spiritual feelings transport tranquility and timelessness, a fulfillment of the wish which Rousseau (and later Goethe) identified as existential: "If only this moment would last forever" (Rousseau 2011 [1782], p. 55). We have already touched on experiences that have strong emotional qualities, especially *relief, awe, sensuality, presence, and liveliness*. What makes feelings of spirituality special and distinguishable from all other feelings are *feelings of connectedness, trust, tranquility, thankfulness, and joy of being.*

The result of connectedness is trust. Whatever conflicts and frictions we may observe in our relationship to nature, this is only possible if we simultaneously trust in successful interactions. Whatever difficulties and problems may confront us, we can only observe or even solve them if many things work simultaneously and we have a, more or less, strong foothold in the present. We must always adjust to the present and synchronize with it, in order to solve problems in it.[116] Furthermore, the present is mostly harmless, most of our problems exist in the past or future. In nature – as we usually experience it – this becomes especially clear to us. *Trust* is a form of resonance to these successful interactions. It gives us the security to encounter special challenges with ease. In nature, we can overcome fixating on problems and place them in a further context of stability and reliability, which cannot be irritated by our tensions and strains. Nature follows its own path, the seasons change, we cannot create the weather, we cannot

---

116. See Huppertz 2000 and the literature referenced there.

move mountains. We experience nature as powerful, steady, reliable, independent. Seasons will return, plants will grow, and the night will end. The fact that we cannot intervene and therefore do not have to intervene, and that we can rely to a great extent on the course of things, creates *tranquility*.

Spiritual *thankfulness* develops when we recognize the foundations of our life in nature and the seemingly self-evident becomes conscious again – the air, water, earth, plants, beauty, diversity, and reliability of nature. It also means thankfulness for our body. Appreciating nature also means appreciating the body when in nature or doing physical work, sports, dance, or during sexual activity. We have not created outer nature nor our inner nature. We have not created all of this. Our thankfulness is directed towards the unknown, and belief gives it a name. The following report shows the coherencies of these feelings in a Christian setting. The narrator, Marie de Brebis, was in grief:

> "Only God's creation saved me; with this I mean the world that He has gifted to us: the flowers, trees, animals, and soil. (…) And so it transpired that I lay for hours in the sun, my cheek leaned against a warm stone, like a lizard. And this warmth that emits from the limestone is soft and lively, and resembles the hand of God. And I could sense the warmth that the stone gave me flow like a spring of life inside of and strengthen me. Hour for hour, I observed the greater celandine, the blessed thistles, the buttercups, until I discovered what transpired inside of them and I loved them equally to humans. Simply because I required life around me, in order to stay alive myself. I layed myself down in the middle of a herd of sheep, I breathed in the smell of the wool, I drank milk directly from the udder, I allowed myself be completely entranced by the smell. (…) I always knew that plants, animals, and even stones have the same origin as us. We are all similar and we are all a part of creation. I also believe that the good Lord is much closer to them than to us, because he prefers the fragile and vulnerable, which requires more life. That is why I could only find the strength to wait and hope amidst God's creation, where it is warmest." (Signol 2007, p. 38-39, own translation, GZ).

Finally, *joy of being* accompanies our existence, as Rousseau noted:

> "The feeling of existence stripped of all other affections is in itself a
> precious feeling of contentment and peace which alone would be
> enough to make this existence prized and cherished by anyone who
> could banish all the sensual and earthly impressions which constantly
> distract us from it and upset the joy of this world. But most men, being
> constantly stirred by passion, know little of this state, and, having only
> experienced it imperfectly and briefly, they have only a vague and
> confused idea of it, which gives them no sense of its charm."
> (Rousseau 2011 [1782], p. 56).

This feeling of existence is a mood which is not dependent on any
specific object or event, except a sense of being-in-the-world; the feeling of
being in an easy, playful, aimless contact with nature or other people and
our self. Gernot Böhme named it "happiness to be" (Böhme 2006), I prefer
"joy of being".

13.3. Interpretations of Spiritual Experiences of Nature

13.3.1. Limits and Significance of the Interpretation of Spiritual
Experiences

Spiritual experiences are only described as such, if they can be brought into
relation with one's own life, so if they are personally significant. This may
be possible without verbal communication in regard to others or myself,
simply because the experience affects my thoughts and feelings without
being articulated. But it is at least desirable that this takes place in a comprehensible form for both the parties concerned and their social environment. We cannot avoid formulating our experience in some manner, if we
wish to give them meaning, consciously integrate them into our life, reflect
on them, and share them with others.

The need for communication, passing things on, and power has lead to
us commanding over innumerable spiritual interpretations, which in turn
influence experiences. One may consider such interpretations and examinations of them unnecessary, and they often probably are for individual

spiritual seekers. However, considering the many highly problematic interpretations of spiritual, especially mystical, experiences by fundamentalist or fascist movements, a general dismissal would mean not facing a dispute with such currents. False interpretations of spiritual experiences – within and aside from religions – were and are one of the main sources of violence and human rights violations.

A common objection is that spiritual experiences are inherently indescribable, especially if they are accompanied by unio mystica, an experience of ego dissolution, a dissolution of the subject-object structure, disappearing into an unnameable primal ground, etc. Therein lie several misunderstandings. First, it is trivial that experiences cannot be described and (as a rule) only approximations, indications, metaphorical descriptions, etc., are possible. This is also true for the taste of a banana, the smell of the ocean, the touch sensation of moisture, or the sound of a clarinet. Experiences must be undergone, and we learn practical instructions and advice from them. I have termed it "triviale Unsagbarkeit"[117] ("trivial ineffability", own translation, GZ). However, it is central to some spiritual experiences that people who are undergoing them do not think of or interpret the world at that moment, and instead are exclusively in "direct" contact with it. The ineffability of this experience is crucial for them and in this sense "affirmative".[118]

Some forms of meditation are supposed to lead to dedifferentiation of perception. Immobilization, closed eyes, silence, and introvertive attention aid this process. The experience of interactivity thereby disappears, and self-experience is greatly reduced. Strong focuses over a longer period of time have a similar effect. Focusing on an object, task, or goal leads to a reduction of self-experience to an observation or activity. Dedifferentiation can be continued to the dissolution of any sense of self, for example in form of feelings or bodily feelings. The resulting circumstances are then termed immersion ("samadhi"), "self-dissolution". "unio mystica", etc. Similar experiences of dedifferentiation can also be undergone through trance,

---

117. Huppertz 2015.
118. Huppertz 2015.

hypnosis, the consumption of drugs, or ecstatic conditions. There are many overlaps between hypnotic induction and some meditation practices (focusing, sensory deprivation, ritualization, social cooptation, monotony, authoritarian settings, suppression of a critical consciousness). Immersion has its value as an intermittence of thought, perception, and feeling routines, and of course simply because it can feel wonderful, provided that feelings such as happiness and tranquility are not eliminated, which is indeed a goal of such practices.[119] It may well be that afterwards we regard the world with different and fresh eyes, and that a consciousness for the relativity of our experiences and interpretations accompanies us.

Every formulation of an experience as subjective is unproblematic now. As long as someone does not claim its general application in form of a practice or insight one cannot object to it. It simply does not make sense to deny that someone sees colors, animals, or angels that other people do not see, or if they claim to hear voices or see the mother of God. One cannot argue over sensory impressions, bodily feelings, dreams, visions, etc., so long as it is not advocated as an assertion on a mutually shared world. The decisive difference occurs when somebody does not just state that they heard a voice and instead claims that a known or unknown person really said this or that, the mother of God was in a certain place, etc. Now the speaker refers to a mutually shared reality and will perhaps act accordingly. This may now concern us. If they, for example, believe to have received the mission from an actually existing God to convert the world, jump out of a window, stop traffic, or blow up an airplane, we should indeed argue with them, or rather stop them from implementing their plans.

All statements that begin with "I believe" are similarly immune to discussions as are references to spiritual experiences. Here we can discuss the consequences of actions, etc., but not the contents themselves. Through its classification as belief, the speaker has shielded the contents from criticism. I have referred to such statements as "arational".[120] Statements to which someone adheres to even though they can be disproven would be irrational, for example because they reject experience, logical reasons, or

119. See the Matti-Satipatthana-Sutra from the Buddhistic Pali canon in Seidenstücker 2005, p. 345-378.
120. Huppertz 2009, p. 69 et seq.

proven knowledge on principle ("irrationalism"). However, someone who speaks of a belief has already made it clear that they cannot or do not want to provide convincing arguments, neither in the sense of a mutually sharable experience nor in the sense of a conclusion. If they could, they would not have to believe. This statement would be a devaluation of belief, which can only lose here. A belief which can be justified is as senseless and valueless as a detailed justification of love.[121]

13.3.2. Humans and Nature – Otherness, Unity, or Relationship?

All interpretations of spiritual experiences in nature are based on assumptions on the relationship between humans and nature, or culture and nature. It is not possible to represent the diversity of interpretations of the relationship between humans and nature here, but the contextualization of a continuum of closeness and distance, or rather more or less identity, of humans and culture seems to create some clarity in my opinion. Since both interpretations, as I wish to show, are unsatisfactory, it offers itself to understand the possibility of spiritual experiences in nature as a specific form of structuring relationships. These three positions cannot be ascribed to a specific religion. In Christian traditions, for example, all three depictions of the relationship of humans and nature exist: otherness, unity, and relationship. Here, the idea exists that humans should subdue the earth, a conception which moves solely on the pole of non-identity between humans and nature. In this conception, nature itself cannot be a source of spiritual experiences. In contrast, the Christian perception of nature as God's creation is close to the concept of unity between humans and nature. As humans are part of God's creation as well, humans and nature are at least identical in this regard. The leveling of the difference between nature and humans however remains the exception in Christianity, because Christianity – as all monotheistic religions – is based on significant differences (God/ humans, God/ nature, humans/ nature). The third way can be found in the conception of nature as a creation which can be trusted and through which God provides for humans, and is neither identical with humans or a tangible

---

121. Nussbaum 2001, p. 51-52. Also beautifully expressed in "Liebst du um Schönheit" ("do you love for beauty", own translation, GZ), a poem by F. Rückert, set to music by G. Mahler.

God. This position allows room for spiritual experiences that include the otherness of nature.

The problem of the interpretation of spiritual experiences in nature becomes clear, if we first turn to the extreme poles of complete otherness or complete identity.

Let us begin with the interpretation of the relationship between humans and nature which assumes *otherness to the greatest extent.* In a world shaped by technology and science, it is a familiar experience that nature is emptied of all aesthetic, atmospheric, metaphorical, personal, existential, or even spiritual meaning. Science and technology require none of this.[122] These interactions are markedly regulated and limited. However, emotional and spiritual experiences do indeed appear on its margins – for one, if scientist or technicians experience the narrowness of their approach: time and time again, nature emerges as a great mystery or a vast manifold, and the narrowness of one's own actual and possible knowledge becomes clear. Especially scientists are open toward this borderline experience. Furthermore, natural scientists gain insights into unfamiliar dimensions of nature, immense variety, and unbelievably complex – and in certain regards perfect – creations of systems. They probably marvel more than other people, and we marvel with them when they present their findings to us. Even marveling over the fact that all of this even exists is understandable here.

The otherness of nature can also be described as a very personal emphatic experience. Then nature is not only "inexpressive", but also "does not express anything to us". It seems uninvolved, alien, indifferent, senseless. This perception of the strangeness and senselessness is an interpretive frame which is jarring, as W. Szymborska shows, especially against the backdrop of the usual meaningful approaches toward nature:

122. Networks in which the agent cannot easily be defined also develop in science and technology (Belliger&Krieger 2006, Roßler 2016). Pure objectivity is an illusion in scientific approaches as well, as science is only possible by intervening into natural processes and reorganizing them – with experiments, tools, laboratories, scientific institutions, discourses, paradigms, and theories.

View with a grain of sand

We call it a grain of sand,

but it calls itself neither grain nor sand.

It does just fine without a name, whether general, particular, permanent,
passing,

incorrect, or apt.

Our glance our touch mean nothing to it.

It doesn´t feel itself seen and touched.

And that it fell on the windowsill is only our experience, not its.

For it, it is no different from falling on anything else with no assurance
that it has finished falling or that it is falling still.

The window has a wonderful view of a lake, but the view doesn´t view
itself.

It exists in this world

colorless, shapeless,

soundless, odorless, and painless.

The lake´s floor exists floorlessly, and its shore exists shorelessly.

Its water feels itself neither wet nor dry and its waves to themselves are
neither singular nor   plural.

They splash deaf to their own noise on pebbles neither large nor small.

And all this beneath a sky by nature skyless In which the sun sets
without setting at all and hides without hiding behind an unminding
cloud.

The wind ruffles it, its only reason being that it blows.

A second passes.

A second second.

A third.

But they´re three seconds only for us.

Time has passed like a courier with urgent news.

But that´s just our simile.

The character is invented, his haste is make-believe, his news inhuman.

Szymborska, W.: *View With a Grain of Sand. Selected Poems.* Orlando: Harcourt Brace & Company; 1995 [1962] [translated from Polish, GZ].

This ascetic design of the relationship with nature is a form of perceiving nature which respectfully releases nature to itself.[123] In it "one abstains as far as possible from one's own interests, puts acquired knowledge aside, and at first does not want to be with anything else other than that which is being observed" (Goldstein 2013, p. 20, own translation, GZ). "It is about understanding the world and gaining intuition, not athletic performance and self-experience adventures" (p. 15). This devotion allowed natural scientists to be ready to adjust their conceptions of time periods, developments, and diversity to nature. But especially from this devotion to nature, natural scientists can develop intense personal resonances and experiences of freedom and luck.[124]

---

123. Martin Seel (1996) referred to this as the contemplative aspect of the "aesthetic of nature". However, we understand contemplation in nature differently in this book, as we understand it to be tracing personal, existential, and spiritual meaning in nature experiences.

124. As Jürgend Goldstein (2013) writes about Maria Sibylla Merian, Wilhelm von Humboldt, Charles Darwin, or Jean-Henri Fabre. Using Humboldt as an example: he "does not have a commission, is not accountable to anyone, does not – unlike Columbus 300 years ago – have to find gold or slaves. He may look, measure, collect, write" (p. 119, own translation, GZ). For him, this activity means an escape from the narrow and paralyzing homeland, as he wishes to find freedom ("nature however is the realm of freedom", cited from Goldstein, p. 118, own translation, GZ) and exhaust his personal

The otherness of nature can also take a form which tears people out of their usual environment – majesty. The experience of nature requires that one takes the individual personal resonance to experiences in nature seriously and formulates them, which presumably first occurred in the Middle Ages – approximately in the 13th century -, a time in which individualization gained currency in everyday life.[125] The experience of nature first appears later, during early Enlightenment in the 17th and 18th century.[126] The perception of majesty implies an elevation of the subject. It must be able to perceive and endure the majesty of nature. It simultaneously experiences its own limits, as well as its possibilities. Occasions are woods, mountains, oceans, starry skies, etc. There are many interpretations of majesty in the course of natural history. There is a tension between whether the extreme otherness of nature is experienced more as horrible, ugly, and threatening, or if it is perceived as wonderful, harmonic, and beautiful. Romanticism, in which majesty plays an important role, is familiar with all variations on the level of poems and literature. Sublime nature is irrational, mysterious, chaotic, horrible, dangerous, bewitching, but also wonderful, felicific, homely, filled with incomprehensible beauty, harmony, and perfection. Places of longing are hidden by the bustle of everyday life, can be found in the wilderness, the interior of the earth, the night, and in the past.[127]

---

opportunities. Due to this, nature experiences serve not only the acquisition of knowledge for Humboldt, but also cause awe, happiness, feelings: "The ability to think and to feel therefore stand in obvious harmony. The larger the cognitive capacity, the deeper the feeling. The first is a means, the latter the purpose. Nature must be felt; he who only sees and abstracts from it can divide a lifetime in the crowded life of the glowing tropical world, plants, and animals, he will believe he is describing nature, but always remains estranged from it himself" (cited from Goldstein 2013, p. 122 et seq., own translation, GZ).

125. Ariès&Duby 1990.

126. Hoeps 1989, Pries 1989a.

127. Affirmativeness towards majesty is similarly dangerous as affirmativeness towards the mystical. Majesty has a power from which humans can hardly withdraw and cannot see through. Rudolf Otto derived the term "numinous" as the characteristic of the holy from majesty (Otto 1979 [1917]). What is easily overlooked in the creation of terms is the social constructive participation by those who are fascinated by majesty (Huppertz 2007). If one ascribes majesty solely to the side of the object and identifies it with natural entities or cultural or political events, one easily overlooks leeway of reflection and criticism and the political dimension of the topic, for example in German history ("the German forest", "the German oak tree", cult of the body, and mass demonstrations) or powerful religious enactments. Christine Pries underlined the difference "between a critical and a metaphysical accentuation of majesty" (Pries 1989b, p. 28, own translation,

As diverse movements and authors as dark romanticism, Heinrich von Kleist, Sigmund Freud, Theoder W. Adorno, Hans-Richard Brittnacher, authors of post-modernism, the wilderness movement, and nature pedagogy have ensured and continue to ensure that inner and outer nature survive as challenges, a realm of the untameable, wayward, terrifying, and resistant.

Let us now turn to the opposite pole, the *unity of humans and nature*. It is surprising how many people involved in the environmental movement and of outstanding merit are of the opinion that the differentiation between humans and nature is only due to a limited perspective. Both supposedly belong to a greater whole, in which differences disappear. Only a limited ego hinders us from perceiving this supposed unity and acting accordingly. I have already discussed the ethical problems of this position in chapter 12. "The holistic argument is by far the most popular argument outside of professional philosophy, for instance in the deep ecology, ecofeminist, and new-age movement, and it is often – as it is confused – not considered worth a philosophical discussion" (Krebs 1997, p. 362, own translation, GZ). But even if the success of the holistic position is not due to its arguments, it is then founded on the credibility of the commitment of its representatives and a spiritual aura, which turns them into a sort of core belief of a movement. The commitment and the merit of those who hold these views are explicitly not questioned in the following criticism.

As already shown in the chapter on ethics, a holistic perspective assumes that not only a great unity of nature or the universe exists, but that it also represents an absolute value. Therefore, insight and practice are about "overcoming the division between humans and nature" (Dunde 1989, p. 99, own translation, GZ). The unity lies in a "source of existence",

---

GZ): "The place of the unrepresentable must not be filled, "majesty" not actually be redeemed, as it for example happened in fascism. This inevitably leads to terror. When majesty is spoken of, in no way is a monumentality akin to fascism meant (..). The empty pathos and the bombast of fascism are attempts to "embellish" the implicit incommensurability of majesty and prematurely dissolve its unsettling power in harmony. Not majesty, but such transformations of majesty into beauty encourage fascism. On the contrary, majesty is the category that faces totalitarianism by demanding the endurance of contradictions and fostering a culture of dissent, instead of promising reconciliation" (Pries 1989b, p. 30, own translation, GZ).

"source of the world", or a "source and unity of existence" (Kalff 1994, p. 191 et seq., own translation, GZ). The founder of "deep ecology", Arne Naess, speaks of "self-realization" (1995, p. 80) and ties into Hindu concepts: "I want to give it an expanded meaning based on the distinction between a large comprehensive Self and and narrow egoistic self as conceived in certain eastern traditions of *atman*. This large comprehensive Self (with a capital `S´) embraces all the life forms on the planet (and elsewhere?) together with their individual selves (jivas)" (ibid.). Naess' understanding of life explicitly refers "to what biologists call 'not-living': rivers (watersheds), landscapes, ecosystems" (p. 68). From a pantheistic Christian perspective, Emerson sees humans and nature connected through spirituality and the inexhaustible power of a source (see introduction). From a Mahayana-Buddhist perspective, Mark Coleman speaks of the "the essential unity or commonality that is a thread throughout everything in the universe" (Coleman, 2006, p. 79) or of a "oneness with all of life" (p. 80). For Joana Macy and Molly Young Brown, the universe consists of hierar-chically ordered "holons"[128]: a holon "is both a whole in its own right, comprised of subsystems, *and* simultaneously an integral part of a larger system" (Macy&Brown 1998, p. 42). "They [life scientists, M. H.] dis-covered that these wholes – be they cells, bodies, ecosystems, or even the planet itself – are not just a heap of disjunct parts, but are dynamically organized and intricately balanced 'systems', interdependent in every moment, every function, every exchange of energy and information" (p. 40). The natural systems cooperate harmoniously, because the character of nature is harmonious. In the end, it is about a deification of nature and thereby human beings, or in other words neither about nature or culture: "Earth takes on a presence in our consciousness, not unlike the presence of gods and goddesses in the lives of our early ancestors" (p. 44).

Angelika Krebs attempted to breakdown the "notoriously ambiguous (…) sentence 'humans are a part of nature'" (1997, p. 362, own translation, GZ). "One can roughly discern three meanings: (1) the ontological thesis of identity, (2) the eudaemonistic thesis of harmony, and (3) the thesis of dependency" (p. 362, own translation, GZ). "Ontological identity" means

---

128. Term and theory date back to Wilber 2011 [1995].

that humans and, for example, living beings, but also plants and landscapes share the same mode of being. This "can hardly be meant in a literal sense" (362), as humans act, unlike a bacteria or an earthquake. At best one could speak of gradual transitions or commonalities, but according to Krebs this is something entirely different than identity. Sadly, the sentence on the unity between humans and nature is really meant ontologically. This thesis of a mutual mode of being is founded on natural science theories (like quantum physics or general systems theory) or the cited metaphysical ideas of a comprehensive source, network, or something similar.[129] I will limit myself to a few objections:

From an epistemological perspective it is impossible to make statements in regard to "the whole". We could only capture the universe if we could step outside of everything and stop time. It was an achievement of the Enlightenment, which is often criticized for its presumptuousness, to reflect on the conditions and limits of human reason. Human knowledge is limited by categories of reason, body, technology, history, language, media, and time. The conditions and limits of reason are the topic of philosophy since Kant, but even more so in 20th century philosophy (phenomenology, philosophy of body, linguistic philosophy, structuralism, post-modernism, philosophy of science). Science does not have an interest in "nature", "the whole", or "the universe. Individual sciences, on the basis of their different paradigms (premises, techniques, methods, institutions, terms), research their individual objects and cannot be reduced to one another. "Metaphysicians and physicalists have both equally attempted to invalidate this perspectivity of human perception through a unitary perspective" (Mutschler 2002, p. 15, own translation, GZ). But psychology cannot be reduced to neuro-biology, nor can biology be reduced to physics. Furthermore, no universal language or theory is conceivable in which all scientific knowledge could be formulated[130]. The consequences of these diverse insights

---

129. Usually in reference to Hinduism, Mahayana-Buddhism, (neo)Platonism, a general truth to all mystical experiences (philosophia perennis), or theories of a universal consciousness in the tradition of trans-personal psychology.
130. S. Welsch 1996, 2012, Gabriel 2013. The criticism of the idea of a holistic position does not have to lead to a constructivist or relativistic position. Gabriel connects a criticism of holistic cognition with a radical criticism of constructivist theory and argues for a "new realism". Welsch (2012) also argues the "universal truth" of human cognition

can only be speculated on. We are inherently unable to overcome the relativity, perspectivity, and discursivity of our knowledge.

It is not more sensible to derive general statements on the nature of the world from "general systems theory". It is a method, not a statement on certain content matter. If we use a ruler we do not believe that the world only consists of distances. Systems analyses are only applicable to certain aspects of system elements, never to their entire complexity (see chapter 7). Furthermore, systems can only exist through dissociation. They can only exist if they are not connected with everything. They must make a selection due to their internal structure and, in their individual manner, selectively come into contact with the complexity of the exterior world. The nervous system, for example, can only function if signals are only transferred with a certain strength and summation. If everything was connected with everything in the brain, we would permanently suffer from epileptic seizures or we would hear noise when processing optical signals.

Of course there are developments that have far-reaching consequences, for example global warming. That glaciers suffer from global warming as do the inhabitants of Pacific islands does not mean that the inhabitants of the islands are causally, cognitively, or emotionally related to glaciers. If "connectedness" is only understood as being subjected to the same influences in different ways, the term is trivialized.

Many people resist the influences of international corporations and data collection. According to the "everything is connected with everything" theory this is not only completely pointless, but also undesirable. Does the contemporary popularity of such theories, which refer to "Buddhism", not also have to do with the international circulation of data, commodities, and people? Is it a coincidence that holistic ideas are especially popular in Silicon Valley and that Steve Jobs was regarded as a spiritual messenger? Holistic conceptions of nature and information are joined in the idea of

---

as an evolutionary necessity, without claiming that there must be "*the* perspective on the world" (p. 130, own translation, GZ).

global networking.

The second interpretation of the sentence "humans are a part of nature" suggests that a fundamental identity of human and natural interests exists ("eudaemonistic theory of harmony", own translation, GZ), "that a good human life can only be had with the flourishing of the good in nature, or even constitutes itself through this" (Krebs 1997, p. 263, own translation, GZ). I have already criticized this thesis under the aspect of nature ethics. Krebs vehemently summarizes the concerns over "false harmonism" (p. 363, own translation, GZ): "If 'fascism' is understood as a doctrine which seeks to convince people that their benefit lies in the flourishing of the whole, then the accusation of ecofascism is not unjustly leveled against the supporters of the eudaemonistic theory of harmony" (p. 363, own translation, GZ).

Indigenous peoples, who supposedly lived – or live – in harmony with nature, are often cited as an argument for the possibility of a harmonious fusion of nature and culture in a harmonious whole. Both existing indigenous cultures and prehistoric cultures are included in this conception (hunters and gatherers, but not agricultural societies with which urban life began). The closeness to nature was and is unquestionably greater with these populations, but there is little evidence that this closeness generally means more friendliness towards nature, or even humans. Sometimes ecological interpretative and behavioral patterns, and in some cases pronounced destructiveness towards nature can be found in these cultures, which even led to the ruin of their own existential foundations. Furthermore, many behavioral patterns of such cultures towards foreign peoples or tribes and towards their own population, especially towards weaker members of society like children, the elderly, and often also women, rigorously breach our sense of morals.[131] But this sense is first aroused by differentiated ethnological and archaeological studies, and can only be numbed by extreme cultural relativism. The construction of "indigenous people" itself can only be understood as a wish to idealize, and also as an attempt to criticize dominant culture in the manner that has been popular since

---

131. Edgerton 1994, Helbling 1999, Anderson 2013.

Rousseau. Even if one lays this intention aside, indigenous peoples are civilized peoples who try to assert themselves with and against nature, and thereby often harm other tribes, members of their own tribe, or nature because they do not know and cannot do any better.

According to Angelika Krebs, the third meaning of the sentence "humans are a part of nature" is simply that humans and nature have an interdependent relationship. This is undeniable. There are countless mixes and interrelations between natural and cultural processes. Our book describes such interdependencies on the practical level and the level of experience. In their own way, systemic functional analyses lead to the recognition of the relationships between culture and nature. However, phenomenological and systemic analyses must always be newly achieved. The ecological view is of greater importance for appropriate nature ethics, environmental education, and environmental policies. It also suggests that we arrive in nature and can feel at home.

13.3.3. The Meaning of Mindfulness for the Spiritual Search in Nature – Farewell and Arrival

Spirituality always includes a certain radicalism, as it questions and broadens the coordinate system of our everyday life. It relativizes our daily life, with all of its worries and routines, in order to integrate it into a broader view of the world and life later on. When we question people about their spiritual experiences they usually refer to "borderline situations" (Jaspers, own translation, GZ), situations in which the "and so on" of everyday life (Schütz, own translation, GZ) was broken and existential topics became perceptible. They speak of births and deaths they have witnessed, or of experiences of unusually deep happiness in love or nature. These reports are often accompanied by strong feelings. Intimacies are broken and simultaneously a new evident nature is experienced, as if one glanced behind the backdrop, as if a true word had been spoken, as if one had learned to see again. In the second part of this chapter I have shown how nature experiences can lead to such experiences. The otherness of nature plays as big a role in this, as does the connectedness that we experience with it.

So spiritual experiences are often caused by especially strong events or situations. However, less dramatic situations can shift the backdrop of our life as well. This is where mindfulness starts. Mindfulness has a spiritual potential in itself.[132] The spiritual potential of mindfulness lies in the characteristics of deconstruction, openness, and receptivity. The deconstructivist attitude leads to familiar modes of thought, feeling, and behavior, related to the environment or one's own identity, losing importance in the experience of the present. They do not thereby become false or superfluous, but move into the background. To actively turn against them would not be progress, but would only replace it with a new interpretative pattern. We would be captured within this conflict and would not really have new experiences.[133] If one consistently follows the path of Mindfulness to the end, even the most self-evident categories of sense and reason dissolve. The familiar experience of time, space, self, the care structure of existence (Heidegger), and even actively representative existence can be suspended. This is sometimes accompanied by fear, but more frequently by a feeling of release and intense happiness.[134]

Formulated in a positive manner, deconstruction leads to an openness towards new, and under circumstances fundamentally new, experiences such as timelessness or a flowing relational self, which resonates in this situation. The third potentially spiritual characteristic of mindfulness is receptivity or readiness to receive. In the end, spiritual experiences cannot be specifically acquired or worked towards, and instead are a gift or a grace which the seeker encounters along his or her journey. They are rendered easier through rituals and meditation practices, or God-given. Christianity does not think any differently then Islam or Zen-Buddhism in this regard. The ways of life that especially make spiritual experiences possible are deeply connected to receptivity: encounters with people, dances, art, journeys, love, sexuality, rituals or liturgies, meditations, overwhelming existential events, and nature experiences.

---

132. Huppertz 2009, p. 79 et seq.
133. This logic is especially stressed in Zen-Buddhism, in unsurpassed clarity by Ta Hui (Cleary 1977). Also see Huppertz 2015.
134. Many examples of this can be found in Huppertz 2015 and the literature that is cited there.

Of course, no explicit concept of mindfulness is necessary for spiritual experiences. Some occur spontaneously, some in religious or spiritual contexts. But all of these ways of life will only lead to spiritual experiences, if they are sufficiently connected to implicit mindfulness in the manner in which it has been described. However, an explicit concept of mindfulness can be helpful. Provided the practice of mindfulness is supposed to lead to spiritual experiences, a longer, more intense, and more regular practice of it is usually necessary. Even if, in principle, all of the exercises we have presented in this book make spiritual experiences possible (some more, some less), this is especially true in regard to the contemplative exercises, which also take more time. From the specific aptitude of mindfulness towards spiritual experiences we can conclude: the more mindful the attitude, the less spectacular nature experiences have to be. What counts is sensitivity and attitude:

> "A student complains to his Zen master that he has the feeling that his master is keeping something from him that could bring him spiritual enlightenment. 'Master, I believe that you are withholding a decisive indication from me on the path to absolute enlightenment.' The master denies this accusation. In the evening they were both hiking in the mountains, when the master stood and said to his student: 'Do you smell the mountain laurel?' The student affirmed this. The master replied: 'You see, I am not withholding anything from you.'" (Kuhn Shimu 2013, p. 104-105, own translation, GZ)

As does mindfulness, nature suggests an attitude of deconstruction, openness, and receptivity. Therein lies a specific fit. Can we understand why spiritual mindfulness is especially supported by nature, and vice versa the attitude of mindfulness answers to spiritual impressions of nature and being in nature?

The experiences described in section 13.2 are pervaded by a double movement. I refer to it as "farewell" and "arrival". The movements of farewell from the bustle of everyday life and changes in living environments have already been thoroughly described. This can occur within a half an hour or only after being in nature for weeks. Existential topics which seemed securely buried beneath the activities of daily life can arise – as insecurity, as an encounter with the abysmal aspects of life. If we get off the wheel of everyday life and follow the path of deconstruction for a while, then sooner or later our consciousness for the fundamental contingency – the unpredictability and uncontrollability – of our lives will increase. Clifford Geertz summarized this in the following way: "This contingency is the issue of spirituality and religion" (Geertz 1973). Nature supplies us with these cognitively, emotionally, and morally borderline experiences in abundance. Spiritual mindfulness in nature answers with acceptance. It does not wish to provide any metaphysical messages. It does not want to define the universe or know if and how everything is connected to everything. Buddha presumably saw this the same way, as he accorded great importance to mindfulness as a spiritual practice and refrained from metaphysical speculations.[135] But what it can offer is "opinion and feeling":

> "It [religion] does not wish to define the nature of the universe and explain it in metaphysical terms, it does not wish to develop and finalize it like morals by virtue of the freedom and divine arbitrariness of humanity. Its nature is neither thought nor action, and instead opinion and feeling. It wishes to examine the universe, wishes to reverently listen to it in its own representations and actions, wishes to be seized and filled by its direct influences in childlike passiveness."
> (Schleiermacher 1969 [1799], p. 35, own translation, GZ)

The peculiar aspect of the encounter with nature is: the more we say farewell, the more we arrive. Nature welcomes us with open arms. Deconstruction goes hand in hand with connectedness, openness finds a footing, and receptivity is rewarded with diversity, sensuality, as well as personal and existential meaning. This outcome is not self-evident if we consider how ascetic spiritual searches are often designed. Ascetic traditions of spirituality urge saying farewell, but arrival is often postponed to the afterlife or conceived of as deliverance from the vale of tears of life. But spiritual nature experiences thrive on the arrival in the present, which is an intense physical, sensual, and emotional experience. The practice of mindfulness in nature does not lead to an abyss, instead we sink into moss, allow

---

135. Bronkhorst 2000, Batchelor 2001, Huppertz 2009.

ourselves to fall into the clouds, or marvel at the sight of mountains.

> "The more restless, uncertain, and opposed modern existence be-
> comes, the more passionately it demands from us to set our sights to
> new levels, which lie beyond our ideas of good and evil, and which
> we have otherwise forgotten. I do not know of anything else in visible
> nature which has the characteristic of earthly heavenliness as do the
> snowy firn landscapes, anything which already expresses 'heights' in
> its colors and forms. Those that have enjoyed it long for it like they do
> for deliverance, for that which is simply different than the ego, with its
> murky unrest and North German lowlands, and where the torment of
> will is halted." (Simmel 1992 [1895], p. 94, own translation, GZ)

If we aimlessly engage nature we find ourselves in the middle of a polyphonic concert of sensual experiences, discoveries, playfulness, impressions, metaphors, and existential analogies, as we have described them in this book. If we react with sensibility and presence, our resonance will convey a feeling of liveliness that allows for our emotional and cognitive wishes to rest. And if we are open towards the intrinsic values of nature, we will find moral orientation and our life will become more meaningful. In the end, even mindful existence in nature can evolve to an intrinsic value.

This is the answer of mindfulness in nature to the existential challenges described by Clifford Geertz. In it, at least three voices can be heard: the attitude of mindfulness, nature itself, and lastly, but most importantly, the encounter of humans and nature in the spirit of mindfulness and on the basis of the naturalness of humans. We cannot be receptive, open, connected, etc., outside of interactions and relationships. We cannot even be free, as freedom requires conditions it can refer to. We need an opposite that we can mindfully encounter, open ourselves to, and that in turn affects us, and therefore cannot be identical to us. But they only become a spiritual experience, if we also reward these specific nature experiences a personal existential meaning in the sense of a foundational expansion of our horizon. This can occur within and outside of religious living environments and discourses. As all interpretations that raise a claim on truth, our spiritual interpretations can be criticized in regard to their ability to aid the understanding of the world and existence. They are not above rationality or ethics. But every spiritual interpretation will only be convincing for as long as it is carried by experience. We do not need to draw this experience from ourselves, it develops through mindful encounters with nature. We do not need to pull ourselves out of the swamp by our hair. These encounters with nature can neither be reduced to nature, nor to culture, nor to anything else. Spiritual mindfulness in nature is a creative process.

Bibliography

Abram, D.: *The Spell of the Sensuos. Perception an Language in a More-Than-Human World.* New York: Vintage Books; 1996.

Altner, N.: *Achtsam mit Kindern leben. Wie wir uns die Freude am Lernen erhalten.* München: Kösel; 2009.

Amthor, W.: Jean-Jacques Rousseaus Pflanzen-Lesen. Wissenschaft und Belehrung aus Leidenschaft. In: Amthor, W., Hille, A., Scharnowski, S. (Hgg.) Wilde Lektüren. Festschrift für Hans-Richard Brittnacher zum 60. Geburtstag. Bielefeld: Aisthesis Verlag; 2012.

Andermann K., Eberlein U. (Hg.): *Gefühle als Atmosphären: Neue Phänomenologie und philosophische Emotionstheorie.* Berlin: Akademie Verlag; 2011.

Anderson, E. N.: Culture and the Wild. In: Kahn P. H., Hasbach P. H (Eds.): *The Rediscovery of the Wild.* Cambridge: The MIT Press; 2013.

Ariès, P., Duby, G.: Geschichte des privaten Lebens. Bd. 2 [Duby, G. (Hg.)]: *Vom Feudalzeitalter zur Renaissance.* Frankfurt a. M.: S. Fischer; 1990.

Baier, K.: *Nicht-Üben.* Obergrafendorf: Diotima-Presse; 2001. http://homepage.univie.ac.at/karl.baier/texte/pdf/nicht_ueben.pdf

Baier, K.: *Meditation und Moderne.* Würzburg: Königshausen& Neumann; 2009.

Bäumer, B.: *Vijnana Bhairava. Das göttliche Bewusstsein.* Frankfurt a. M.: Insel, Verlag der Weltreligionen; 2008.

Batchelor, S.: *Buddhismus für Ungläubige* [orig.: Buddhism Without Beliefs]. Frankfurt a. M.: Fischer; 2001.

Bayrische Forstverwaltung: *Waldpädagogischer Leitfaden nicht nur für Förster;* Bayrisches Staatsministerium für Ernährung,

Landwirtschaft und Forsten; 2010.

http://www.stmelf.Bayern.de/wald/waldpaedagogik/
veroefentlichungen/005832/index.php.

Beck, C.: *Die Geschichte der "Heil- und Pflegeanstalt Illmenau" unter Chr. Fr. W. Roller (1802– 1878)*, Diss. Univ. Freiburg 1983.

Beck, T., Karn, S.: Einleitung. In: Föhn, M., Dietrich, C. (Hg.): *Garten und Demenz*. Bern: Huber; 2012.

Belliger, A., Krieger D. J.: *ANThology: Ein einführendes Handbuch zur Akteur-NetzwerkTheorie*. Bielefeld: Transcript; 2006.

Berthold, M., Ziegenspeck, J.: *Der Wald als erlebnispädagogischer Lernort für Kinder,* Lüneburg: Edition Erlebnispädagogik Lüneburg; 2002.

Bestle-Körfer R., Stollenwerk A., Heinlein K.: *Sinneswerkstatt Landart: Naturkunst für Kinder,* Münster: Ökotopia; 2010.

Bibelriether, H.: *Natur Natur sein lassen.* In: Prokosch, P.: *Ungestörte Natur – Was haben wir davon?* – Tagungsbericht. 6 Umweltstiftung WWF Deutschland, P. 85–104, Husum; 1992.

Binswanger, L.: *Grundformen und Erkenntnis menschlichen Daseins.* Zürich: Niehans; 1953.

Bögeholz, S.: *Qualitäten primärer Naturerfahrungen und ihr Zusammenhang mit Umweltwissen und Umwelthandeln.* Opladen: Leske und Budrich Verlag; 1999.

Böhme, G.: *Anthropologie in pragmatischer Hinsicht. Darmstädter Vorlesungen.* Frankfurt a. M.: Suhrkamp; 1985.

Böhme, G.: *Für eine ökologische Naturästhetik.* Frankfurt a.M.: Suhrkamp; 1989.

Böhme, G.: *Natürlich Natur. Über Natur im Zeitalter der technischen Reproduzierbarkeit.* Frankfurt a. M.: Suhrkamp; 1992.

Böhme, G.: *Atmosphäre. Essays zur neuen Ästhetik.* Frankfurt a. M.:

Suhrkamp; 1995.

Böhme, G.: *Anmutungen. Über das Atmosphärische.* Frankfurt a. M.: Suhrkamp; 1998.

Böhme, G.: Phänomenologie der Natur – ein Projekt. In: Böhme G., Schiemann G. (Hg.): *Phänomenologie der Natur.* Frankfurt a. M.: Suhrkamp; 1997.

Böhme, G.: *Das Glück, da zu sein.* In: II. Jahrbuch für Lebensphilosophie (Hg. Kozljanic, R. J.). München: Albunea Verlag; 2006.

Bolay, E., Reichle, B.: *Waldpädagogik Teil 1: Theorie,* Handbuch der waldbezogenen Umweltbildung, Hohengehren: Schneider-Verlag; 2007.

Bolay, E., Reichle, B.: *Waldpädagogik Teil 2: Praxiskonzepte,* Handbuch der waldbezogenen Umweltbildung, Hohengehren: Schneider Verlag; 2011.

Bollnow, O. F.: *Das Wesen der Stimmungen.* Frankfurt a. M.: Kostermann; 1995 [1956].

Brämer, R.: Grün tut uns gut. Daten und Fakten zur Renaturierung des Hightech-Menschen. In: Brämer, R.: *Natur subjektiv – Gedanken zur Natur-Beziehung in der Hightech-Welt.* http://www.natursoziologie.de; 2008.

Brämer, R.: Zurück zur "Natur"? Ein natur-kulturkritisches Essay zur neuen Naturliebe. In: Brämer, R.: *Natur subjektiv – Gedanken zur Natur-Beziehung in der Hightech-Welt.* http://www.natursoziologie.de, o. J.

Bronkhorst, J.: Die buddhistische Lehre. In: Bechert, H. (Hg.): *Die Religionen der Menschheit Bd. 24: Der Buddhismus I. Der indische Buddhismus und seine Verzweigungen.* Stuttgart: Kohlhammer; 2000.

Brooks, C.: *Sensory Awareness: The Rediscovery of Experiencing.* Santa Barbara: Ross Erikson; 1983.

Brown, L. R.: Ecopsychology and the Environmental Revolution: An Environmental Foreword. In: Roszak T., Gomes M. E., Kanner A. D. (Eds.): *Ecopsychology. Restoring the Earth. Healing the Mind.* San Francisco: Sierra Club Books; 1995.

Buber M.: Ich und Du [1923]. In: Ders. *Das dialogische Prinzip.* Gütersloh: Gütersloher Verlagshaus; 1999.

Buber M.: Zwiesprache [1929]. In: Ders. *Das dialogische Prinzip.* Gütersloh: Gütersloher Verlagshaus; 1999.

BUND Friends of the Earth Germany: *Wildnisbildung,* ein Beitrag zur Bildungsarbeit in Nationalparken, Stand 25.2.2002. http://www.gfnharz.de/sites/wildnisbildung.pdf

Chadwick, P.: *Person-Based CognitiveTherapy of Distressing Psychosis.* Hoboken: John Wiley & Sons; 2006.

Chawla, L.: Spots of Time: Manifold Ways of Being in Nature in Childhood. In Kahn, P. H., Kellert, S. R.: *Children and Nature: Psychological, Sociocultural, and Evolutionary Investigations.* Cambridge, Massachusetts, London: MIT Press; 2002.

CH-Waldwochen: *Naturerlebnis Wald, Gemeinsam mit Kindern und Jugendlichen im Wald, verweilen, entdecken, spielen,* Zofingen: CH-Waldwochen; 1996.

Cleary, C.: *Swampland Flowers: The Letters and Lectures of Zen Master Ta Hui.* New York: Grove Press; 1977.

Coleman, M.: *Awake in the Wild. Mindfulness in Nature as a Path of Self-Discovery.* Novato: New World Library: 2006.

Corleis F., Stoltenberg U., Duhr M.: *Schule: Wald: Der Wald als Ressource einer Bildung für eine nachhaltige Entwicklung in der Schule.* Lüneburg: Verlag Erlebnispädagogik; 2006.

Cornell, J.: *Listening to Nature.* Nevada: Dawn Publications 1987.

Cornell, J.: *Sharing nature with children: the classic parents' and teachers' nature awareness guidebook.* Nevada: Dawn

Publications; 2006.

Cornell, J.: *Sharing Nature. Nature Awareness Acitivities for all ages.* Nevada City: Crystal Clarity Publishers; 2015.

De Haan, G. & Harenberg, D.: *Bildung für eine nachhaltige Entwicklung,* Materialien zur Bildungsplanung und Forschungsförderung. Heft 72, Bund-Länder-Kommission, Bonn, 1999.

De Haan, G.: *Gestaltungskompetenz als Kompetenzkonzept für Bildung für nachhaltige Entwicklung* in: Bormann, I., de Haan, G. (Hg.): Kompetenzen der Bildung für nachhaltige Entwicklung, Wiesbaden: Verlag für Sozialwissenschaften; 2008.

De Haan, G.: *Zugänge zu einer Bildung für nachhaltige Entwicklung. Stand und Perspektive in Deutschland.* Tagung: Nachhaltige Entwicklung macht Schule – macht die Schule nachhaltige Entwicklung? Bern; 2002.

Dunde S. R.: *Spirituelles Erleben der Natur. Die Einheit von Mensch und Natur erfahren.* Düsseldorf: Econ; 1989.

Edgerton, R. B.: *Sick Societies: Challenging the Myth of Primitive Harmony.* New York: Free Press; 1992.

Eggman, V., Steiner, B.: *Baumzeit, Magier, Mythen und Mirakel, Neue Einsichten in Europas Baum- und Waldgeschichten.* Zürich: Werd-Verlag; 1995.

Einwanger, J.: Workshop *"Mut zum Risiko"* Tagung ERBINAT – Forum, Männedorf /Schweiz am 30.03.2012.

Ellenberger, H. F.: *Die Entdeckung des Unbewussten: Geschichte und Entwicklung der dynamischen Psychiatrie von den Anfängen bis zu Janet, Freud, Adler und Jung.* Zürich: Diogenes; 1985.

Emerson, R. W.: *Nature.* In: Emerson, R. W.: Nature and Selected Essays. New York: Pinguin Books; 2003 [1836].

Erxleben, A.: Einheimisch werden in der Natur – Untersuchung zur

Wirkung ursprünglichen, ganzheitlichen Lernens in Wildnisschule als Beitrag zur Umweltbildung, Diplomarbeit zur Erlangung des Grades eines Dipl.-Ing. (FH) Landschaftsnutzung und Naturschutz, Fachhochschule Eberswalde; 2008.

Fachgruppe Arbeit mit dem Pferd in der Psychotherapie: Psychotherapie mit dem Pferd. Beiträge aus der Praxis. Bremen-Oberneuland: Pferdesport Verlag Rolf Ehlers; 2005. Fachkonferenz Umweltbildung Schweiz: http://www.education21.ch/sites/default/files/uploads/pdf-d/akteure/netzwerke/Fachkonferenz- UB_Positionspapier_1.pdf.

Fingerhut J., Hufendieck R., Wild M. (Hg.): Philosophie der Verkörperung. Frankfurt a. M.: Suhrkamp; 2013.

Fischer, J.: Verstehen statt Begründen. Warum es in der Ethik um mehr als nur um Handlungen geht. Stuttgart: Kohlhammer; 2012.

Fischer, J.: Zwischen religiöser Ideologie und religiösem Fundamentalismus. Zu einem Irrweg evangelischer Ethik. In: Evangelische Theologie, 1/2014, P. 22–40.

Fischer, J.: Der Verlust der Wirklichkeitspräsenz. Zu Ronald Dworkins "Religion ohne Gott". In: Evangelische Theologie, 2/2015, P. 120-135.

Fischer-Rizzi, S.: Mit der Wildnis verbunden, Kraft schöpfen, Heilung finden. Stuttgart: KOSMOS Verlag; 2007.

Flade, A.: Natur psychologisch betrachtet. Bern: Huber; 2010.

Frischknecht-Tobler, U., Nagel, U., Wilhelm, S.: Wie Kinder komplexe Systeme verstehen lernen. Beiträge zur Didaktik des systemischen Denkens und des systembezogenen Handelns in der Volksschule. Schlussbericht. Pädagogische Hochschulen Zürich und Rohrschach; 2008.

Gebhard, U.: Erfahrung von Natur und seelische Gesundheit.In: Seel, H. J. (Hg.): Mensch – Natur: Zur Psychologie einer problematischen Beziehung. Opladen: Westdeutscher Verlag; 1993.

Gebhard, U.: Naturverhältnis und Selbstverhältnis. In: Gebauer, M., Gebhard, U.: Naturerfahrung. Wege zu einer Hermeneutik der Natur. Zug: Prof. Dr. A. Schmidt Stiftung; 2005.

Gebhard, U: Kind und Natur, die Bedeutung der Natur für die psychische Entwicklung. Wiesbaden: Springer Verlag; 2013 [1994].

Gebhard, U.: Tierbegegnung und seelische Entwicklung von Kindern und Jugendlichen. Vortrag an der BAGLOB Tagung Bundesarbeitsgemeinschaft Lernort Bauernhof, 22. Februar 2013 in Altenkirchen.

Geertz, C.: Religion as a Cultural System. In Geertz, C. The Interpretation of Cultures. New York: Basic Books; 1973.

Gergen, K. J.: Relational Being. Beyond Self and Community. Oxford: Oxford University Press; 2009.

Goepfert, H.: Naturbezogene Pädagogik. Weinheim: Deutscher Studienverlag; 1988.

Goldstein, J.: Die Entdeckung der Natur. Etappen einer Erfahrungsgeschichte. Berlin: Matthes & Seitz; 2013.

Goldsworthy, A: Rain sun snow hail mist calm: Photo works by Andy Goldsworthy. The Henry Moore Centre for the Study of Sculpture, LeedsCity Art Gallery and Northern Centre for Contemporary Art, Sunderland: 1985. http://www.goldsworthy.cc.gla.ac.uk/extracts/.

Goldsworthy, A: Stone, New York: Viking Press; 1994.

Goldsworthy, A: Wood. New York: Viking Press; 1996.

Gorke, M.: Schweitzers Ethik der Ehrfurcht vor dem Leben als Wegbereiterin einer holistischen Umweltethik. Gemeinsamkeiten und Unterschiede. In: Hauskeller, M. (Hg.): Ethik des Lebens. Albert Schweitzer als Philosoph. Zug: Prof. Dr. A. Schmidt Stiftung; 2006.

Greiffenhagen, S., Buck-Werner, O. N.: Tiere als Therapie. Neue Wege in Erziehung und Heilung. Mürlenbach: Kynos; 2007. Groh R., Groh D.: Die Außenwelt der Innenwelt. Zur Kulturgeschichte der Natur 2. Frankfurt a. M.: Suhrkamp; 1996.

Groh R., Groh D.: Weltbild und Naturaneignung. Zur Kulturgeschichte der Natur. Frankfurt a. M.: Suhrkamp; 1991.

Grossheim, M.: Atmosphären in der Natur – Phänomene oder Konstrukte? In: Sieferle R. P., Breuninger, H. (Hg.): Natur- Bilder. Wahrnehmungen von Natur und Umwelt in der Geschichte. New York: Campus; 1999.

Guéguen, N.; Meineri, S.: Natur für die Seele, die Umwelt und ihre Auswirkungen auf die Psyche. Berlin, Heidelberg: Springer Spektrum; 2013.

Gugerli-Dolder, B., Frischknecht-Tobler, U.: Umweltbildung Plus, Impulse zur Bildung für nachhaltige Entwicklung. Verlag Pestalozzianum an der Pädagogischen Hochschule Zürich; 2011.

Gunia, H., Huppertz, M.: Das Darmstädter Modell: Psychotherapie von Menschen mit einer Borderline – Persönlichkeitsstörung in einem ambulanten Netzwerk. In: Psychotherapie im Dialog 4/ 2007.

Güthler, A.: Erlebniswerkstatt Landart: Neue Naturkunstwerke für Klein und Gross. Aarau und München: AT Verlag; 2011.

Güthler, A.; Lacher, K.: Naturwerkstatt Landart: Ideen für kleine und grosse Naturkünstler, Aarau und München: AT Verlag; 2005.

Habermas, J.: Die Herausforderung der ökologischen Ethik für eine anthropozentrisch ansetzende Konzeption. In: Krebs A. (Hg): Naturethik. Grundtexte der gegenwärtigen tier- und ökoethischen Diskussion. Frankfurt a. M.: Suhrkamp; 1997.

Häfele, A.: Landart für Kinder: Mit Natur-Kunst durch die Jahreszeiten, Mülheim an der Ruhr: Verlag an der Ruhr; 2011.

Halbig, C.: Der Begriff der Tugend und die Grenzen der Tugendethik. Frankfurt a. M.: Suhrkamp; 2013.

Halemeyer, R.: Die Pflege und Behandlung Geisteskranker im "Waisenhaus" zu Pforzheim von der Mitte des 18. Jh. Bis zur Gründung der Anstalt Illmenau. Diss. Univ. Freiburg; 1966.

Han, B.- C.: Duft der Zeit. Ein philosophischer Essay zur Kunst des Verweilens. Bielefeld: Transcript; 2009.

Hauff, V. (Hrsg.): Unsere gemeinsame Zukunft. Der Brundtland Bericht der Weltkommission für Umwelt und Entwicklung. Greven: Eggenkamp; 1987.

Hauskeller, M.: Atmosphären erleben. Berlin: Akademie-Verlag; 1995.

Hauskeller, M.: Biotechnology and the Integrity of Life: Taking Public Fears Seriously. Farnham: Ashgate; 2012.

Hauskeller, M.: Verantwortung für alles Leben? Schweitzers Dilemma. In: Hauskeller, M. (Hg.): Ethik des Lebens. Albert Schweitzer als Philosoph. Zug: Prof. Dr. A. Schmidt Stiftung; 2006.

Hauskeller, M.: Versuch über die Grundlagen der Moral. München: C. H. Beck; 2001.

Heerwagen, J., Orians, G.: The ecological world of Children. In: Kahn, P., Kellert, S.: Children and Nature: Psychological, Sociocultural, and Evolutionary Investigations. Cambridge, Massachusetts, London: MIT Press; 2002.

Heidegger, M.: Sein und Zeit. Tübingen: Max Niemeyer; 1979 [1927].

Helbling, J.: Der Einfluß religiöser Vorstellungen, Normen und Rituale auf die Ressourcennutzung einfacher Gesellschaften am Beispiel der Cree und der Maring. In: Sieferle, R. P., Breuninger, H. (Hg.): Natur-Bilder. Wahrnehmungen von Natur und Umwelt in der Geschichte. New York: Campus; 1999.

Hepfer, K.: Philosophische Ethik. Eine Einführung. Göttingen: Vandenhoeck & Ruprecht; 2008.

Hoeps, R.: Das Gefühl des Erhabenen und die Herrlichkeit Gottes: Studien zur Beziehung von philosophischer und theologischer

Ästhetik. Würzburg: Echter; 1989.

Hofstetter U., Schatanek, V.: BNE Planungshilfe, http://www.stadt-zuerich.ch/naturschulen; 2014.

Hoppe, J. R.: Bedeutung von Naturerfahrungen für die psychologische Entwicklung von Kindern, in: Schemel, H.- J. (Hrsg.): Naturerfahrungsräume. Bonn, Bad Godesberg; 1998.

Huebner, K.: Wissenschaftliche und nicht-wissenschaftliche Naturerfahrung. In: Großklaus, G., Oldemeyer, E. (Hg.): Natur als Gegenwelt. Beiträge zur Kulturgeschichte der Natur. Karlsruhe: von Loeper Verlag; 1983.

Huppertz, M.: Schizophrene Krisen. Bern: Huber; 2000.

Huppertz, M.: Mystische Erfahrung und Trance. In: Amthor W., Brittnacher, H., Hallacker, A. (Hg). Profane Mystik? Berlin: Weidler; 2002; P. 23–50.

Huppertz, M.: Die Kunst der Wahrnehmung in der Psychotherapie. In: Hauskeller, M.: Die Kunst der Wahrnehmung. Beiträge zu einer Philosophie der sinnlichen Erkenntnis. Zug: Prof. Dr. A. Schmidt Stiftung; 2003.

Huppertz, M.: Wissen und Können in der Psychotherapie, in: Psychologik 1, Freiburg, München 2006. http://www.mihuppertz.de/texte-zum-download.

Huppertz, M.: Spirituelle Atmosphären. In: Debus, S., Posner, R. (Hg.): Atmosphären im Alltag. Bonn: Psychiatrie-Verlag; 2007. Download. http://www.mihuppertz.de.

Huppertz, M.: Achtsamkeit – Befreiung zur Gegenwart. Paderborn: Junfermann; 2009.

Huppertz M.: Achtsamkeitsübungen. Experimente mit einem anderen Lebensgefühl. Paderborn: Junfermann; 2011.

Huppertz, M.: Anthropologische Psychiatrie und achtsamkeitsbasierte Therapie. http://www.mihuppertz.de/texte-zum-download, 2012.

Huppertz, M.: Meditation und Psychiatrie. Über die Verseelung und Vergeistigung der Meditation. In: Renger, A., Wulf, C.: Meditation in Religion, Therapie, Ästhetik, Bildung. Paragrana -Zeitschrift für Historische Anthropologie, 1/ 2013. [2013a]

Huppertz, M.: Wo bleibt die Zeit? Achtsamkeit, Zeiterleben und seelische Gesundheit. Vortrag im Rahmen der "Tage der seelischen Gesundheit" in Darmstadt am 11.10.2013. Anhang: Die Zeitlichkeit der Achtsamkeit. http://www.mihuppertz.de/texte-zum-download. [2013b]

Huppertz, M.: Die Bedeutung der Achtsamkeit für die ethische Intelligenz von Unternehmen. In: SEM/ Radar, 13. Jg. 1/ 2014a.

Huppertz, M.: Erleuchtung – Erlebnis und Einsicht. Zur Struktur von Erleuchtungserfahrungen aus Sicht der Phänomenologie und der Kognitionswissenschaft. In: Renger, A.: Erleuchtung. Kultur- und Religionsgeschichte eines Begriffs. Freiburg: Herder; 2015.

Huppertz, M., Saurgnani, S., Schneider, S.: Ein pluralistisches Achtsamkeitskonzept für die therapeutische Praxis. In: Verhaltenstherapie und psychosoziale Praxis, 2/2013, P. 381–397. http://www.mihuppertz.de/texte-zum-download. [2013]

Institut for Earth Education Deutschland, http://www.earth-education.org.

Jäger, M: LANDART gestalterische Naturpädagogik, Modul Gestalten mit Gruppen in der Natur, SILVIVA für Umweltbildung und Wald und ZHAW Zürcher Hochschule für angewandte Wissenschaften, Life Sciences und Facility Mamagement, IUNR Institut für Umwelt und Natürliche Ressourcen; 2011.

Jakoby, H.: Jenseits von ,Begabt' und ,Unbegabt'. Hamburg: Heinrich-Jacoby / Elsa-Gindler Stiftung, Christians Verlag; 2004 [1945].

Joller, K: Naturerfahrung mit allen Sinnen, ein Praxisbuch mit vielen Übungen. Aarau und München, AT Verlag; 2008.

Jullien, F.: Treatise on Efficacy: Between Western and Chinese

Thinking. Honolulu: University of Hawaii Press; 2004.

Jung, N.: Auf dem Weg zu gutem Leben. Die Bedeutung der Natur für seelische Gesundheit und Werteentwicklung (Bd.2). Opladen: Budrich UniPress; 2012.

Jung, N.: Mensch – Natur – Gesellschaft: Was ist ganzheitliche Umweltbildung? Einführung in die Sektion, in: FH Eberswalde (Hrsg.) Neue Wege-Alter Standort 175 Jahre Lehre und Forschung in Eberswalde. Die Festschrift. Eberswalde: FH Eberswalde; 2005.

Jung, N.: Natur im Blick der Kulturen. Naturbeziehung und Umweltbildung in fremden Kulturen als Herausforderung für unsere Bildung (Bd.1). Opladen: Budrich UniPress; 2011.

Jung, N.: Psychotope – zwischen Mensch und Natur. Greifswald; 2008. http://www.natursoziologie.de/files/14-jungpsychotopevers2_1411281042.pdf.

Kahn, P. H., Hasbach, P. H.: The Rewilding of the Human Species. In: Kahn, P. H., Hasbach, P. H. (Eds.): The Rediscovery of the Wild. Cambridge: The MIT Press; 2013.

Kahn, P. H., Hasbach, P. H.: Introduction. In: Kahn, P. H., Hasbach P. H. (Eds.): The Rediscovery of the Wild. Cambridge: The MIT Press; 2013.

Kahn, P. H.: Children's Affiliations with Nature: Structure, Development, and the Problem of Environmental Generational Amnesia in Kahn, P. H., Kellert, S. R.: Children and Nature: Psychological, Sociocultural, and Evolutionary Investigations. Cambridge, Massachusetts, London: MIT Press; 2002.

Kalff, M.: Handbuch zur Natur- und Umweltpädagogik. Theoretische Grundlegung und praktische Anleitungen für ein tieferes Mitweltverständnis. Tübingen: Ulmer Verlag; 1994.

Kalff, M.: Kinder erfahren die Stille, Freiburg, Basel, Wien: Herder Verlag; 1998.

Kals, E., Platz, N., Wimmer, R.: Emotionen in der Umweltdiskussion.

Wiesbaden: Deutscher Universitäts- Verlag; 2000.

Kals, E., Schuhmacher D., Montada, L.: Naturerfahrungen, Verbundenheit mit der Natur und ökologische Verantwortung als Determinanten naturschützenden Verhaltens. In: Zeitschrift für Sozialpsychologie 29.5-19, 1998.

Kaltwasser, V.: Achtsamkeit in der Schule, Stille-Inseln im Unterricht: Entspannung und Konzentration. Weinheim und Basel: Beltz; 2013.

Kaplan, R., Kaplan, S.: The Experience of Nature: A Psychological Perspective. Cambridge University Press; 1989.

Katcher, A.: Animals in Therapeutic education: Guides into the Liminal State, in Kahn, P. H., Kellert, S. R.: Children and Nature: Psychological, Sociocultural, and Evolutionary Investigations. Cambridge, Massachusetts, London: MIT Press; 2002.

Kellert S. R.: Experiencing Nature: Affective, Cognitive, and Evaluative Development in Children in Kahn, P. H., Kellert, S. R.: Children and Nature: Psychological, Sociocultural, and Evolutionary Investigations. Cambridge, Massachusetts, London: MIT Press; 2002.

Klinkenberg, N.: Achtsamkeit in der Körperverhaltenstherapie.Ein Arbeitsbuch mit 20 Probiersituationen aus der Jacoby/ Gindler-Arbeit. Stuttgart: Klett-Cotta; 2007.

Kohler, B., Lude, A.: Nachhaltigkeit erleben, Praxisentwürfe für die Bildungsarbeit in Wald und Schule. München: OEKOM; 2012.

Krebs, A.: Naturethik im Überblick. In: Krebs, A. (Hg): Naturethik. Grundtexte der gegenwärtigen tier- und ökoethischen Diskussion. Frankfurt a. M.: Suhrkamp; 1997.

Kriebel, H. J.: Wie lerne ich Spurenlesen? Norderstedt: Books on demand; 2007–2010.

Kruse, L.: Katastrophe und Erholung – Die Natur in der umweltpsychologischen Forschung. In: Großklaus, G., Oldemeyer,

E. (Hg.): Natur als Gegenwelt. Beiträge zur Kulturgeschichte der Natur. Karlsruhe: von Loeper Verlag; 1983.

Kuhn, K., Probst, W., Schilke, K.: Biologie im Freien. Hannover: Metzler; 1986.

Kuhn Shimu, S. T.: Das Tao der Worte. Darmstadt: Schirner Verlag; 2013.

Künzli-David, C.: Zukunft mitgestalten. Bildung für eine nachhaltige Entwicklung – Didaktisches Konzept und Umsetzung in der Grundschule. Bern: Haupt Verlag; 2007.

Kyburz-Graber, R., Halder, U., Hügli, A., Ritter, M.: Umweltbildung im 20.Jahrhundert – Anfänge, Gegenwartsprobleme, Perspektiven, hrsg. von Klaus Schleicher, Umwelt Bildung Forschung, Band 7, Münster, New York, München, Berlin: Verlag Waxmann; 2001.

Lakoff, G., Johnson, M.: Metaphors We Live By. Chicago: University of Chicago Press; 2003.

Lederbogen, S.: Tiere in der Therapie psychisch kranker Menschen: Ein Überblick über den Einsatz von Tieren in der stationären Psychiatrie. Hamburg: Diplomica Verlag; 2012.

Leopold, A.: A Sandy County Almanach and Sketches Here and There. London, Oxford, New York: Oxford University Press; 1969 [1949].

Linden, S., Grut, J.: Healing Fields.Working with Psychotherapy and Nature to Rebuild Shattered Lives. London: Frances Lincoln Limited; 2002.

Löwith, K.: Das Verhängnis des Fortschritts. In: Band "Bad Wildunger Hochschulwochen" Nr. 28. Bad Homburg, Berlin, Zürich: Verlag Dr. Max Gehlen; 1960.

Louden, R. B.: On Some Vices of Virtue Ethics. In: American Philosophical Quarterly, Vol. 21, No. 3 (July, 1984), pp. 227-236. Stuttgart: Reclam: 1998 [1984].

Louv, R.: Last Child in the Wood. Saving our Children from Nature-

Deficit Disorder. Chapel Hill: Algonquin Books of Chapel Hill; 2008 (updated and expanded).

Louv, R.: The Nature Principle. Human Restoration and the End of Nature-Deficit Disorder. Chapel Hill: Algonquin Books of Chapel Hill; 2011.

Lude, A.: Naturerfahrung und Umwelthandeln – Neue Ergebnisse aus Untersuchungen mit Jugendlichen. In Unterbrunner, U.: Natur erleben. Innsbruck, Wien, Bozen: Studienverlag; 2005.

Lude, A.: Naturerfahrung und Naturschutzbewusstsein. Innsbruck: Studienverlag; 2001.

Ludwig, S.: Elsa Gindler – von ihrem Leben und Wirken: Wahrnehmen, was wir empfinden. Hrsg.: Heinrich- Jacoby/ Elsa-Gindler-Stiftung. Bearb.: M. Haag. Hamburg: Christians; 2002.

Ludwig, T.: Basis Kurs Natur- und Kulturinterpretation Trainerhandbuch. Bildungswerk interpretation, Werleshausen, 2012. http://www.interp.de.

Ludwig, T.: Einführung in die Naturinterpretation. In: Alfred Toepfer Akademie für Naturschutz – Mitteilungen 1/2003, Schneverdingen, 2003. http://www.interp.de.

Ludwig, T.: Natur- und Kulturinterpretation – Amerika trifft Europa in: Natur im Blick der Kulturen, Opladen: Budrich UniPress; 2011. http://www.interp.de.

Ludwig, T.: Natur- und Kulturinterpretation – ein zeitgemäßes Konzept? In: Bund Heimat und Umwelt – Wege zu Natur und Kultur, Moser Druck+Verlag, Rheinbach, 2010. http://www.interp.de.

Luhmann, N.: Funktion und Kausalität. In: Ders.: Soziologische Aufklärung, Bd. 1. Opladen: Westdeutscher Verlag; 1970.

Macintyre; A.: After Virtue. London: Duckworth; 1997 [1981].

Macy, J., Brown, M. Y.: Coming Back to Life. Practices to Reconnect Our Lives, Our World. Gabriola Island: New Society Publishers:

1998.

Manstetten, R.: Selbstlos töten im Namen des Einen. Mystik und die Ausrottung des Bösen in der Welt. In: Bonheim, G., Regehly, T. (Hg.): Mystik und Totalitarismus. Berlin: Weißensee-Verlag; 2013.

Mayer, J.: Die Natur der Erfahrung und die Erfahrung der Natur. In: Gebauer, M., Gebhard, U.: Naturerfahrung. Wege zu einer Hermeneutik der Natur. Zug: Prof. Dr. A. Schmidt Stiftung; 2005.

Meyer-Abich, K. M.: Physiozentrisch lebt sich's gesünder. Begründung der Umweltethik aus der Praktischen Naturphilosophie. In: Köchy, K., Norwig, M. (Hg.): Umwelt-Handeln. Zum Zusammenhang von Naturphilosophie und Umweltethik. Freiburg: Karl Alber; 2006.

Minkovski, E.: Die gelebte Zeit. Salzburg: Müller; 1971/1972 [1933].

Moser-Patuzzi, S., Jettenberger, M.: Das Draußen im Drinnen erleben. Naturerfahrungen im Pflegealltag. Mülheim an der Ruhr: Verlag an der Ruhr; 2014.

Muir, J.: The Mountains of California. In: Ders.: Nature Writings. New York: Literary Classics of the United States, Inc.; 1997 [1894].

Müller- Schöll, T.: Das Erdschützerprojekt, Pädagogik für eine lebenswerte, friedliche Zukunft. Esselbach: Erdschützer Verlag; 2010.

Müller, R.: Die geheime Sprache der Vögel. Aarau und München: AT Verlag; 2011.

Mutschler, H.-D.: Naturphilosophie. Stuttgart: Kohlhammer; 2002.

Myers, O., Saunders C.: Animals as Links toward Developing Caring Relationsships with the Natural World. In: Kahn, H. P. Jr., Kellert, S. R. (Hg.): Children and Nature. Cambridge, Massachusetts, London: MIT Press; 2002.

Naess, A.: The Deep Ecology Movement. Some Philosophical Aspects. In: Sessions, G. Deep Ecology for the Twenty-First Century. Boston, London: Shambala; 1995.

Neels, K.: Nachhaltige Entwicklung als Leitbild der Bildungsarbeit an Umweltbildungseinrichtungen, Entwicklung eines Profils am Beispiel des Besucherzentrums für Natur- und Umwelterziehung "Drei Eichen" (Buckow/Märkische Schweiz), Diplomarbeit, Fachhochschule Eberswalde; 2003.

Neuberger, K., Putz, M.: Zu den Wurzeln der Gartentherapie im internationalen Kontext. In: Deutscher Verband der Ergotherapeuten (Hg.): Gartentherapie. Idstein: Schulz-Kirchner; 2010.

Niebrügge, A.: Wildnis. Ideengeschichte und Argumente für Wildnisschutz aus ethischer Sicht. Saarbrücken. VDM Verlag Dr. Müller; 2007.

Niepel, A., Pfister, T.: Praxisbuch Gartentherapie. Idstein: Schulz-Kirchner; 2010.

Nussbaum, M. Aristotelian Social Democracy. In: R. B. Douglas, R. B., Mara, G., Richardson, H. (Ed.). Liberalism and the Good. New York: Routledge; 1990.

Nussbaum, M. Non-Relative Virtues: An Aristotelian Approach. In: Martha Nussbaum, M., Amartya Sen. The Quality of Life. Oxford: Clarendon Press; 1993.

Nussbaum, M. Why Practice Needs Ethical Theory. Particularism, Principle, and Bad Behavior. In: Burton, S.J. (Ed.). The Path of the Law and its Influence. Cambridge: Cambridge University Press; 2000.

Olbrich, E., Otterstedt, C.: Menschen brauchen Tiere: Grundlagen und Praxis der tiergestützten Pädagogik und Therapie. Stuttgart: Franck Kosmos; 2003.

Ott, K.: Umweltethik zur Einführung. Hamburg: Junius; 2010.

Otto, R.: The Idea of the Holy. London, Oxford, New York: Oxford University Press; 1958 [1917].

Pohl D. T.: Naturerfahrungen und Naturzugänge von Kindern,

Dissertation zur Erlang des Grades eines Doktors der Erziehungswissenschaften der Pädagogischen Hochschule Ludwigsburg 2006. http://opus.bsz-bw.de/phlb/volltexte/2006/2812/.

Pottmann-Knapp, B.: Tiergestützte (Psycho-)Therapie. Saarbrücken: AV Akademikerverlag; 2013.

Poyet, M.: Ideenbuch Landart: 500 Inspirationen für Naturgestaltungen rund ums Jahr. Aarau und München: AT Verlag; 2008.

Pries, C. (Hg.): Das Erhabene. Zwischen Grenzerfahrung und Größenwahn. Weinheim: VCH Verlagsgesellschaft; 1989a.

Pries, C.: Einleitung. In: Pries C. (Hg.): Das Erhabene. Zwischen Grenzerfahrung und Größenwahn. Weinheim: VCH Verlagsgesellschaft; 1989b.

Renz-Polster, H., Hüther, G.: Wie Kinder heute wachsen. Natur als Entwicklungsraum. Weinheim, Basel: Beltz; 2013.

Rehmann-Sutter, C.: Über Relationalität. Was ist das "Ökologische" in der Naturästhetik? In: Hauskeller M., Rehmann-Sutter C., Schiemann G.: Naturerkenntnis und Natursein. Frankfurt a. M.: Suhrkamp; 1998.

Rosenberg, M. B.: Life Enriching Education. Encinitas: Puddle Dancer Press; 2003.

Roszak, T., Gomes, M. E., Kanner, A. D. (Eds.): Ecopsychology. Restoring the Earth. Healing the Mind. San Francisco: Sierra Club Books; 1995.

Rossler, G.: Der Anteil der Dinge an Gesellschaft und Kognition. Sozialität – Kognition – Netzwerke. Bielefeld: Trancript; 2016.

Rousseau, J.-J.: Reveries of the Solitary Walker. Oxford: Oxford University Press; 2011.

Roszak, T.: Ecopsychology: Restoring the Earth, Healing the Mind. Oakland: Sierra Club Books Publication; 1995.

Schatanek V., Elkharassi H.: Sahara: Tiere, Pflanzen, Spuren. KOSMOS Naturführer; Stuttgart: KOSMOS; 2006.

Schatanek, V.: Welchen Wert haben Naturerfahrungen in der Kindheit?, in Dossier: Erfahrungsfelder und Standards für den Frühbereich, Arbeitsversion der Stadt Zürich, https://www.stadtzuerich.ch/ssd/de/index/volksschule/ publikationen_broschueren/dossier_ fruehbereich.html.

Schatanek, V., Schneider, R., Häberling, D.: Naturschulen 2010, Bildungskonzept der Zürcher Naturschulen Beiträge für die Förderung der Naturbeziehung und für eine Bildung zur nachhaltigen Entwicklung, Grün Stadt Zürich; 2010. https://www.stadtzuerich.ch/ted/de/index/gsz/angebote_u_ beratung/ naturschulen/naturpaedagogik_undbildungskonzept.html.

Schauma, S.: Landscape and Memory. New York: Knopf: 1995.

Schiemann, G.: Phänomenologie versus Naturwissenschaft. Zum Verhältnis zweier Erkenntnisweisen. In: Böhme, G., Schiemann, G. (Hg.): Phänomenologie der Natur. Frankfurt a. M.: Suhrkamp; 1997.

Schleiermacher, F.: Über die Religion. Reden an die Gebildeten unter ihren Verächtern. Stuttgart: Reclam; 1969 [1799].

Schmitz, H.: System der Philosophie Bd. III , Teil 2: Der Gefühlsraum. Bonn: Bouvier; 1998 [1969].

Schmitz, H.: Leib und Gefühl, Materialien zu einer philosophischen Therapeutik. Paderborn: Junfermann; 1992.

Schreier, H.: Gespräche über Bäume. In: Gebauer, M., Gebhard, U.: Naturerfahrung. Wege zu einer Hermeneutik der Natur. Zug: Prof. Dr. A. Schmidt Stiftung; 2005.

Schweitzer, A.: Aus meinem Leben und Denken. Frankfurt a.M.: Fischer; 2011 [1931].

Seel, M.: Eine Ästhetik der Natur. Frankfurt a. M.: Suhrkamp; 1996.

Seidenstücker, K.: Buddha – Die Lehren. Paderborn: Voltmedia; 2005.

Sieferle, R. P., Breuninger, H. (Hg.): Natur-Bilder. Wahrnehmungen von Natur und Umwelt in der Geschichte. New York: Campus; 1999.

Sieferle, R. P.: Einleitung: Naturerfahrung und Naturkonstruktion. In: Sieferle, R. P., Breuninger, H. (Hg.): Natur-Bilder. Wahrnehmungen von Natur und Umwelt in der Geschichte. New York: Campus; 1999.

Signol, C.: Marie de Brebis: Der reiche Klang des einfachen Lebens. Eine Biographie. Stuttgart: Urachhaus; 2007.

Simmel, G.: Alpenreisen. In: Ders.: Aufsätze und Abhandlungen 1894–1900. Frankfurt a. M.: Suhrkamp; 1992 [1895].

Simmel, G.: Philosophie der Landschaft. In: Ders. Philosophie der Landschaft. Stühlingen: Mahler; 2014 [1913].

Sloterdijk, P.: Der Zauberbaum. Frankfurt a. M.: Suhrkamp; 1987.

Stern, D. N.: The Interpersonal World oft the Infant. A View from Psychoanalysis and Developmental Psychology. London: Karnac Books; 1985.

Stevens, J. O.: Awareness: Exploring, Experimenting, Experiencing: Gestalt Therapy with Children Adolescents and their Families. Gouldsboro: Gestalt Journal Press; 1971.

Stoltenberg, U.: Mensch und Wald: Theorie und Praxis einer Bildung für eine nachhaltige Entwicklung am Beispiel des Themenfelds Wald. München: Oekom; 2009.

Surrey, J. L.: Relational Psychotherapy, Relational Mindfulness. In: Germer, C. K., Siegel, R. D., Fulton, P.R.: Mindfulness and Psychotherapy. New York, London: Guilford; 2005.

Szymborska, W.: View With a Grain of Sand. Selected Poems. Orlando: Harcourt Brace & Company; 1995 [1962] [translated from Polish].

TAYLOR, P.: The Ethics of Respect for Nature. In: Environmental Ethics 3 (1981), p. 197-218.

Tellenbach, H.: Geschmack und Atmosphäre. Salzburg: Müller; 1968.

Thoreau, H. D.: Walking. In: Thoreau, H. D.: Walking & Other Essays. American Classics Library, n.d. [1851].

Thoreau, H. D.: *Walden and Other Writings. New York: Bantam Books; 1983 [1854]*.

Thoreau, H.D.: The Journal 1837 – 1861. New York: New York Review of Books; 2009.

Thoreau, H. D.: *Wild Fruits: Thoreau´s redicovered Last Manuscript. New York: W. W. Norton & Company; 2001*.

Tieck, L.: Franz Sternbalds Wanderungen. Stuttgart: Reclam; 1966 [1798].

Tilden, F.: Interpreting our Heritage, Chapel Hill: The University of North Carolina Press; 1977.

Timmerman, P.: It is dark outside. Western Buddhism from the Enlightenment to the global crisis. In: Batchelor, M., Brown, K. (Ed.): Buddhism and Ecology. London, New York: Cassell Publishers Limited; 1992.

Trommer, G.: Naturbildung – spürsames Bewildern des zivilisierten Menschen. Festschrift für Prof. Dr. W .Janßen. Flensburger Universitätszeitschrift 5, S. 77–92; 1998.

Trommer, G., Noack, R. (Hrsg): Die Natur in der Umweltbildung, Perspektiven für Grosschutzgebiete. Weinheim und Basel: Beltz; 1997.

Trommer, G.: Schön wild! Warum wir und unsere Kinder Natur und Wildnis brauchen. München: Oekom; 2012.

Trommer, G.: Ein Psychotop entsteht. Wildniserfahrungen mit Studenten. Nationalpark 4/ 98:611 1998.

UNESCO: World declaration on Higher Education for the twenty-first Century: Vision and Action; 1998. http://www.unesco.org/education/educprog/wche/

declaration_eng.html

Unterbrunner, U.: Natur erleben, Neues aus Forschung & Praxis zur Naturerfahrung, Forum Umweltbildung (Hg.): Universität Salzburg, Innsbruck/Wien/Bozen: Studien Verlag; 2005.

Van Matre, S.: Earth Education, Ein Neuanfang. Lüneburg: The Institute for Earth Education; 1998.

Vernooij, M. A., Schneider, S.: Handbuch der tiergestützten Intervention. Wiebelsheim: Quelle & Meyer Verlag; 2013.

Victoria, B.: Zen at War. Lanham: Rowman & Littlefield; 2006. Weber, A.: Mehr Matsch. Kinder brauchen Natur. Berlin: Ullstein; 2011.

Wilber, K.: Sex, Ecology, Spirituality. Boston, London: Shambala; 1995.

Wolter, A.: Stellenwert der Tiefenökologie in der Umweltbildung, Diplomarbeit Fachhochschule Eberswalde; 2004.

Wüst M., Michel, S., Heller, S.: Handbuch der Vogelexkursionen: Tipps, über 100 Methoden und Musterexkursionen für Exkursionsleitende und Lehrpersonen. Zürich: Bird Life Zürich; 2012.

Young, J., Haas, E., McGown, E.: Coyote´s Guide to Connecting with Nature. Shelton: Owlink Media; 2010.

Made in the USA
Monee, IL
16 September 2021